Walter Waddington Shirley

Royal and other historical Letters illustrative of the Reign of Henry III

Walter Waddington Shirley

Royal and other historical Letters illustrative of the Reign of Henry III

ISBN/EAN: 9783337171414

Printed in Europe, USA, Canada, Australia, Japan

Cover: Foto ©ninafisch / pixelio.de

More available books at **www.hansebooks.com**

INSPIRATIONAL LECTURES

AND

IMPROMPTU POEMS.

DELIVERED BY

W. J. COLVILLE.

AUTHOR OF "BERTHA: A ROMANCE OF EASTER-TIDE," &c., &c.

WITH

PERSONAL SKETCH OF THE SPEAKER.

London:

PRINTED BY
JAMES BURNS, 15, SOUTHAMPTON ROW, W.C.,
LONDON.

NOTICE TO READERS.

THE following Inspirational Lectures and Poems were, with three exceptions, delivered in Neumeyer Hall, London, during April, May, and June, 1884. Arrangements were made to secure thirteen Lectures and Poems, at the commencement of the series; the other five were reported and secured for publication as follows.

Lady Caithness desired the publication of the remarkable utterances delivered in her *salon*, in Paris, and very kindly defrayed the cost of their reporting and publication. A gentleman greatly interested in the question of Re-embodiment, secured a report of the lecture given on that subject, in Neumeyer Hall, Sunday afternoon, June 1. A lecture given on "Progress and Poverty" elicited much interest, but it was not reported, as it contained very similar ideas to that on "What is Property?" given in Leeds, August 14; that lecture found place in this Volume. The closing lecture, on "Atlantis," was reported *verbatim* as it fell from the lips of the speaker, in Neumeyer Hall, Sunday evening, June 29, 1884, a kind friend defraying the expenses. Thus eighteen Lectures and Poems are embodied in the following pages, while the original intention was only to report and publish thirteen.

The poems, with one exception, were all given publicly in Neumeyer Hall, at the close of the morning or evening services. That following the lecture on "What is Property?" was given in Psychological Hall, Leeds, and being peculiarly suitable was attached to the lecture on the Land Question, in print.

Each Lecture and Poem has been revised by the speaker, through whose hand the inspiring spirits can always correct reporter's or typographical errors, one of W. J. Colville's spirit guides having been, when on earth, actively engaged in literary labour of that particular kind.

These observations are made in justice alike to the public at large and those kind friends through whose generosity *verbatim* reports of W. J. Colville's utterances on special themes have been secured. Should this Volume meet with an extensive sale, a second collection of W. J. Colville's Inspirational Utterances will shortly appear.

CONTENTS.

IMPROMPTU POEMS.

ERRATUM.—Page 229: for "Black Forest" read New Forest.

PERSONAL SKETCH OF W. J. COLVILLE.

IN presenting this Volume of Discourses and Poems to the public, it may be interesting to all readers, especially to those who have neither seen nor heard the Lecturer, to be made acquainted with a few facts concerning him.

It is quite beyond us, in the brief space at our disposal, to do more than present a few salient points of interest to the reader, without any attempt at elaboration. Plain facts are always valuable and interesting, and as phrenology and physiognomy have commanded a considerable share of the attention of thoughtful people of late, a word-picture of a celebrated personage is often an illustration of the truth of these sciences.

In the very early spring of 1877, W. J. COLVILLE was first introduced to Mr. Burns, the publisher of this volume. At that time he was about 18 years of age, and had enjoyed very few educational advantages; nevertheless his inspired oratory was so remarkable, that after hearing him speak once in the drawing room at the Spiritual Institution, the Editor of THE MEDIUM considered himself justified in hiring a short-hand writer to take down W. J. Colville's oration, at Doughty Hall, on the following Sunday evening. That lecture and many others were soon after published in THE MEDIUM, and the name of W. J. Colville soon became a household word with all English-speaking Spiritualists.

The story of his sudden and singular discovery of his mediumistic powers has often been told, and is doubtless familiar to many who will read this record, though it will be new to others.

On the 24th of May, 1874, Mrs. Cora L. V. Tappan (now

Mrs. Richmond) spoke in the Concert Hall, West Street, Brighton. W. J. Colville, who was then under 16, and knew nothing whatever of Spiritualism (though he was extremely interested in liberal religion, and was at that time an active member of a Unitarian congregation, though as a professional singer he frequently officiated in the choirs of churches of widely different theology) was attracted by the unusual announcement that a lady, described on the placards as a "trance medium," would lecture upon "Spiritualism, under influence of her spirit guides," and also give "an impromptu poem on a subject chosen by the audience."

Attending the meeting on the evening in question, he became conscious of spirit presence during Mrs. Tappan's inspired invocation. He distinctly remembers seeing a misty form behind the speaker, the outlines of whose features he could clearly trace, while throughout the oration and poem his attention and gaze were rivetted upon the speaker, he feeling all the time under a most agreeable spell, as though some very pleasant change were about to take place in himself and his surroundings.

No sooner had he returned home than he astonished all at the supper table, by asking in a deep bass voice if the company present knew anything about Spiritualism, telling them that if they did not they would show their wisdom if they refrained from abusing it. (The conversation had turned on Spiritualism, through W. J. Colville having told the folks at the table, that he had been to hear a Mrs. Tappan instead of going to a church as usual.) "Well," said a lady present, "you say that Mrs. Tappan gives impromptu poems on any subjects the audience may give her; if there are any spirits here, let them influence you and give us a similar test; and that will be a test if you give a poem, as we know you have never displayed the slightest poetical genius, and do not even care to read poetry." The words were hardly out of the lady's mouth, when W. J. Colville's features underwent a complete transformation, and, in a girlish voice of very peculiar tone, he expressed his readiness to improvise on any suitable theme.

He describes his sensation at the time in the following words, which we have from his own lips: "I suddenly felt myself lifted in the air. I seemed to have an enormous head and a very small body. My lips seemed to be moving mechanically, under the pressure of some influence over which I could exert, and could will to exert, no power whatever. I heard some one commenting upon a poem, and then I sat down and finished my supper, and wondered if I had not been to sleep. That was my first experience as a medium for speaking, though from my earliest childhood I had had spiritual experiences, and constantly felt, saw, and heard beings around me, who were not in material form."

After that first striking example of inspired utterance, W. J. Colville was constantly requested to display his phenomenal abilities, in the drawing-rooms of the aristocracy and gentry. About that time, or soon after, he was the subject of many very successful mesmeric experiments, though he was never really subject to the influence of more than one person, a young gentleman of extraordinary psychological power and very attractive personal appearance, to whom W. J. Colville continued devotedly attached from the first moment of their meeting till circumstances, over which neither of them had the least control, separated them, doubtless at the right time, as this loss of his dearest friend opened the way for our Lecturer's prominent appearance before the public at large.

All through his public career, which has been a very striking and eventful one, W. J. Colville has relied entirely upon the guidance of his invisible friends. He assures all that they have never deceived and never once led him to make a move he afterwards repented. The only occasions when he has acted unwisely have been when he has not taken or acted upon the advice of his unseen directors, whom he regards as his dearest friends, and between whom and himself the closest bonds of sympathy always exist.

Sometimes while speaking he is quite unconscious, at other times he hears everything that is said, but his own mind never interferes with the controlling spirit. No one can listen to his utterances for any length of time, without discovering traces of the distinctive individuality of the various spirits who constitute his band of guides. At times the style is argumentative, and the lectures are closely reasoned in plain, forcible language, adapted to hard-headed thinkers and controversialists; at other times the language is singularly flowery and poetic, and the subject matter is idealistic or transcendental; while the answers to questions upon hundreds of different subjects, which are constantly being given both publicly and privately through this remarkable instrument of the Spirit-world, give evidence of a reservoir of intelligence somewhere, which appears inexhaustible.

Though W. J. Colville is admirably adapted for introducing Spiritualism to new hearers and in places where its claims have never been fairly presented to the public, and while he excels in dealing with almost every topic of public interest, his great power has been chiefly manifested in long engagements in one place, as in the case of his lengthy ministrations in Berkeley Hall, and other places in the city of Boston, U. S. A. The more one hears him the more one wishes to listen to what he says (or rather to what his guides have to say through him), and it is only when he has the opportunity of following up a train of thought, by a long series of concatenated lectures, that the full greatness of his abilities as an orator begins to dawn upon the listener. Of course all lectures are not of equal value, and conditions have something to do with their delivery, though not nearly so much as with the majority of mediumistic orators.

W. J. Colville cannot be called an uncultured or illiterate person, though he never received any education beyond that obtained in a preparatory school, and he was never either an apt scholar nor a regular attendant when he was getting his education. He has, however, considerable natural abilities, has keen perceptive faculties, but not a very good memory. He can be very agreeable in private life, when he chooses to exert himself to please, but very often persons, who desire to intrude upon his privacy or force themselves upon his notice, find him absent-minded and indifferent to their desires.

In personal appearance he is decidedly attractive, though one would not call him singularly handsome. His manners, when he is in a happy mood, are pleasant and polite. He can converse fluently and entertainingly upon his travels and experiences in the world, and often manifests a large amount of genuine humour, not always unmixed with satire. He is five feet seven inches in height, not very stout, singularly well-built, though by no means powerfully organized. His features are finely chiselled. He has a fine head, expansive brow, expressive blue eyes, fair hair and a very clear skin.

The leading phrenological indications of character seem to

be *Conscientiousness*, manifesting itself in a devout reverence for the moral sense of every individual, a hatred for shams and artifices, and a singular breadth of thought and toleration for everybody's convictions, no matter how singular they may appear to the world. *Benevolence*, expressing itself in a desire to help everybody, without however any particular feeling of regard for relations or fellow countrymen. *Ideality*, manifested in an appreciation of everything beautiful in nature and art, and a great belief in the influence of the beautiful to elevate the human race. *Causality*, evidenced in a determination to know the why and wherefore of all things as far as possible. These four organs seem exceptionally prominent, while Mirthfulness, Self-esteem, Approbativeness, Combativeness and Cautiousness, are all quite sufficiently developed. Continuity, Amativeness, Philoprogenitiveness, and some others are conspicuous by their absence rather than by their presence.

W. J. Colville is a natural Theist: he could not be an Atheist were he to try ever so hard to give up his faith in a Supreme Intelligence. He is a born Spiritualist, and finds it as hard to comprehend Materialism as Materialists find it difficult to discover the reasonableness of Spiritualism. Though fond of music, ritual and all the accessories of ostentatious systems of religion, he has a hatred of all sectarian limitations, and perhaps his intense love of liberty is after all his dominant characteristic. He is quite willing that all others should enjoy their freedom, but he must have his own. He makes a bad servant, but a kind and considerate master. He is not tyrannical or aggressive, but very impatient of all restraint, and therefore succeeds far better on an independent basis than as the hireling of a society.

As an author, W. J. Colville has made a great name, both in England and America. He wields a graceful and a facile pen, but declares himself utterly unable to excel in any literary enterprise, without the assistance of his spirit friends. He has a splendid voice, both for speaking and singing, clear, resonant and penetrating, capable of giving great expression to all he essays to interpret. As an instrumental musician he would never rise into celebrity, by reason of his lack of application to study, it being quite unnatural to him to work in any direction which requires a special effort of his own mind. This trait would be a weakness in many, but in him it is a source of strength, as with his peculiar gifts and sensitive organization, he is now often able to speak at length three times on a Sunday, and five evenings in the week, to large public audiences; also frequently to sing in public, accomplish a great deal of literary work, and take a large amount of out-door exercise without apparent fatigue.

His chosen companions are vigorous young men, and he has a great love of animals, from whom he says he gets more good than from any other quarter. Dogs are his especial favourites, with whom he is always on terms of mutual confidence and affection. He is kind and considerate to children, but has no faculty for training them, until they are approaching maturity. He seems entirely destitute of appreciation of wedded bliss, and, though thoroughly domesticated from childhood, is utterly unfit to enter the married state; and, indeed, he assures us he cannot understand the attraction of the sexes, except theoretically.

He is almost always in the enjoyment of excellent health, and finds his work a pleasure, and is evidently peculiarly cut out by nature to do exactly the work he is so ably performing.

With these few introductory remarks, we refer the reader to the Lectures.

CHARLES BLACKIE MONCRIEFF.

INVOCATION.

O THOU unchanging Spirit! who alone canst never change, while all things change around Thee; Thou who art at the centre of all being, where perfect repose remains in its undisturbed serenity for ever: the generations of men coming and going upon the little planet earth are ever seeking to find Thee out to perfection, and are always failing in their search, because Thou alone art Infinite, and all they are finite. Spirits released from the bonds of flesh still search for Thee, but they to full perfection ne'er discern Thee, for they also are less than infinite; and as Thy perfect Mind and Will govern all things, inimitably and unerringly, from age to age, we can but seek to know Thee more and more, by contemplating the vastness, the majesty, the order, the beauty of Thy creation. We know not how souls at first received their birth from Thee; we cannot fathom the eternal abyss of Thy wisdom and Thy love, but Thy spirit is ever teaching us that the pure in heart shall see Thee, and the experiences of our own souls confirm the heavenly teaching. We come to Thee upon this day, when thousands upon thousands are congregated to dwell upon Thy love in providing means of salvation for man from sin and its consequences. We have gathered in this place to-day, that we may learn of Thee, Thou who art Thyself the Creator, Sustainer, Saviour and Redeemer of men; and we come to Thee as children to a gracious Father and a tender Mother: not to appease Thine ire or supplicate Thee to be gracious, but to strive to remove whatever impediments stand between us and a knowledge of Thyself. We know not all Thy laws, we keep not all we know; we need angelic, yea, divine strength to perfect and sustain us; and as the fair spring flowers open wide their petals to receive the light, as human eyes and ears are ever ready to welcome the sights and sounds of spring-time, and receive new baptisms of nature's lovliness and joy, so may we spiritually open every avenue of our being to receive Thy Light, and by it be blessed indeed for time and for eternity. AMEN.

LONDON LECTURES, 1884.

I.

WHAT THE WORLD NEEDS TO MAKE IT HAPPY.

WE have chosen, as the subject upon which to open up this Course of Lectures, "WHAT THE WORLD NEEDS TO MAKE IT HAPPY." This theme we have not idly or accidentally selected, but have thoughtfully made choice of it as a fitting introduction to all we may have to say in subsequent Discourses.

In order to make ourselves plain to our hearers, it is very necessary that we should at the outset of any special course of teaching, lay down very plainly certain general principles, upon which we intend to build, certain cardinal propositions which it will be needful for you to keep plainly before you, as our subjects unfold themselves in orderly sequence.

We start with the search for Happiness, and lay it down as a central affirmation, that every human spirit, either in this world or any other, seeks happiness: and that happiness can only be found in what may be truly termed a life of spiritual perfection.

The trite saying: "Virtue is its own reward, vice its own punishment," is ever true. But—What is virtue? What is vice? Can we point to any one on earth and say: Behold! he is altogether virtuous, or to any one else and exclaim: Behold! he is altogether vicious? We cannot pronounce any one wholly good, neither can we pronounce any one wholly happy; we can pronounce no one wholly evil, neither can we pronounce any one wholly miserable. Virtue and vice, happiness and misery, are on earth, at least, but relative terms. Absolute happiness and absolute virtue belong only to those celestial or deific states of being, where souls having completed their probationary progress enjoy uninterrupted felicity, as the result of unpolluted integrity and unsullied charity.

The search for happiness is purely natural and thoroughly justifiable. It is so universal that it is shared by all sentient beings without exception. Only very occasionally do we meet one who even professes to be indifferent to happiness; and this indifferentism is so morbid and unhealthy a thing, that we instinctively recoil from it, and cannot be made to see any virtue, beauty, or religion in it. Many persons' religious views are, however, so gloomy and pessimistic, that they wage incessant warfare against the natural and legitimate indulgence of our love of the beautiful, and our desire to enjoy ourselves and to see others enjoying themselves around us. The Puritans, for instance, considered not only dancing, theatricals, and evening parties, but even instrumental music and all other songs than sacred ones, sinful. They proposed to regard the earth as a dreary wilderness, a wretched waste, an arid desert, a vale of tears in which all the elect of God should appear among their fellows with sober countenances, and be known as saints by the gloominess and rigour of their conduct and appearance.

No doubt Cromwell's soldiers, who destroyed all the costly and exquisite works of art they could lay their hands upon, were actuated in part, at least, by a laudable protest against idolatry, which they wished to stamp out, root and branch, through the length and breadth of the land, but an insolent reactionary wave of feeling and action can be only temporarily healthful; it is in itself a storm, a scourge, a pestilence, a consuming fire which sweeps and burns everything before it, and like John the Baptist, who preached repentance only, like Carlyle who did little else than expose the wrongs and injustice in the world, it can never be more than a necessary precursor of some truth yet to dawn, which could never make its advent were it not for the hard and crude preparation which a sturdy iconoclasm has made for it.

Dr. Watts, tinctured with Puritanism though he was, and introducing into his hymnology many verses teaching the severest Calvinistic doctrines, has nevertheless made himself memorable as the author of these beautiful and justly-celebrated lines, forming part of a really charming and inspiring hymn :—

"Religion never was designed to make our pleasures less."

But the contexts very positively show that Dr. Watts' idea of pleasure is not that of the worldling, who speaks of enjoyment as though it were inseparable from expensive living and noisy recreation. He takes the ground that all our true joys must spring from that celestial world towards which we are all tending, and that before we rise to the immortal state beyond the stream of death, a reflected glory from the realms of bliss may light our pathway here, and cause us to enjoy, in anticipation at least, much of the happiness which will be uninterruptedly ours in a higher state of being than the present.

/ It is quite an open question, whether this constant living in the future is practically best or not. The best thinkers of this age are not usually averse to Mr. Moncure D. Conway's theory of an "Earthward Pilgrimage;" though, on the other hand, if earth be all, it is extremely unsatisfactory, as it raises many hopes it never gratifies, and constantly mocks us with delusive dreams of a fruition which can never come. The middle ground between two extremes is ever the wisest and safest stand to take; the golden mean is ever the most desirable position. We need the prospect of results to nerve us to noble endeavours here and now, and we need to give assiduous attention to the duties of the present hour, or we shall never qualify ourselves for future happiness, which is after all but the harvest of life's seed-time here below. /

We find ourselves in conflict perpetually with two directly opposite schools of thought, both of which contain many great and good men and women, with whom personally we have no quarrel, but the fallacy or incompleteness of whose theories we feel bound to expose; as false theories of life are only too likely to give rise to erroneous modes of living, as we cannot expect a conscientious supporter of any theory not to be influenced by that theory in his daily conduct. The Church has always laid immense stress upon mere belief. Believe and be saved, disbelieve and be damned, has been for ages the watchword of orthodoxy. Liberal thinkers very naturally and reasonably object to this wholesale condemnation for eternity as well as time, of all who do not believe the Church dogmas, or place reliance upon a personal saviour and redeemer in the person of Jesus Christ. But though we sympathize most warmly with all who dissent from doctrines their reason cannot accept, we can nevertheless see the rise of the doctrine that salvation is the result of faith, in a very natural experience of human life. The doctrine has its analogy in the affairs of material life. Take an instance: one of you desires to go from London to New York, and you persistently sail in an easterly instead of a westerly direction. You have got into your head that New York lies east from London, and so long as you believe this you will go on sailing east and getting farther and farther away from your desired destination. Some one points out to you your mistake, and causes you to see, acknowledge, and rectify your error, with this result: you at once change your course completely, you convert yourself, or you are converted through the instrumentality of the person who has made you see your error and rectify it, and henceforth you sail west instead of east, and in due time arrive at your journey's end and find yourself safely landed in the port where you desire to be.

You can readily multiply instances to prove that a right faith is necessary to a right life, and that as works are necessary to spiritual growth, and works largely depend on faith, faith may be necessary as a cause while works are its natural effects. The temperance advocate may go on preaching against the use of alcohol, but people will go on manufacturing and drinking it till they see it to be an evil; you may talk as much as you will about temperance legislation and enforced abstinence under penalty attached to disobedience, but laws cannot be passed until people are disposed to pass them, and even if passed while generally unpopular they will be to a great extent evaded, disregarded, and in many cases openly defied. Moral suasion and mental advancement will accomplish in this country far more in a single week than coercive measures in twenty years. People are no longer the children in understanding they were in the dark ages, no longer can they be governed by fear, and made to live soberly because they fear the chastisement of an outraged sovereign. The culture of the intellect and the development of the moral sense in the individual, constitute the pride and glory of the nineteenth century, and all preaching to be lastingly effective must be addressed to the souls and intellects of men, to their sense of right and of utility, not to their craven dread of punishment, or their debasing fear of a divine or human tyrant./

The search for happiness is universal, the instinct of self-preservation is naturally implanted in every living creature: and as no instinct is given to us for naught, as no natural impulse is in itself sinful or unworthy, it is surely justifiable on the part of us all, to do all that in us lies to promote our own happiness and welfare as well as that of others. The mistake has been to regard a purely natural animal instinct as an evidence of supernatural grace. Perhaps no text has been more frequently spoken from in Christian pulpits than this: "What shall we do to be saved?" It has formed a fruitful topic for innumerable tracts and sermons of the most rhapsodic and exciting kind, and yet the occasion of that question being originally asked, by the keepers of the prison where Paul and Silas were confined, according to the Acts of the Apostles, does not necessarily justify the immense stress which evangelical divines invariably lay upon it. We are told that there was a fearful earthquake which caused great alarm to the jailors, and that through its instrumentality and also by the aid of spirit-power, the fettered disciples had their chains broken and were themselves set free. The superstitious and terrified officers of the law shrieked out to the delivered captives: "What shall we do to be saved?" and received the answer: "Believe on the Lord Jesus Christ and ye shall be saved, and all your households." The salvation referred to by Paul and his companion was, undoubtedly, salvation from that fear which made life burdensome, and in the event of a sudden natural upheaval, a burden almost too heavy to be borne.

/ The fear of death is one of the greatest curses of humanity. It arises no doubt from the inscrutable mystery which ever enshrouds man's future, and also from the sense of unpreparedness for life beyond, which oppresses every heart when conscious of duties unfulfilled and time and opportunities for improvement and amendment wasted. Remove all fear of death and of the hereafter from the minds of men, and you have done for the world what ages of work in every other direction could never accomplish. Can intelligent, thinking people be happy or feel any security, with the awful dread of eternal misery constantly hanging over their heads?/ Can any sane and cautious individual erect a homestead at the base of Etna or Vesuvius, and feel contented and secure when at any moment a volcanic eruption may bring death and desolation to himself and all he holds most dear. The fear of death has been and to a large extent still is the nightmare of the world. To assuage this terror and calm this fear, rivers of blood have been outpoured in vain; human as well as animal sacrifices have been offered upon the altars of all religions. Christianity has not been exempt from the terrible charge of murder: the heretics burnt at the stake by Catholics and Protestants alike; the bloody wars engaged in; the cruel massacres perpetrated to appease the wrath of an offended deity, render sickening the pages of history, which record the progress of a religion avowedly under direction of the heavenly Prince of Peace. We condemn no one system more than another; we find fault with no one class of persons more than with others; we attribute much, though not all of the iniquities perpetrated in Religion's sacred name, to the terrible dread of divine wrath, which has so overwhelmed men's minds that they have made frantic attempts to appease the offended Sovereign of the Universe, by slaughtering upon altars dedicated to His name whatever the devotee most highly prized or dearly loved. In this age of the study of comparative theology, we are obliged to place side by side the glories and defects of all the religious systems of the world, so far as we able, and with what result? Surely we are forced to the conclusion that no one system of religion has a monopoly of truth or a monopoly of error, but that all systems have been defiled, even from their inception, with the fearful thought of an angry God and some dreadful outpouring of His wrath in the world to come.

We have just celebrated the Thirty-sixth Anniversary of the advent of Modern Spiritualism, and in addresses appropriate to the occasion have endeavoured to ennumerate some of the most important advantages of Spiritualism to the world. First and foremost among these advantages do we place the revelation Spiritualism makes of the hereafter, and the immense influence it has exerted in freeing the human mind from that enslaving fear of death, which is so widespread and so terrible in many instances. Spiritualism may have intoxicated those who have been too suddenly brought under the searching beams of its stupendous light; some may have been so elated with its consolations, so blinded with its revelations, that so much light has made them dizzy, and they have staggered and fallen by the wayside, while the enemies of Spiritualism have rejoiced over their temporary bewilderment, and proclaimed with the voices of trumpeters, that Spiritualism leads its victims to immorality or the madhouse. But to the great majority of those upon whom its light has shone, its warnings have been equal to its promises, and its faithful delineations of sorrow as well as joy in the spirit-world, have led to sober reflections upon the responsibility attached to human life, and the inevitable results in the future of all acts committed, words spoken, and thoughts encouraged here. Spiritualism is, after all, the only system that can effectually overcome that unfounded or exaggerated fear of death, which is so prevalent in the world, and so direful in its consequences to humanity. No amount of Atheism, Materialism or Agnosticism can do anything more than leave the future life an utter blank, an impenetrable mystery. To disbelieve in a future life, or to doubt there is one, proves nothing; and in the absence of proof to the contrary, orthodoxy may be true after all.

Before we can effectually refute the false theories of our orthodox brethren, we must first prove what there *really is* beyond death; we must clasp hands across the mystic river with our brethren gone before, for only when we can explore the land where they are dwelling, and bring tidings to the world concerning the Realm of Spirit, have we positive, definite knowledge wherewith to silence doubt and put to flight erroneous theories. In the absence of definite knowledge concerning the life after death, any theory may be true; we can never displace an error unless we have a fact to put in its place, which renders it (the error) an impossibility. Let all our teachers remember this when they pour out tirades of abuse against those who differ from them, and hold up to ridicule the opinions and doctrines of others. To prove others wrong is not to prove yourselves right; you must prove that something is true; prove an affirmation, ere you can dethrone an error or destroy a superstition. No error is completely overturned except by a truth, which renders it impossible. You are falsely accused, for instance, of committing some misdemeanour, in a certain place, at a certain time. How is the accusation to be refuted and your reputation restored? Simply by your proving where you really were at that particular time, and if it can be shown to the satisfaction of the court, where you were at that moment, common sense declares you could not have been elsewhere. You have thereby saved your character and escaped fine or imprisonment.

/ Agnosticism is an improvement upon Orthodoxy, in a purely negative sense: it deadens the fear of hell, but who shall say that the sceptic is not oftentimes the most miserable of men? He tells you he does not believe this, that, and the other; but can he *prove* anything to the contrary? What certainty can he have that the very things he denies may not be realities after all. Knowledge not ignorance, certainty not doubt, gives real and lasting happiness, and no one can be said to be truly happy until he has some satisfactory philosophy which can stand by him in foul weather as in fair, never leaving him in his hours of loneliness, depression and well-nigh despair.

Far be it from us to assert that a knowledge of phenomenal Spiritualism is necessary to this result. There are intuitive evidences of the justice of God and the real nature of life here and hereafter, which need no phenomena to make them more secure: but how any thoughtful and affectionate person can be satisfied or happy when he holds orthodox opinions concerning the future, is more than we can imagine. /

A few years ago we knew a lady who had seven children, all of whom she professed to love very dearly. Three of these children were converted, according to her belief, and were members of Christian churches; the other four were "yet in their sins." Two of her sons, both of them "unconverted," were engaged in very dangerous business, and at any moment might be hurried into eternity. This lady said she fully believed that if either or both of her sons should die in their then condition, they would go to hell and remain there for ever; while she and her three other children were secure of heaven. Was this woman concerned about her unconverted children? Apparently not; she dwelt so much upon her own personal security that she paid little heed to the moral state of her sons in peril of eternal doom. And why should she? She professed to love God, and bow in all things to His will. One of her favourite texts, when questioned on this matter, was: "Shall not the judge of all the earth do right? But what is right, if it is not that which is increasingly revealed to man through the moral sense, with growing brightness age after age, as right? Are we to take certain isolated texts and distorted views of Scripture, and cling to them with a death-grip, when they outrage our every sense of rectitude, and at the same time flatly contradict the precept and example of that Great Teacher whom Christendom acknowledges as God made manifest in flesh? Callousness, indifferentism, selfishness: Is this religion? To be satisfied with safety for oneself when others are in danger: Is this nobility? Such consummate selfishness, according to the Gospels, led to the doom of Dives, for whom the cleansing fires of a spiritual Gehenna were necessary to the bringing out of his latent regard for the welfare of his brethren who yet remained on earth. We are told in the Lives of the Saints, that many a holy man has been so overcome when contemplating the wicked in futurity, that though the weather was bitterly cold, his cell unwarmed, and himself most thinly clad, he became so heated with intensity of feeling that the perspiration streamed down him in torrents; and if poor, frail, fallible, imperfect man can be so deeply touched at the mere thought of the sufferings of his fellow-beings, can we for a moment dare to blaspheme the Eternal, by imagining that he can regard as eternally right that which we in our imperfect charity cannot bear to so much as consider with complacency for a single instant?

This brings us to a point where we wish to say something concerning the nature of Happiness in the Spirit Spheres. We are constantly asked if friends in the higher life know how their loved ones suffer on the earth, and in adjacent spheres; if so, can they be happy? Many prevailing conceptions of the spirit-world are remarkably incorrect. Orthodox theories teach that all who die in Christ are instantly at rest, immediately translated to some fair and glorious world where they will sorrow and sigh nevermore. Happiness, however, in the spirit-world depends, as it does on earth, upon inward growth and harmony. Nothing can give us happiness unless we have developed within us power to appreciate and enjoy. A box at the opera is of no use to a deaf man, or to one who cannot enjoy the music. A ticket to a flower show, or a picture gallery, is of no possible service to one who is blind to form and colour, or who has no regard for floral and artistic beauties. Enjoyment is ours when we have earned the right, and developed the power to enjoy, but no sooner. Death is the great emancipator, who sets us all free by his mystic touch, to find our own level: but death does not endow us with either knowledge or spiritual development; these are not consequent upon his icy touch. Happiness in the material world is dependent upon knowledge and contentment, upon usefulness and symmetry, upon ability to discover the use of life, and the disposition to employ every energy in the performance of some useful tasks, which, while they do not overtax or strain the mind, constantly and harmoniously employ its every capability./

Work has been too often associated with the fall of man; we hear that labour is a curse, and that if our first parents had not transgressed the command of God in Eden, 6000 years ago, we should have enjoyed a physical immortality of luxurious indolence and ease. But neither work nor death came into the world by sin, which is any deliberate breaking of a Divine command or natural law; work and death are alike necessary to the evolution of higher and ever higher states of being, and correct views of both work and death (for both are inevitable) are in our opinion essential to the most perfect unfoldment of human nature here and hereafter.

We have already spoken of the fear of death as one of the greatest blights and curses of the world, and have asked you to consider well the importance of a spiritual revelation which explains the part played by death in the evolution of ultimately perfect states of being. We have only to study natural science, to learn how vegetables died, and animals died, before primeval man could walk this planet; and as there can be no discordance between the word and works of Deity, that cannot be a true message from the Infinite, which in any way falsifies the message from the Eternal, which he delivers to us through the agency of his magnificent creation. / We have now to inquire: Is not work as inseparable from human happiness as it is from human usefulness? Our answer is an unqualified affirmation. Work and happiness are inseparable. Idleness and misery go hand-in-hand, and if we are truly intent on making ourselves and others happy, we shall carefully see to it that as far as can be, every human being is usefully and appropriately employed.

We hear in these days a great deal about the sin of

drunkenness. You organize vast Temperance organizations, Blue Ribbon Armies, &c., &c., but do the great masses of temperance advocates, sincere and philanthropic though they may be, weigh sufficiently the significance and importance of the view of the subject taken by Henry George, and many other earnest social revolutionists? Henry George's remedy for every ill is "*Land Nationalization.*" You may not all agree with him in his views upon land distribution, but no really earnest thinker can fail to coincide entirely with his views on Home influence. Mr. George very truly says, that while intemperance is the cause of a vast amount of misery, intemperance is oftener produced by unhappiness at home than unhappiness at home is produced by intemperance. The mind naturally seeks comfort and recreation somewhere. If after the toil and worry of the day, your husbands, fathers, brothers, sons, and lodgers come home to an uninviting substitute for a home, can you expect them to remain sober and steady, and stay at home when they have practically no home to stay in?

We are constantly being asked to point those outside the Spiritual Movement to Churches, Hospitals, Orphanages, &c., erected and sustained by Spiritualists. We are told that the immense Charitable Institutions of England and America are the pride and glory and direct outgrowth of Christianity. If they are, let us credit Christianity with having done *some* good, but let us strive to accomplish yet more good than our Christian brethren have accomplished. *Our* work must be to create and sustain bright and happy homes, and we shall never have these till work is regarded as an honour, instead of a dishonour, while all useful occupations, and those who engage in them, are placed on a footing of rational equality, equally honoured and equally respected. Every sincere and conscientious worker should be regarded as a necessary part of human society; so soon as this is, so soon we shall, perhaps, begin to understand what is really meant by that "Christ" about which we hear so much as a person, but which the early Christians regarded as a body of faithful and united workers, of whom Jesus was the head. But as the foot cannot say to the hand, nor the eye to the ear: I have no need of thee; as members veiled and unseen are as necessary to the whole frame as ever the most conspicuous and ornamental can be, so in an ideal state of society, he who cleanses the streets and he who discourses eloquently on matters pertaining to religion; she who with broom in hand sweeps clean the kitchen and she who with piano or easel makes vocal or beautiful the drawing-room, must be accounted as absolutely necessary, the one to the other, and both to all. Imagine Mr. Gladstone deprived of the assistance rendered him by the sons and daughters of toil! He would have to spend all his time and strength in making provision for his material wants. With what result? He would be unable to devote time, talent and energy, as he does now, to the affairs of State. Mr. Gladstone's tailor, baker and cook are just as essential to his Parliamentary eloquence as he is himself.

We throw this fact into especial prominence, to enforce the dignity of labour, and to do what in us lies to reconcile all persons to their state in life, no matter what it may be. There are many who complain of drudgery, and sigh for more exalted stations. We hear no end of grumblers, finding fault with their work, and sighing over its uselessness. They are clerks, or servants, or agriculturists, or housekeepers: their days are all spent in making up parcels, and delivering them, in weighing out provisions, in cleaning rooms, and mending clothes. To what end is all this turmoil, this worry, this unceasing strife? Martha, in the kitchen, is disposed to envy Mary, seated at the footstool of some great teacher, drinking in words of inspiration as they fall from his heaven-anointed lips; but has Martha any reason to complain? (If Mary's is the "better part," it is only so because Mary has attained to such a height of spirituality, that she can enjoy the sublimity of the Great Teacher's utterances. If Martha's mind were as receptive to spiritual things as Mary's, she might enjoy equal communion with a master-mind, intuitively, if not outwardly. And this brings us to that point where we see practically illustrated the utter impossibility of simply local heavens and hells, conferring happiness or misery upon their occupants.

Let us take the case of a modern Martha and Mary. A pattern Martha is a born housekeeper; one who is never so happy as when she is dusting and sweeping, baking, ordering, superintending. Her house is her palace, and she is the happy and active queen, never so content as when she is controlling all things under her, and making them serve her purpose. The pattern Mary is a student: she is always engrossed in artistic and literary occupations; her mind is not on the kitchen, but on the study. Let these two women change places. and they would be out of their native elements. As well try and make fish fly in the air and birds swim in the water, as put these women in each other's places. The housekeeper's happiness is as a housekeeper. If it be genuine and enduring it consists in this, that she realizes the necessity of the work in which she is engaged. She does not, like Martha of Bethany, trouble herself about providing a great many more dishes than her guests require, neither does she attach such supreme importance to domestic affairs that she loses sight of the value of higher and more directly spiritual pursuits. She rather takes into account the relative value of diverse occupations, realizes her own ability to fill a certain niche in the great temple of humanity; and she fills her niche admirably, knowing that even though a humble and minor one, if it were left unoccupied all the rest of the building would be unfinished, and, perhaps, insecure. The pattern Mary never despises her sister's occupations, never looks down on those less educated, and less interested in æsthetic pursuits than herself. She acknowledges her indebtedness to her Martha-like sisters, and they—if they are intelligent, humane women—return the compliment, and let the Marys see how indispensable they are to them, and to all the brethren.

The secret of a happy life, is that the liver feels himself or herself to be engaged in some useful, necessary and elevating work: and if at times life's burdens press very heavily, and the load seems almost too grievous to be borne, the tried spirit takes comfort with two blessed assurances: one is, that whatever we do faithfully as our contribution to the world's store, blesses some one; and the other is, that all our sufferings while they have a vicarious have also a personal value. When we have learned all the lessons that can be taught us by temptation, suffering and trial, we shall know no more of trials and temptations. Every sorrow is a part of our education, and no one can ever be truly resigned to life, until he feels that every burden imposed upon him is both for his own and others' good.

Our last thought carries us beyond the realms of time and sense, beyond the murky shades of material existence, to the beatified spirits whom we call angels or celestial beings, who, while they are cognizant of human sorrow, are not made sad by it, and while they mingle even in the life of the hells, are not contaminated thereby. One of the greatest drawbacks to Spiritualism in the feeling of many is, that it teaches that the loved ones who have gone to the spirit-world, are not so fully at rest as orthodoxy has said they were. It is difficult for some minds to reconcile the discrepancy between the doctrine of perfect happiness in the angelic spheres, and the acquaintance with human misery which angels must have if they are ministering spirits to those yet on earth. Of course, it is needless to declare that we know of progression beyond the grave, and that all happiness is measurable and increases with the spiritual development of the individual; but when happiness is complete, malice, hatred, and all uncharitableness are completely eliminated from the breast of the perpetually happy spirit. That spirit is never exacting, never self-seeking, always working for others' good, bestowing no single thought on self-aggrandizement. Such a spirit has attained to the celestial degree of life. He may not know everything; an infinity of knowledge may yet be his to grasp, but wishing no ill to any, loving all tenderly and truly wherever he goes—be it even into haunts of deepest crime—he remains pure as the light, which shining into the foulest dungeon is uncorrupted still.

Spirits who have not yet fully out-grown their moral imperfections, are like water—they can be polluted; those who have overcome every temptation and conquered in the fray, are like the pure unsullied light—go where they will they are forever unsullied. Their sight and knowledge of human misery does not really distress them, because they have themselves passed through it, reaped its advantages, and have therefore learned how essential it is to the rounding out of character and development of the moral nature. The angel is like the friend on a mountain-top, while you, his charge, are in the valley. You cannot see more than a step before you; he see the fair pastures and the glorious homes ahead. He does not weep over your lot, he does not pity you or condole with you; he spurs you on over the Hill Difficulty, through the Valley of Humiliation, on to the Land of Beulah, and at length to the Celestial City.

When one can look at life with angel's eyes, and see its

purpose and its outcome, then good-bye to every repining word and discontented mood. If we would be truly happy in this or any other world or life, we must strive earnestly to bless rather than to be blessed, to confer happiness rather than to obtain it, and in so doing we shall develop a Kingdom of Heaven within us, which we can carry with us wherever we go, as our unfading source of joy for ever and ever.

We leave with you for your consideration a new motto: "Strive to be a Glow-worm!" while we leave it to yourselves, in your quiet hours, to work out the meaning of the precept.

IMPROMPTU POEM.

THE CROSS-BEARER.

I ASKED of the angels, bright and fair: what work have you for me?
I told them, the heaviest cross I'd bear, to set my brethren free
From their load of want, and pain, and care. But the angels answered me:
"We call you not to bear such cross; there's your burden, can you see
That tiny cross, so near the ground, which is among the rushes found."

I gazed with wond'rous great amaze upon that cross so small;
For I had asked a mightier task—I had asked the angels all,
Some great and glorious work to do, that should startle all mankind:
And when I raised that tiny cross, surprised its weight to find
Far heavier than I thought 'twould be, life's burdens great and tall,
I prayed the angels to exchange my load for one less small.

For, said I, Oh! if I may but take a burden of precious gold,
Its very glory will bear me up; that heavier cross I'll hold
Most willingly, and bear it thro' the desert, bleak and wild,
But give me not this tiny cross, so heavy for a child;
Yet so unlovely 'tis withal, its beauty none can see,
And, if I bear it, what reward will ever come to me?

A meek-faced angel, clad in robes of dazzling, snowy white,
With coronet of lilies fair, and jewels, sparkling bright,
Bowed down with kind and tender smile to me, her erring child,
And said, "You but deceive yourself; this cross, that you despise
And think so lowly, yet will yield a harvest passing good,
Flowers and fruits, most beautiful, will spring from that bare wood!"

"But," said I, "Angel! may I not some glorious burden bear?
Behold those martyrs, radiant-browed, with glorious light for hair!
Behold philanthropists who stand among the highest there,
Where all the spirits look so bright—what burdens did they bear?
Oh! may I not, like them, go down to the weary earth below,
And carry e'en the heaviest load, that I like them may grow?"

Straightway, as tho' with fairy wand, the angel touched my eyes,
And showed to me the earthly life of those in Paradise;
And one, more bright than all the rest, advancing close to me,
Revealed her work in earthly form, when she in drudgery
Had toiled and slaved, both night and day, to keep a cellar clean,
Protect twelve children from the frost, while scarcely could she glean,
By honest industry, enough to keep fire in the grate,
To feed and warm the helpless ones who on her toil must wait.

"And was that all?" I then enquired, "That God did ask of thee,
So gifted, beautiful, and wise, of such divine degree;
Wert thou not numbered 'mid the throng of those the world counts great,
And did not Emperors and Kings adorn thy form in state,
And summon thee to palace halls, to sing thy songs so grand,
Or hang thy pictures on their walls, o'er all some mighty land?"
"Nay," answered she, "it was not so; my spirit highest rose,
When far from grandeur and display, it dwelt 'mid human woes."

Then to the angel straight I turned—To my wise and gentle guide,
And eagerly did take from her, from yonder paradise,
The lowly cross I bore on earth throughout a life of pain,
Till I, by blessing other lives, the heavenly spheres might gain.

This little story from the spheres, I bring to you to-day,
That while on earth in want and toil your spirits need to stay,
This blessed truth may buoy them up, above the clouds of pain:
The lowliest workers oftentimes the heights of heaven gain!

BENEDICTION.

God grant that all, both high and low, as men count low and great,
May follow Charity's blest law, and find heaven's pearly gate;
And then with earthly journeys o'er, where every trial doth cease,
May each and all, at God's right hand, enjoy eternal peace!

II.

SEVEN STEPS TO SPIRITUAL PERFECTION.

(*Delivered, Good Friday, April* 11*th*, 1884.)

GOOD FRIDAY has always been consecrated in the Christian world to solemn commemoration of the sufferings and death of that great hero of the Gospels, Jesus the Christ, around whose memory so much affectionate devotion clusters, wherever persons are to be found who can appreciate loyalty to conviction under the most trying circumstances possible, conscientious, steadfast, unselfish devotion to truth and the highest interests of humanity, no matter to how great an extent self-sacrifice may be necessary to the maintenance of this unswerving and God-like integrity.

The hero of the Gospels has been deified quite naturally. His deification is as easy to be accounted for as the simplest forms of hero worship. (Veneration is an organ of the human brain quite as indispensable to man's being as any other organ can be, and the cultivation of the religious instinct should always be included in every scheme of education, which lays any claim to being perfect or even good.) Objection may be made by Secularists and others to the use of the Bible in public schools supported by public money, and indeed to every form of teaching that can with any degree of truth be denominated sectarian, but widely as persons may differ concerning every non-essential, (the great essentials of character are everywhere insisted upon as necessary to the best and happiest life on earth, whether people believe or disbelieve in consciousness hereafter.)

The beauty of the moral character of Jesus can never be overestimated; criticize his conduct on certain exceptional occasions as you will, these exceptions the more strikingly prove the rule, and show him to us all the more conspicuously in his accustomed robe of gentleness and humility. If he occasionally gave way to impetuosity or hastiness of temper, if he once in a while seems arrogant and self-asserting, these few and occasional blemishes in a character usually extraordinarily near perfection, make the general features of the character all the more prominent and remarkable.

We know quite well that there are many in these days who will tell you that Jesus is a myth; that no such man ever existed, or that if he did exist, contemporaneous history is silent concerning him, and therefore nothing whatever can be with certainty attributed to a man who, if not a myth, was an almost unknown personage during his earthly lifetime. Did we teach the necessity of belief in Christ as indispensable to salvation; did we regard the Gospels as final and in the highest sense authoritative on all subjects of which they treat; did we pledge ourselves to accept everything and reject nothing put forward as truth by the Evangelists; did we acknowledge no other court of appeal than the Scriptures; did we, as our orthodox friends are apt to do, weigh and measure all things by the biblical standard, to the shutting out of all modern inspiration,—we might find a difficulty in treating of the influence of Jesus upon the world, unless we could prove with certainty, not only the fact of his personal existence but also the miraculous manner of his life, death and resurrection. Having, however, taken no such premises as our orthodox brethren take, our task is very much lighter than theirs; as it is ours to deal with the character as it stands out in history, independent of any special theories concerning the original, while it is theirs to refer to Jesus as "very God of very God, begotten of his Father before all worlds were made."

Let us consider the character of Jesus as we would that of any other man, or of any great hero of romance. Some people are very anxious to draw hard and fast lines between works of fact and works of fiction, and between what is founded on fact and what is purely imaginative. No clear lines can ever be traced in these cases. Fact and fiction are so interwoven, so mysteriously interblent, that it is impossible to say where one leaves off and the other begins. So-called fiction is often fact in a fancy costume, as facts are not materially altered by change of time and place, or by any alteration whatever in the mere garb in which they are presented to the public.

No one can write higher than his experience or inspirations carry him, and no one can be inspired with anything beyond the experiences of the inspirer. Sometimes, if you are novelists, you will find yourselves making ideal characters, by taking parts of a great many characters which are real to you in your experiences through life, and throwing them together till they form your hero or heroine. Sometimes, if you are mediumistic, you will write almost automatically; you will at least follow some impulse so strong that it is practically irresistible. Frequently these inspirations come to you from spiritual beings who, when they lived on earth, underwent exactly the experiences of which you find yourselves compelled to write. The theory of Inspiration needs liberalizing and unfolding; it is so narrow in many minds that it leads multitudes of intelligent persons to taboo the facts of spiritual communion altogether.

These remarks, bearing somewhat upon the "Theological Conflict" in which many of you have been interested lately, we have merely introduced to let you perceive as plainly as possible the views we take of mere disputations concerning what is historical; when we have practically to deal with great propositions of a moral character, which neither lose nor gain anything in the estimation of true philosophers, by being connected with or disassociated from any particular country, period, or personage.

"Seven Steps to Spiritual Perfection" is the topic we have announced for this morning, and as the churches throughout the length and breadth of the land are at this time considering the seven last sentences or words of Jesus on the cross, we intend to take these up very briefly, one by one, and see what spiritual truth they may contain, and what important lessons they may be capable of conveying to those who study them.

We ask you, in imagination, to put yourselves in the place of those who witnessed the wondrous spectacle of the crucifixion of an innocent man between two malefactors, whose only crime was his too plain-speaking concerning matters which it was to the interest of the priests and civil rulers to have kept quiet, that power might remain vested exclusively in their own hands. There is nothing improbable in the story told by the Evangelists. Crucifixion was a Roman mode of punishment, and Judea was at one time a Roman province, under Roman jurisdiction. The putting to death of a heretic, who was also in insurrection, is not difficult to realize, when the tragic end of Socrates and martyrs innumerable is still on record.

We are told concerning Jesus, that on the Sunday before his Passion, he was triumphantly introduced into Jerusalem, accompanied by the hosannas of the multitude, and the adoration of the very people who only five days later would shout: "Crucify him, crucify him!" The incidents are so graphically portrayed, that if any one should style the Gospels romances, they must admit that they are not only most cleverly written, but that they abound in telling portraits of human nature, as it is all the world over and in all periods of human history.

(Popular applause is no criterion of real merit, and no spiritual worker should ever be anxious for it. Very often applause is granted to mediocrity and withheld from exceptional talent; because while a multitude are ready to appreciate commonplaceness, only the very few are, among prepared minds, ready to benefit by a supernal revelation of truth.)

The great struggle in the closing days of the life of Jesus, seems to be between the old Messianic idea of a deliverer interpreted materially and interpreted spiritually. The orthodox party among the Jews was determined to literalize every prediction of the olden prophets, therefore, whenever they were disposed to regard Jesus as an inspired teacher, they tried to make him a king. Their ideas of atonement, or redemption, were eminently vicarious or substitutionary, for no matter how sunk in materiality and injustice they might be, they constantly expected a man to rise up among them of the house and lineage of David, who should put himself at the head of an army which should soon discomfit all the enemies of Israel, and lead his victorious troops to a complete triumph over the Romans, to whom the Jews considered it a great disgrace to be in bondage. The spiritual, or reform party, contended for an interior or moral interpretation of the Law and Prophets. They declared that all prophecies were made conditionally, that they referred to Israel only so far as Israel obeyed the divine law; for should Israel rebel against Jehovah, then her doom was certain, and even greater, because of the opportunities and advantages she had had over all the other races of mankind.

Great opportunities necessarily imply great responsibilities. If you have ten talents, you must account for ten; but if only two are entrusted to you, then only two more than these are you expected to win. The unprofitable servant was not upbraided because of his slender endowments; he had one talent, but used none, and for this reason he was cast into outer darkness, where there is weeping and gnashing of teeth.

(Jesus taught the unpopular doctrine of the divine impartiality. The God whom he worshipped and revealed was a Universal Parent, not the leader and patron of one single privileged clan. Strange though it may seem, there is a deep-rooted prejudice in the human mind against any philosophy which teaches that God and his laws respect no one person or nation more than another. Teach divine favouritism; teach that some persons are elect, or that some will be rewarded for efforts which are not recognised in others; teach that those who have not encountered the manifold temptations of life shall, on the score of simple abstinence from sins they have had no inclination to commit, enter the highest heavens immediately they leave their material frames, and you may count upon a large congregation of Pharisees, who will applaud you to the echo, and adore you for your orthodoxy; but preach the highest truth which appeals to your inmost sense of right, and your followers will surely be in a minority, and if you live where freedom is not secured by law, you stand a great chance of meeting the fate of many a true reformer, who has consulted conviction rather than policy.

Jesus had boldly told the most reputable and influential citizens of Jerusalem that they were "whited sepulchres." He had boldly rebuked them for their long prayers and fastings, which they thought must surely win the favour of heaven and pardon for all their sins.) He had turned out those who bought and sold in the courts of the Temple, where it was customary to take advantage of the ignorance of those who came from the country, to offer sacrifices in the holy city, and did not know the marketable value of the birds and animals kept for sale to those who visited the temple from the surrounding country.

Some people have found fault with the harshness displayed by Jesus on this occasion, but righteous indignation against wrong is in no sense inconsistent with universal charity. No one who is truly charitable can see a wrong and not endeavour to redress it; no one imbued with a strong sense of justice, and having a concern for the welfare of others, can fail to express indignation at a course of action which pauperizes those in humble circumstances, taking a mean and unjust advantage of their necessities and ignorance; for the very concern for these people will lead to a vigorous protest against such courses of action as do harm to the multitude, and increase the ill-gotten gains of haughty and tyrannical monopolists. (Laxity of morals, and indifference to the wrongs of others, can be no part of charity, as true charity can never be unjust, and true justice can never be uncharitable.)

We are told that the first words uttered by Jesus on the cross were: "Father! forgive them, for they know not what they do." In these words human sin is attributed to human ignorance, and the plea for forgiveness is based upon the ignorance of the wrong-doer.

Now, are we justified in attributing sin to ignorance in all cases? Is not very much evil resultant from deliberate wrong desire? We may argue the point as we will, and arrive, perhaps, at widely divergent conclusions in some instances, but all moralists bent on improving society, must agree that our work is to remove evils, not to punish evil-doers; except by the administration of such chastisement as is indispensable to the overcoming of the love of evil in the heart of the wrong-doer.

(We can scarcely go too far in applying the doctrine of Necessity to all persons except ourselves, because we cannot tell what their temptations may have been, how hardly they have struggled to overcome, and how futile their best endeavours may have been. We can know something of ourselves, and our own experiences; our moral sense is given to us as a lever to lift us higher, and it is never necessary to believe in an offended Deity, to account for the existence and activity of the moral sense, or conscience, within man. This conscience is the voice of the soul, pleading to be delivered from carnal bondage. Matter is a prison-house for the soul, until such time as the spirit has vanquished it; then it becomes the ready tool and obedient vassal in the hands of its rightful controller.)

To attribute human sin to ignorance, and to style it folly, is quite rational, even should we take the worst possible view of human nature, and consider man at his lowest as being utterly selfish, actuated by no motives higher than concern for personal welfare. (Even were we all consummately selfish, we should have no interest in committing crime or depredation, did we really know what was necessary to our own individual welfare. No adage is truer than that old and oft-quoted one: "Virtue is its own reward; vice its own punishment." We are confronted with the mystery of pain and evil in the world, and often ask: Are these things reconcilable with the perfect wisdom and love of the Supreme Being, about which we hear so much? Absolute, positive, or eternal evil cannot be reconciled with a Supreme Being of infinite justice, as there can be but one absolute, positive, eternal, or primal state of being in the universe. If it be good, there can only be relative and temporal evil; if that primal state be evil, then goodness must have begun in time, and must be destined to expire with the lapse of ages.)

The Persians endeavoured at one time to account for the coexistence of good and evil by what is known as a system of Dualism. They worshipped Ormuzd and Ahriman conjointly. Ormuzd was said to be the Creator and Source of light and good, while Ahriman was regarded as the Fount of darkness and evil; but there cannot be in nature two such rival powers; and this the most enlightened among the Persians clearly saw when they foretold the ultimate and complete subjugation of evil to good and darkness to light, as only Good and Light are positive existences in all the boundless realms of space.

The importance of Universalism can never be overestimated, as it has a direct moral bearing upon every theory of reform and act of life. We know full well that many Materialists and many Calvinists are most excellent people, and their efforts are exceptionally praiseworthy in many instances, as they rise above their respective deities in their daily conduct. The God of Calvin is an angry, capricious spirit, whose tyranny far outweighs his graciousness; the "Nature" of the Materialist is a soulless force, a blind destiny, an inexorable fate, possessing neither justice nor compassion. We cannot but admire the philanthropy of persons who are better than their creeds, but these very persons exemplify in their own lives the fallacy of their theories. In them goodness of heart certainly does atone for errors of the head; but where is the profound thinker who does not desire to see a true and lasting union, on a rational and moral basis, effected between the affections and the intellect? We are well aware that sectarian efforts can never accomplish this. Denominational Universalism in America is considered by some stagnant or at best but slightly progressive; still it is admitted on every hand that Hosea Ballou, Murray and many other brave pioneers who fought manfully for the doctrine of universal salvation, at a time when to avow one's belief in the boundlessness of the love of God was to awaken in its direst fury the almost fiendish wrath of bigoted adherents to the system of Calvin, in New England, have exerted a vastly wider influence upon the thought of America, and indeed upon the whole civilized world, than any sectarian scheme could possibly have done, no matter how successful. The very idea of the universality of God's fatherhood and man's brotherhood, must have a tendency towards the unification of human interests and sympathies. If we are all fellow travellers to the same goal, all fellow sufferers, fellow pilgrims, all regarded with equal kindness by the Eternal Mind, we must, surely, unless we utterly fail to inwardly realize what we outwardly profess, be stimulated to such efforts for the promotion of the general good of the human family, as may make the self-denying love of a saviour something infinitely more to us than a beautiful dream, a lovely fairy tale, an ancient legend of singular pathos, or, what is much less, considered morally, a mere relic of ancient superstitions and phantasies.

In due course during this series of Lectures, we shall devote an hour to a special consideration of the presumed zodiacal origin of Christianity, and shall proceed to show how utterly incomplete and unsatisfactory are theories of "equinoctial christolatry," which pretend to account for the Gospel narratives. We do not deny that the very ancient Egyptians, or even that pre-historic races, had their conceptions of Deity, their belief in incarnate deities, and their theories of rewards and punishments after death, and that Christianity, even in its original simplicity, that the religion of Jesus itself perpetuated many old-world ideas, and endorsed many ancient precepts.

The beauty of the religion of Jesus is its eclectisism and its catholicity. Were it a distinct revelation, utterly separated by impassable barriers from all other religions, it would not have answered to the spiritual and social needs of mankind; neither would it have promoted unity of sentiment and universal toleration among men. God can have no favourites. A Hottentot or a Negro must be quite as sacred in the eyes of Infinite Goodness as a polished Anglo-Saxon. The barbarian and the civilizee, the Jew and the Gentile, are alike precious in the sight of Infinite Love and Wisdom; and he whose painful death all Christians commemorate to-day, taught nothing more plainly than the absolute impartiality of the Eternal Mind. It is quite erroneous to suppose that the idea of God's fatherhood originated with Jesus, or that his teachings were in all instances more than sweet echoes from many an old refrain; but what we have to consider to-day is not so much the antiquity or the origin of a precept, as the intrinsic value of a command or example itself.

The old bases are shifting; we tremble for the fate of those who repose confidence in miracles and testimony only, for so obscure is the testimony and so bewildering the explanations of miracles, given by those who would make religion stand or fall upon the basis of authority of an ecclesiastical kind, that every fresh scientific discovery and every new development of advanced thought in any community, deals another blow which the old fortresses and bulwarks of sand cannot resist, without being severely shaken and often well-nigh shattered by the magnitude of the billows which assail them. But when we build upon the rock, how different it is with us! How coolly and bravely we can watch the fury of the storm, and smile upon the breakers as they spend their strength and fury in futile efforts to remove our edifice, whose foundations are upon the rock of ages; nay, within that rock, imbedded in the very nature of the Power which governs and sustains the universe. We can afford to be patient and sweet-tempered, when we know that our opponents must necessarily take up our positions eventually; but the most lovely disposition is apt to become soured by repeated endeavours to champion a doomed and a dying cause. The majesty of the Gospel hero was never so conspicuous as when impaled upon the cross: he, in all the sublimity and invincibility of conscious rectitude, does not defy or malign but compassionates, forgives, and prays for his enemies. A truly great character can never stoop to feel resentment against personal enemies, though righteous indignation against wrong is never inconsistent with the divinest and deepest charity.) Jesus does not say one solitary word against his persecutors; the utmost he expresses is compassion and sorrow for their weakness and their folly. The burden of his prayer is: O Father! do not make them suffer for the wrong they have done to me. It would intensify my agony a thousand-fold, were I to feel that my accusers should suffer because they have thus in their blindness put me to grief and shame.

In one light, at least, this prayer may be regarded as sentimental simply, but the sentiment is so pure, so lofty, so worthy of a celestial spirit, that though it is from one standpoint open to possible criticism, it leads us at once to another point in our subject, intimately associated with the general topic; and that is, to an inquiry into the uses of suffering. We may ask, with all reverence, was that prayer of Jesus answered, or must it be refused acceptance at the throne of justice? Our answer is two-fold, and perhaps at first sight paradoxical. The prayer was answered doubtless in the spirit, but in the letter it must be denied, in so far as this, that the penalty due to sin can never be cancelled, never can be borne for one by another; because the penalty itself is a necessary part of the scheme of redemption from the love and practice of evil to the love and practice of virtue.

Take the case of your own children. These words may reach some tender, loving parents, whose very affection for their offspring compells them to be stern. Your boy wishes to play truant, but you force him to school, not because you are unmoved by his tears and entreaties to be allowed to play, but because in your superior wisdom and better judgment, you foresee most disastrous consequences resulting in the future from an encouragement of an unhealthy propensity, to make work subordinate to play, and amusement the sovereign good of existence. You have a very dear child, who sometimes steals, sometimes acts deceitfully, sometimes is disobedient or untruthful, and though it grieves you to the heart to punish her, you chastise her because you plainly see that unless she is made to suffer for her errors, she will go on repeating them. (It is not necessary for you to judge motives, it is never just to put the worst construction upon the conduct of anyone. Give everyone the benefit of the doubt; you had far better err on the side of leniency than too harsh criticism, and it is indeed true that we often help to make people what we consider them already to be. Still, though it is both uncharitable and unjust ever to attribute human sin and folly to the worst motives which can possibly actuate the transgressor, we have to grapple with an evil which if unsubdued will cause the perpetrator of such evil an incalculable amount of suffering in the future.

Our view of Deity presents the Eternal to us as a Being of perfectly pacific and complacent justice, the serenity of whose nature can never be disturbed by a single jarring sentiment; who knows neither passion, pride, anger nor love of glory; a Being who, instead of creating a universe for his own glory, as men count glory, created it out of pure beneficence, and governs it by laws, which when fully understood will be admired and loved by every conscious being.)

Spinoza suggests that this is the only possible universe, while the laws governing it are the only possible laws, and while we cannot take our stand with Spinoza in all his deductions, we nevertheless can trace in such a declaration, a very vivid glimpse of the divine character, as revealed in the persons of the purest minds with whom we have ever associated, or of whom we have ever heard. (We deem no conception of the Divine character so high as that which treats of God as a perfect Unit, in whose all-embracing Justice, Love and Wisdom—like two hemispheres—are blended into one eternal orb of light. When we speak of the world, do we speak of the Eastern hemisphere, or of the Western only: do we not speak of both together? Two hemispheres are necessary to one sphere. A sphere cannot exist apart from two hemispheres, but hemispheres can be conceived of apart from spheres.

Now, it seems to us that Justice is, and ever must be, the perfect sphere of Deity. Ask us for a definition of Justice, and we define it as Love and Wisdom: no more Love than Wisdom, no more Wisdom than Love. This thought concerning Justice would not only revolutionize all orthodox theories of the object and nature of future punishment; it has power also to completely re-model every law and institution having for object the correction of social sinners. To remit penalty, to do away with chastisement, is the height of cruelty; but to adjust all penalties to the needs of mankind, to so improve prisons that a prison is transformed into a school and palace of industry, is surely to keep clearly before us the only two justifiable reasons for submitting any to the pain of incarceration, *viz.*, the reformation of the offender and the protection of society.)

If Jesus intended to petition his Heavenly Father to remit the penalty necessarily consequent upon transgression, he was humane but not wise; but if he intended by the utterance of such a prayer aloud, even in the hearing of his bitterest persecutors, to set an example of perfect forbearance, and to present to the world a philosophy of evil worthy of the deepest consideration and world-wide application, then his wisdom and humanity are alike revealed, and his example is indeed worthy of all imitation, so long as sin and sorrow continue to perplex mankind. The words of the dying are invariably treasured as no other utterances are. There is a sanctity about the final scene of earthly life, which invests the chamber of death with a peculiar and most touching solemnity; and were we to see no other good in the death of Jesus than the inspiration to human forbearance, arising from the record of this first sentence of Jesus on the cross, so wide reaching may be the benefits of that single sentence, that to utter it under such circumstances would explain for ever the utility of the tremendous sacrifice on Calvary.

Vicarious suffering offers insurmountable obstacles to many who are for ever vainly endeavouring to harmonize the decrees of Infinite Justice with the miserably unsatisfactory theories of life, invented by Orthodoxy on the one hand and Materialism on the other. Both these systems are to us self-evidently false, because they contradict the facts of nature in innumerable instances. The sense of justice, innate in man, the conception of perfect justice and unbounded loving-kindness now becoming more universal day-by-day, are in themselves testimony to the existence of a God, such as neither the orthodox Christian nor the Atheist recognises or has yet found in nature. (When Thomas Paine turned from the lesser Bible to the greater,—when he forsook allegiance to the letter of a volume called the "Word of God," though written by frail and fallible men, no one knows just when or how, and turned to the sublimities of the universe, and found a perfect God revealed through Nature, compelling him to become a Deist, he believed in so large a revelation that he could never narrow his mind to accept a smaller revelation. in the ecclesiastical sense of its being miraculous or special,—people called him, and many still call him, an infidel. If to be faithful to the moral sense and unfaithful to the traditions of the elders, is heresy or infidelity, then Jesus was an arch-heretic, an arch-infidel, and was put to death by Roman soldiery at the instigation of Jewish Pharisees, because God was to him greater than Cæsar, and the living spirit of the ever-speaking Eternal, of more value than Rabbinical interpretations of what constitutes divine revelation.

Whenever one rises to so broad and lofty a conception of truth that puny minds cannot explore the whole of one's horizon, then that spiritual discoverer is pronounced either a blasphemer or insane. It is mere absurdity to say Jesus was either God or an impostor, because he made himself equal with God. He did nothing of the kind. To say that he did is to agree with his blind and fanatical persecutors, and utterly fail to grasp the spiritual meaning of those words of his which unfold a doctrine of the divine indwelling, utterly beyond the comprehension of those whose mental eyes are so dim, that at best to use a Gospel metaphor, they "see men as trees walking." The very fact of Jesus addressing a Power superior to himself, and calling that power The Father, is proof positive to any common-sense critic, unwarped by theological prejudice, that Jesus believed devoutly in a God, who was his God as well as the God of the rest of mankind, his Father as well as the Father of all humanity.)

Throughout the Gospels according to Matthew, Mark, and Luke, the phrase "son of man" is constantly employed by Jesus when speaking of himself. It is only in the fourth Gospel, which commences as no history or biography would ever commence, that he seems to be conscious of his own importance, and to be working in any way for his own glorification. (The fourth Gospel is both a Grecian and a Gnostic document, and savours so conspicuously of the Platonic doctrine concerning the *Logos*, that any student familiar with the classics can trace a decided parallel between Platonism and Johannism. Gnosticism made its advent, it is true, after the introduction of Christianity into Europe, but such an advent of Gnosticism was but a reappearance of a very ancient school of philosophy.

The much vaunted Agnosticism of to-day, is of course the

only possible system which can be correctly speaking an antidote to Gnosticism, as Spiritualism is an antidote to Materialism, Atheism an antidote to Theism, and *vice versa*. Socrates was most certainly condemned to drink the hemlock, by reason of his determination to enlighten the Athenian youth concerning the inner meaning of the prevailing Mythology. Jesus was to Galilee what Socrates was to Greece; both teachers conformed to the scholastic as well as the universal mode of conveying instruction. Jesus spake to his immediate followers in parables which he interpreted to them only, while to the multitude he taught in parables which he did not interpret, because had he done so he would have been, to use his own powerful Kabalistic language, "casting pearls before swine," and giving "holy things to dogs." Though up to a certain point Jesus adopted the classic method in the conveyance of spiritual truth, he aroused the ire of the priests and scribes against him by reason of his persistent attempts to enlighten all men upon the mysteries of the Kingdom of Heaven: this Kingdom being a kingdom to be established upon the earth, in which spiritual knowledge and power should take the place so long usurped by arbitrary temporal and ecclesiastical despotism.

It is a very open question, indeed, with many, as to whether the universalization of educational advantages tends to the uplifting of a people morally or not. It is open to question, whether illiteracy and morality of a very high order may not and often do not go hand-in-hand. Your boot-black may be a superior boy, morally, to the son of the millionaire, who regards himself as a walking encylopedia during his career as an undergraduate at a university. Be this as it may, ignorance is, without doubt, the fruitful parent of countless abominations, and to fight resolutely against it with might and main, is a plain and imperative duty forced upon all of us by the necessities of society. The very fact that sin can in any case be attributed to ignorance, is sufficient reason for opposing it with all our might; but it is just here, when we are discussing the great need of ridding the world of vice from the prevalent disorders which afflict it so grievously, that we come to a decided point of issue with our conservative brethren. The fear of hell, the dread of God's displeasure, never redeemed or uplifted anybody. Fear is only valuable protectively; it can never be so reformatively, so far as the wrong doer is concerned, as fear, when it acts as a restraining impulse, only deters people from the commission of wrong from motives of cowardice, and cowardice can be no part of religion.

(The religion of Jesus will never be the established religion of this or any other country, until your entire system of correction is altered. Punishment must be a thing of the past, reformation the work of the future. The picking of oakum, for instance, is not a corrective discipline so much as a punitive one. The only proper kind of work for criminals is work of the most useful and appropriate character. Every criminal should undergo a strict and healthy education, fitting them for useful and remunerative positions when the term of their prison discipline has expired. There can be no greater punishment for anyone than that meted out by conscience. Thus, when we leave sinners to their consciences, we place them in that lake of ever-burning fire, from which they cannot escape until they have paid the uttermost farthing; but it should be farthest from our thoughts, ever to seek to make any one suffer needlessly. All genuine corrective discipline is something vastly higher than punishment, as it raises the one who is even a victim to his own folly, and is in itself such salutary discipline that he who undergoes it is for ever after thankful for the sorrow which has worked in him genuine repentance, followed by practical reformation.)

We have dwelt so long upon this first word from the cross, that we fear the remaining six sentences must be passed over almost without exposition. But there is an old saying, that the first step, either upward or downward, is the most important step of all; and if this be true, its truth must be our excuse to-day for consuming so much time upon the first utterance of the seven we have to consider, as it is the key note to them all.

The second utterance to which we shall call your attention, is the answer made by Jesus to the penitent thief: "This day thou shalt be with me in paradise"; prefaced with the emphatic prefix, "Verily, I say unto thee."

The two thieves who were crucified with Jesus on Calvary represent two classes of sinners, very common now as then. One class is composed of those who sin wilfully, the other being made up of those who sin thoughtlessly. The wilful sinner is he who with open eyes refuses to be guided by spiritual light: he loves darkness rather than light; he knows his deeds are evil; he takes delight in sin, and hates the thought of reformation. To such as he apply those awful words concerning the unforgiven and unpardonable sin, Blasphemy against the Holy Ghost, which never *can* be forgiven either in this world or that which is to come.

We believe in innate goodness as well as in innate depravity in man, as you very well know. As you are also aware, doubtless, we do not agree with the Swedenborgian doctrine of the final confirmation of any soul in evil; still, it is a fact which must be admitted on all sides that there can be no reformation, and no forgiveness or sense of forgiveness, until the party who has done a wrong perceives it, and desires to amend and make atonement. The impenitent thief represents those who go out into the spirit-world without a wish to rise; they enter the ranks of those who were disobedient at a former period of special spiritual enlightenment, and have not thrown off their love of evil, through entire dispensations. The Epistle of Peter declares that Jesus went and preached to spirits in prison, who were rebellious in the time of Noah; the Noachian Deluge symbolizing the culmination of a spiritual and temporal cycle.

The Orientals, who comprehend better than Occidentals usually do the procession of dispensations, have calculated the length of each separate Messianic period to be about 2,170 years, during which cycle of time the sun passes through one of the twelve zodiacal signs in the journey around the more distant sun Alcyone, as the earth in its annual revolution accomplishes a passage through one of these signs in every month. It is true that these divisions of the heavenly bodies into zodiacal constellations, is empirical, at the same time these constellations were employed by the *savans* of antiquity to set forth spiritual truths in relation to the earth and the spiritual spheres surrounding it. One thing is evident, *viz.*, the remarkable progress made by the earth, whenever one of these periods reaches its culmination. If the year has twelve months; and three be summer, three winter, three spring, and three autumn; and you know when to expect the longest and the shortest days, seed-time and harvest; if you know when to expect the birth of the lambs and the advent of spring-flowers, and when to make provision against the stormy winds and snows of winter;—is it incredible that the spiritual students of ancient days were able to calculate the length of time that must elapse between the beginning and ending of a cycle or dispensation of time? The larger movements of Spirit are regulated with as nice accuracy as any affairs of earth can be, so that the wise men guided by the Star of Bethlehem (doubtless the pentagram or five-pointed star), to expect the advent of a new dispensation of truth to earth, were led by the twin sciences of Astronomy and Astrology, as well as by that interior light, without which all external calculations would have been devoid of spiritual significance.)

We are told of the repentant thief being led by Jesus with him into Paradise, a term always used to signify a state of expectancy, preparation, education, growth, but not fruition. The disobedient and benighted spirits of a former age, confined in Hades, are made aware of the advent of a new angel to the earth, and so many as are ready to respond to that angel's call, are released from their prisons and updrawn to more spiritual and progressive states. Why went the repentant thief out into these realms with Jesus, but because there is but one way whereby spirits who have committed wrong finally outgrow it, and are released from its consequences? (Has any one been dishonest on the earth? Then his mission to the earth when he influences it from the spirit-side of life, must prevent and counteract dishonesty. Those warnings against dishonour; those impulses which seize you unawares at times, and seem like voices calling you, and hands pulling you away from scenes and acts of perfidy, are literally due to the contact with you of those in spirit, who have suffered from the commission of sins you are liable to fall into. Your guardian angel reaches you through these intermediaries, and they work out their own redemption by preventing wrongs similar to those they have once committed.)

Interpret this story of the penitent thief in the light of this view of spiritual existence, and while it will not endorse the theology, which tells the sinner there is an instant passage for him from the gallows to glory, if he but rely on Christ for pardon, we may assuredly state without the slightest hesitation, that no one can ever even wish to be reformed, without at once being set to work in the spiritual vineyard.

The penitent thief's petition was a very modest one. He

only asked to be remembered by the saviour when he came into his kingdom. He expressed faith in the ultimate triumph of right over wrong. He saw beyond the jaws of death the glorious victory of the spirit over death. He recognised kingship of soul in one who was doomed to a malefactor's death. The very expression, "Lord! remember me when thou comest into thy kingdom," was a marvel of spiritual insight, and proved the speaker of such words to have been already led by the spirit of truth, to forsake evil and to conquer the love of it.

The lesson we draw from this second episode, is an evidence of the second step towards spiritual perfection we may all take as a result of our suffering. Jesus first attributes human sin to ignorance, and prays forgiveness for his persecutors. The forgiving spirit is the base-rock on which all spirituality must rest. The next time he expresses himself, he promises to help a penitent in carrying out his virtuous resolves. He overlooks the past completely, holds out the right hand of fellowship to a fallen brother who desires to rise, and gives him a good new start, lending him his own companionship and assistance.

Do most people act thus magnanimously? A great many well-disposed people take a fallen person to reform, but they let every one know they are performing an act of magnanimity, by taking one who has been a great sinner into their household. No greater mistake, however, can ever be made than talking about the past weaknesses of those you are striving to assist. A penitent is sure to be sensitive enough without having his or her former transgressions made the subject of comment and criticism. Remember always when you have dealings with those who have been led astray, that the less the world knows about their past life the better. Never allude to it, try not to think about it, give them credit for a present desire to live virtuously, and be sure reminders of past folly are always dangerous, unless administered with the utmost kindness and delicacy, by truly wise and sympathetic friends. "Let the dead past bury its dead," and feel that when a sin or weakness has been truly repented of, the thief, no longer in the love of theft, is a thief no longer, and must be treated as an honest and respectable member of society.

The second great step towards perfection of character is,

to forgive wrong and never to pride yourself on having done so to the pain of the penitent.

The third utterance ascribed to Jesus on the cross is: "Woman! behold thy son. Son! behold thy mother." In the narrative before us, we have presented to our minds a touching picture of that love for others and care for their welfare, which ever characterizes the true exemplar of mankind, even in the midst of excruciating bodily torture.

Some, who have prepared themselves for fault-finding and harsh criticism, whenever they open the Bible, have found much fault with the character of Jesus on the score of his undutifulness to his mother, and disregard for her feelings generally. Some have even gone so far as to say, that he was almost entirely lacking in filial love and devotion, and to support such a view they cite a few passages in the authorized English version, which seem at first sight to justify the assumption. For instance, when he was twelve years old, and he had accompanied his mother to Jerusalem at the annual feast, he caused both his mother and her spouse much anxiety by absenting himself from the company, and remaining two days in the temple, disputing with the doctors of the law, hearing them and asking them questions. Then at the marriage feast at Cana of Galilee, when his mother was present, he seems to have spoken disrespectfully to her, though she showed the greatest respect for his commands, and told the servants to do whatever he bade them. On another occasion, when it is said his mother stood without, desiring to speak with him, he gave utterance to that startling question: "Who is my mother?" which would electrify a well-ordered English company, were it put by a son under similar circumstances to-day. These and other instances are among the most prominent examples of the seeming disregard of Jesus for his mother.

Roman Catholics explain these passages differently from Protestants; and in the case of the conduct of Jesus at the marriage feast, the Vulgate makes it appear in quite a different light to King James's version. The Vulgate rendering is: "Woman! (or mother) what is this to thee and to me? Mine hour is not yet come." A priest of the Church of Rome preaching on this, the first recorded miracle of Jesus, would not only exculpate Jesus from all possible charge of incivility to his mother, but might even go so far as to say that though his time for working miracles had not then arrived, he performed this his first public miracle in compliance with his mother's request.

As we have no time to enter into a discussion upon this point to-day, we will content ourselves with offering a very few practical suggestions which seem to grow naturally out of this prolific and attractive subject. First, the conduct of Jesus, when twelve years of age, can be justified in one way, and that a way in which all your children can be justified, if they seemingly disobey or neglect their parents. (A parent must never stand between a child and his sense of right. Honour your father and mother, but do not blindly obey them, as things are not right because your parents do or advise them. There are many circumstances in life, where young people have to decide between their parents and their own conscience; that is, a choice between God and man. If your parents unduly interfere with you and try to force you to neglect duties or effect compromises with conscience, then disobedience of a calm, dignified order is right. And this remark applies also to keeping and breaking law. There is a higher law than the law of the land, and those who disobey the outer to obey the inner law, are only discarding the letter for the spirit, and are therefore not sinners.)

We do not suppose the mother of Jesus ever stood between him and his duty, but his remarkable words: "Wist ye not that I must be about my Father's business," convey very distinctly his supreme conviction that he had a mission which he came into the world to fulfil, and that that must be fulfilled in spite of every possible obstacle. Perhaps he was an ardent, hot-headed boy, an impulsive youth not quite sufficiently regardful at times of his mother's feelings. If this was so, then mellowed and chastened by suffering, how much more beautiful does his character appear on the cross, when thirty-three years old, than when, as an ardent boy of twelve, he doubtless enjoyed confounding the Sanhedrim with his wonderful wisdom.

The thought, however, we wish to bring into especial prominence with reference to his apparent slight of his mother, when he asked: "Who is my mother?" is this: his drawing the attention of the bystanders to a great law of spiritual relationship, entirely overlooked by those Spiritualists and others in the present day, who make of heaven a large family mansion, where aunts and uncles, nieces and nephews, live together in the bonds of physical kinship for eternity. Relationship of spirit is something so much deeper than relationship of body, that it becomes arrant folly to expect to meet and live with all in the spirit-world, to whom you have been related by ties of blood on earth. If there has been a tie of spirit as well as a tie of blood, then you are truly united in the spirit-life, but if there be no such tie of spirit, then all the blood affinity in creation will not unite you, whereas if there be a tie of spirit, no earthly power can ever separate you, except temporarily, and then only in seeming.)

Jesus answered the question he raised. He told who his mother was; she was the one who stood nearest to him in her devotion to his Heavenly Father; she was the one between whose soul and his the deepest bonds of sympathy were found; and there is no reason to doubt that in his case, she who was his physical mother was his closest companion in spirit. But it is not always so. Unnatural mothers who desert their children, those who bear unwelcome children, have not the motherly impulse which binds them as mothers to their offspring. In the spirit-world, while the foster-mother, who has discharged all a mother's duty and shown all a mother's love, will stand much nearer the child she has befriended than his mother after the flesh. (Some people are very anxious about relationships hereafter. If all could realize that a true affection is of the spirit only, and that material kinship has no necessary connection with it, how much more rational would be their conception of true family unions in the hereafter, and on how much more solid a basis would friendships for eternity be seen to stand.)

Another thought which presses in upon us at this time is that of the peculiar regard felt by Jesus for his beloved disciple John, the one whom he singled out from all the rest as his closest companion. He had seventy-two disciples we are told, and twelve apostles, who were his immediate pupils and followers; three out of this twelve, who accompanied him whithersoever he went and were privileged to witness his transfiguration, but only one most intimate friend of all, about whom he was most deeply concerned in the hour of his final anguish, and to whom he confided his mother.

It may seem strange, that the first words of Jesus on the cross were about his enemies and a penitent thief, but these enemies and that thief were in more pressing need than the highly spiritual and devoted mother and friend, who are not mentioned till afterwards; and we may very justly remark, that (no one can really be said to truly fulfil family and friendly obligations aright, unless he first cultivates those loving and compassionate dispositions which make the love of one's enemies possible and practicable. There are people on earth to-day, who love their enemies and would do all in their power to serve them. It is easy to be kind to those who are always kind to you, but kindness to a foe is a glorious triumph of spirit over temptation. Still, though kindness to enemies and forgiveness of injuries must ever constitute a most important part of true spirituality, there are nearer ties binding us to those who are peculiarly with us in spirit, even in the celestial spheres, and the special friends who stand nearer to you than all others on earth, may still be your chosen companions and most intimate associates in the life above.)

The fourth sentence spoken by Jesus on the cross was: "I thirst"; a simple natural exclamation wrung from him by the heat and his sufferings, and yet considered spiritually doubtless expressive of a burning desire to realize the benefits conferred upon the world by his life of humiliation and sorrow. At this point the strength of Jesus seems utterly to fail, and many there are who with cold and callous tongues have slandered the hero of Calvary, affecting to see in this and especially the next and fifth utterance: "My God! my God! why hast thou forsaken me?" evidence that Jesus died in despair. Many and many are the views taken of these mysterious words, but as two are peculiarly prominent in the world at present, we will endeavour very freely to point out the fallacy of both, from our standpoint, while we endeavour, though very imperfectly, to give you our own conscientious interpretation of the passage.

One theory is that of the strictly orthodox school, which teaches that God literally forsook his Son on the cross, because he was there atoning for the sins of the elect, and was made accursed, as the sin of God's people was laid upon him, and he bore it vicariously that they might escape the punishment due to it. This view we set aside as derogatory to the character of the Infinite, and utterly at variance with all truly enlightened views of the nature and object of punishment for sin. The other prevailing theory is a dastardly one: it is that Jesus really died in despair. No language can be too strong to express our deprecation of so wretched a doctrine, for even should you regard Jesus as a deluded man, should you fancy him having made a mistake in surrendering all earthly hopes and pleasures to accomplish an impossible task, you can scarcely question his sincerity, unless your own lives are so paltry that you cannot conceive of real disinterestedness.

No one who ever strives to do his best goes out of earthly life despairing, though apparent despair is often a discipline through which many have to pass ere they can attain to that spiritual eminence from which they can look back upon all the sorrows of time, and be thankful for them all. Jesus no doubt experienced, just before the closing scene in his life's tragedy, a feeling akin to what often causes the most intense pain to multitudes, who are struggling against tremendous odds, and have at last to face the fact that, in a worldly sense, their lives have been failures. To be obliged to suffer, year after year, on behalf of others, and then find yourself at last in a position in which you feel your own impotence most keenly; to go on labouring in a righteous cause, and at length to have to leave the world without seeing any results attending your undertaking, is the bitterest drop of all in the cup of human sorrow, many a true worker has to drink to the very dregs. It is comparatively easy to be brave and gay on the battlefield, with the drums and fifes sounding all around you: the very noise of the cannon, the rushing hither and thither of the men, the excitement of the whole scene makes you forget your danger, or, at least, enables you to put on a brave front and face the enemy; and then the thought that you are fighting for freedom, and may die gloriously for country and for freedom, spurs you on. Your sacrifice seems worth something. You cannot but picture to yourself the benefits to others accruing from your loss and that of your comrades: but some of the world's greatest heroes and heroines have been left to die of starvation in wretched garrets, or have pined to death in gloomy prisons in which they have wasted out their existence with no prospect of release, and no hope of blessing others. Some there are who seem fated with persistent ill-luck; whatever they touch turns to ashes in their grasp; they live only to suffer and be disappointed, and no one seems any the better for their misery. Such experiences are the hardest of all to endure, and to those who in such distress of mind and body cannot see the hand of God in their affliction, and can trace no light beyond the tomb, life is truly a heavy burden, and we do not wonder if, sometimes, such lives end in suicide.)

But Jesus rose above even this his greatest trial of all, impaled upon the cross, without an earthly friend or helper who could aid him: this last and greatest trial seemed all that was needful to complete his earthly work, and enable him to utter his sixth cry, "It is finished!"

How very few there are who can expire with such triumphant words upon their lips! The wail of most at the hour of earthly dissolution is: "It is unfinished." There is so much more to be done, and they have neither time nor strength now to do it; the sun sets and their day's work is not completed, so they dread to appear before their judge with "nothing but leaves" in their hands.

Very often a great and crushing sorrow is the very thing absolutely needed to bring out the full strength and glory of a character, as choice exotics are often forced into bloom by excessive heat, that they may be ready to grace some nuptial board, or appear in the place of honour at some splendid national or religious fête, so there are some spirits whose experiences are akin to those of Adelaide Proctor's heroine, in the story of "A Faithful Soul." (The poetess tells us a spirit was in purgatory, but almost ready to be admitted into paradise, when her thoughts strayed lovingly toward a dear one on the earth, to whom she had confided all her love, and whom she truly believed had responded fully to her heart's affection. She asked permission of her angel guardian to go and console her sorrowing lover, and was told that a thousand years of further purgatorial cleansing would be needed if she did so. She gladly accepted the penalty, so anxious was she to console the object of her love, of whom alone she thought, never of herself. The sight of his infidelity, or inconstency, so grieved her, that within the compass of a single moment of earthly time, her suffering was so intense that it was equivalent to a thousand years of ordinary purgation, in the effects it produced upon her who endured it. This was the final stroke which weaned her from the earth, and in that intense though momentary suffering, she became ready to join the happy souls in paradise. No greater mistake can be made than to suppose that the greatest sufferers are the greatest sinners. Suffering is a part of education, and were we to do without it, we should never be prepared for the happiness which cannot be ours, until the power to realize it has been brought out by pain.)

The seventh and last expression attributed to the Gospel hero is: "Father! into thy hands I commit (or commend) my spirit." This saying is the grandest and loftiest of them all. (Complete submission to the will of the Eternal, means complete and lasting joy. When all the stormy scenes of life are over, and the tired spirit forsakes the failing tenement of clay, happy will it be for each of you, if you can with calm and blest assurance feel that you are but going into a Father's arms, to take your abode in a Heavenly Father's house. How short is earthly life; though it should extend through cycles of time, how brief would it still be when contrasted with eternity! In the stupendous light of the soul's immortality, the importance of all earthly things fades into utter insignificance; and yet earthly life, with all its alternating joys and sorrows, hopes and fears, is necessary to prepare the spirit for the life beyond.)

May you all be so inspired to live in harmony with conscience here, that the change called death may be to all of you a happy exit from scenes of difficulty and imperfect joy below, to larger liberty, deeper love and clearer vision in the Life Immortal!

IMPROMPTU POEM.

A GLIMPSE OF PARADISE.

I beheld a Golden Ladder, in the visions of the night;
I saw bright angel spirits, wing toward the earth their flight;
I saw a golden ladder, as Jacob saw of old,
But the beauty of that ladder, in language ne'er was told.

The Steps were very varied: some seemed so small and low,
That any child might climb them, some were so high, I know
That only conqueror spirits, who'd wrestled in life's fray,
Could put their feet upon them, and tread their mystic way.

The First Step, which I noticed, was where the children play,
As innocent as lambkins, through the bright summer day;
The Second Step was steeper, and youths and maidens there
Were faltering as they trod it, it seemed so high in air.

I scarce could see the Seventh, it merged into the sky,
While oftentimes dark shadows and storm-clouds passing by,
Would whelm the travellers struggling, to reach its glorious height,
But always the pure summit was crowned in Heaven's own light.

Once on the earth I witnessed a child with weary feet,
Seeking to mount this Ladder; he would his mother meet,
And she had gone to Heaven, both priest and nurse did say,
And he was lone and weary, upon life's toilsome way.

His little feet were bruised, by the stones along the road,
His little heart was breaking, his little head was bowed;
But an angel came to guide him, to lead him by her hands,
And safely he was guided to the summit, where he stands.

One day the Ladder trembled, as though a raging storm
Had shaken its foundations, while dark clouds veiled its form;
The lightning flashed, while thunders with their terrific roar,
Convulsed the angry heavens, till the rain did in torrents pour.

Drenched to the skin, so weary, the child still plodded on,
Though frightened by the thunder, he still pressed bravely on;
And he could not see the angel, at times, it was so dark,
But still she held him firmly, though to her voice he could not hark.

I watched him struggling onward, when the storm had spent its power;
Graver and sadder seemed he, yet, like an opening flower,
I watched his dawning courage, his coming manhood's grace,
When he, a noble ruler, might fill a glorious place.

The years rolled by, and upward and onward still pressed he,
Laden at times with sorrow, at times seemed full of glee;
Till one day from the Ladder, his earth-form fell away,
And his happy, radiant spirit passed through the Gates of Day!

Then when those gates were opened, what visions did I see!
Of such serene enjoyment, as passes earthly glee;
The Mother greets her darling, the Child his mother's hand
Presses with true affection, while o'er the blessed land
Not one poor soul is burdened, with the grief ye ofttimes know,
All see results of labour and its blessed purpose know.

There, in that lovely region, where souls begin to see
The accomplishments of earth-life, and sorrow's ministry;
All doubts and dangers ended, they read the power of thought,
And learn by what strange prowess, heaven's flowers to bloom are brought.

Oh! toilworn hands so weary; oh! hearts so full of care;
Oh! well-nigh breaking spirits, with the burdens that ye bear:
Remember earth-life is seed-time, and each loving deed or prayer,
Yea, each gentle thought is a seedling, ye must water and tend with care!

BENEDICTION.

May the angels, who, under the Eternal, keep watch and ward over all men, so guide you all through life's manifold scenes of trial and sorrow, difficulty and danger, pleasure and bereavement, gain and loss, that when this chapter in your soul's experience closes, you may gladly pass to spheres supernal, with songs of joy on your lips and praises to the Infinite for his goodness, in all your hearts forever. AMEN.

III.

THE COMING OF THE KINGDOM OF GOD.

(Delivered in Paris.)

The Second Coming of Christ. The Second Article in the Dominical Prayer. The Progress of Spirits through the Ages. Spiritualism and its Teachings contrasted and compared with those of Theosophy.

THE four subjects upon which we have been requested by the present company to discourse this evening, are each and all of them so vast, comprehensive, and far reaching, that it is impossible to do more in the very limited time at our disposal than simply give you the barest outline of such information as we possess, and opinions which we hold upon these fascinating and most important themes, ranging over a territory so vast, that it may almost be said to comprise the entire area covered by (the Spiritual Philosophy,—a philosophy, let us assure you, which undertakes to offer the only really satisfactory answers which can ever be given to man on earth, in reply to his ceaseless queries regarding the whence and whither of the human spirit.)

We hope at some time (in this city, when conditions are ripe), to give an extended course of lectures upon these and kindred topics, which through the kindness and talent of some of our kind and sympathetic friends, may be translated into the French language, and circulated broadcast over France, shortly after their appearance in English dress; as, though it may appear to the superficial onlooker that the French nation takes little or no deep interest in such matters, pertaining as they do to the immortal destiny of mankind, no one acquainted with the rapid and widely-extended sale of the writings of ALLAN KARDEC, both before and since his passage from earthly to spirit life, can continue to believe that France is not hungering and thirsting for a Spiritual Revelation.

The works of Kardec were initial and preparatory, but he

would be the last of all men, were he here in earthly form, to even permit the idea to go forth that he thought his works perfect or final. Sitting as he did at the feet of wise and enlightened spiritual teachers, he learned never to ignore the province of human reason, and most of all, never to close the door against the conscience or moral sense, which is indeed the true and essential Christ, Word or *Logos* which enlightens every man coming into the world; be he barbarian or civilized, Jew or Gentile, bound or free, Oriental or Occidental, (one Spirit is at the base of all creation, one universal Soul, one Infinite Will, one sovereign Mind, at the centre of the universe; and that supreme, matchless, unique intelligence men call God.

The great beauty of Kardec's philosophy consists in the fact of his always having conscientiously endeavoured to harmonize all life-experiences with the one absolute and essential principle of Justice, which he conceived as Love and Wisdom united in their most perfect forms.) Looking upon all ecclesiastical dogmas and creeds as transitory, he, in common with all truly spiritually-minded men, was constantly expecting and inviting a New Revelation, not to contradict or supplant, but only to explain, continue, and more perfectly unfold the inner meaning of the teachings of the seers and sages of the days gone by. Therefore, "The Spirits' Book," "The Book on Mediums," "Heaven and Hell," "Genesis," and other works by the same author, are all endeavours after the perfect way, the perfect light, the perfect truth. These works have prepared the studious and intuitive among French philosophers, to look for a fuller and more lucid interpretation of the laws of being, than even the spirits inspiring the mediums, whom Kardec assisted to unfold and exercise their gifts, could give at the time when he and they sat regularly together for spiritual communion.

(If it be asked: Why cannot the highest and most perfect truth be given to earth all at once, or at any time and in any place where truthseekers are gathered together? we answer: That whenever the Spirit of Truth is made manifest, every man must hear in his own language of the wonderful works of God; therefore, there must ever be a diversity of tongues, gifts and interpretations, till all have arrived at an equal standard of spiritual perfection. Then will the Babel cease, and one voice only will be heard, and that will speak the universal language of the Spirit, making truth known on earth even as it is known in heaven.

As we have been requested to express a few thoughts concerning the Second Coming of Christ, we must beg of you to consider how it can be possible for the true Messiah to come to any mind, until that mind is prepared to recognise his mission and understand his teachings. Can the sun-light come to you, if you dwell in darkness, immured in gloomy caverns, prisons, or cellars, into which no light can penetrate, because there are no windows to admit it? Can the air make known to you its advent, until the casement or the portals shall be open to receive it? Can the earth bask consciously in solar warmth and light, while she at night-time is turning her face away from the solar orb? Can the stars make known their presence to you, though they shine ever so brightly in the ether space around you, if mists and shadows arise from the earth, engirdling the planet and rendering its atmosphere so dense, that only the blackness is discernible? In the material world analogies abound which clearly and logically portray the means whereby spiritual truths are made manifest or concealed. God, you are told, has always had a chosen people, but the records which inform you that this is so, tell you also that God is no respecter of persons, that there is naught but impartial justice in the divine decrees. Such apparent contradictions as these lead the casual and the flippant reader of the Bible to pronounce it a mass of contradictions, or else to accept it blindly without investigation, as the infallible and entire Word of God. But God's Word can be confined between the covers of no book, however sacred: no institution and no age can enjoy a monopoly of truth, or bask alone in the favour of the Eternal Spirit; but in every age and to all peoples, the divine fiat has gone forth: "Let there be light!" and there was light.

You are told in the first chapter of Genesis, that on the fourth day God made two great lights, and set them in the heavens: the sun to rule the day, and the moon to rule by night: and that he made the stars also. The scientific student of revelation, who is a naturalist, a geologist and an astronomer as well as a theologian, can perhaps believe that not till after what is geologically termed the tertiary period, sun, moon and stars appeared upon the earth, and that in the fourth great epoch of creative energy, God made them appear to earth as the vapours dispersed, and the atmosphere of earth became so clear that they grew visible. But where is the man of letters at the present day, who accepts the Mosaic cosmogony literally, except as a crude and primitive fable or allegory, by means of which the author of the Pentateuch instructed his infantile scholars, who sought from him an explanation of how the world and all the orbs of light sprang into being at their origin.

The first chapter of the fourth Gospel tells us of the *logos* or divine word which was in the beginning, was with God, and which was God, without which not anything was made which was made. This Word or *logos*, a little later on in the same chapter, is described as the light and life of men: as the light which shined in darkness, which the darkness could not comprehend; and as the light which lighteth every man who comes into the world. Then the writer goes on to declare how that light was manifest in personal form, embodied on this planet in the form of the ideal or perfect man: and how that light and life, declaring itself as the essential *ego* or divine individuality, spoke of having existed before Abraham, being older than all the prophets.

This mystical language undoubtedly refers us to a divine indwelling spirit in man, which the Orientals have called the *atma* or Divine Soul. The philosophers of Greece always made a distinction, and that not without a very decided difference, between the animal or rational and the divine soul. The seven principles of being, acknowledged as comprising man in his perfect state by Oriental Mystics and Theosophists, were all acknowledged by the ancients, from whom Scriptures in their modern form have come down to the present day. These seven principles of being include all that the Occultists call elementary spirit, or sub-human life, and all that the Spiritualists declare they hold communion with, when they enjoy blessed and delightful intercourse with "loved ones gone before," and exalted spirits described as guardian angels.

Theosophy and Spiritualism are not and cannot in their essence be irreconcilable, or in any sense antagonistic. They only become so when broad and comprehensive terms are employed to designate limited, contracted, and dogmatic schools of thought. The larger truth may also contain and make plain the lesser, but the lesser can never make false the greater; the fraction may be contained within the sum, but the sum can never be expressed in fractions, as all fractional parts are necessarily separately less than the sum, which is the whole, or all parts united. There is a great and most unfortunate tendency in many quarters, to underrate some truths, so as to bring others into more conspicuous relief. It may be that some particular truths are not at present adapted to certain minds, and that they may as yet be unable to comprehend the perfect unity, which is a salient and necessarily characteristic attribute of all true revelation; but nothing worth gaining is ever gained, and much well worth preserving is hopelessly lost, by any attempt to limit or monopolize the divine outpourings.)

God is infinite, and man is finite. Man is ever circumscribed to a limited area, and can only do so much work, spend so much money, and visit so many places: therefore, an idea of the Divine Being borrowed from human experience in outward life, is always a dwarfed and circumscribed idea. To hear many persons talk of the divinity of Jesus Christ, of the Word of God, of the operations of the Holy Spirit, of the scheme of redemption, the plan of salvation, and other profound spiritual subjects, you would certainly infer that God was a being of the most arbitrary limitations: that he could love just so many but no more; could send his Son in one human form to one world once, to offer to his children salvation, and then at length to judge them, but no more. You would think that God could only write one book, could only work through one institution, and that, if we accept the mission of Jesus, we must regard all other spiritual teachers as deluded or impostors; while to accept the Bible and embrace Christianity, must mean to renounce all other sacred treatises, and separate oneself entirely from all other systems of religion.

(The Christian missionary goes out to Asia to convert the heathen; and by heathen he often means not only the idolatrous, the degraded, and the illiterate, but under the term "pagan" he includes all the most enlightened, spiritual, progressive, and saintly mystics of the Brahman and Buddhistic types. Among heathen philosophers he includes Confucius and Plato, while no two men have left an impression upon the world for good, intellectually, greater than that left by these two noted sages. Still Confucianism and Platonism are insufficient to satisfy the deep yearnings of the human soul. So is Theosophy, as interpreted by Madame Blavatsky, Col. Olcott, and others of its distinguished leaders; as in the midst of the most brilliant intellectual activity there is a dearth of that spiritual food which is the true bread of life, the manna which comes down from Heaven, feeding the soul with the fare of which angels partake, and wherewith even they are satisfied.

The term "Christ" has many meanings to the exoteric student. Sometimes it conveys the idea of a priest or king solely, one who has been anointed with consecrated oil, and ordained by the imposition of apostolic hands to the work of ministry; but the Jesus of the Gospels was not so anointed. According to the Evangelists he came not as a king or priest appointed or ordained of men: his kingdom was not of the terrestrial world. He had no gorgeous jewels, no robes of state, no brilliant retinue, no flattering courtiers at his feet; his followers were fishermen and many common people, who heard gladly though the chief priests and rulers defied him, persecuted him, and at length put him to death. His court was composed of sinners he had converted from the error of their ways, and who from gratitude for so great a blessing were willing to share his toilsome lot, and ease, if might be, the load on his burdened shoulders. His birth was that of a pauper, his death that of a criminal, and yet his name is, according to the New Testament, the one name given unto men whereby they may be saved; the name at the mere mention of which, every knee in heaven and earth must bow.

The Church on earth has been so literal in the construction it has put upon this passage, that whenever the name of Jesus occurs in the service, caps are lifted or heads bent down; but what means the *name*, but the outward expression of the spirit? The name of God signifies not the titles applied on earth to Deity, but the manifestation of divine life in earthly form, and when it is predicted that at the name of Jesus every knee shall bow, the writer of the esoteric document, from which the words are taken, means that divine or celestial expressions of life on earth shall yet so completely dominate all forces and forms of matter, so thoroughly subdue all forms of pride, tyranny, selfishness and imposture, that when the true Golden Age shall have dawned, right will be sovereign instead of might, and those alone accounted highest and most worshipful through whom the spirit of truth is most perfectly made manifest in love.

You will pardon us if, for a moment, we refer you again to the earliest chapters of Genesis, and this time ask you to carefully note the difference between the man (mankind), male and female, created in the first chapter, and the Adam, formed in the second. This Adam was the first spiritual messenger, of whom the Jews had preserved any written record. He was to them the first man, the source whence they derived all their characteristics as a peculiar people. This the esoteric Jews fully understood, while the ignorant and bigoted believed all Gentiles were sons of Eve, by the serpent, while they (the Jews) were sons, by Adam; and this in a certain sense the Talmud teaches, only the Talmud being itself an esoteric book, can never be correctly interpreted by literalists, as the letter never does more than constitute a veil or covering for the inner meanings conveyed to the initiated, by means of those very veils which conceal them from the vulgar.

Christ is called the second Adam, in the Epistles; and it is declared that, as in Adam all die, even so in Christ shall all be made alive. But "Christ" is here a title applied to the Spirit, and especially given to Jesus by the writers of the New Testament, as the most perfect manifestation or expression of the Spirit witnessed upon earth. If all must die in Adam the first, all be alive for evermore in Adam the second, then a distinction is made between the simply rational and the inmost or divine soul; the former in and of itself is not immortal, the latter lives for ever, and is like Melchisedek, who was the symbol of the soul to Abraham, without beginning of days or end of life. Thus our considerations of this subject cause us to arrive at this conclusion, *viz.*, the soul is alone immortal. Outer personalities, astral bodies, all may be but shells, envelopes, or derivations, but in them is no life *per se.* The essential unit of life is eternal and immortal, has an unbroken consciousness through all the ages, and is indeed the breath of God in man, the candle of the Lord, the spark from heaven's eternal fire, individualized for ever.

In Kardec's Philosophy, and in that of Roustaing, great stress has been invariably laid upon the doctrine of Re-Incarnation—not a particularly happy word, as it does not convey the idea of spiritual embodiment anything like so clearly as the term Re-Embodiment, now more generally made use of by advanced spiritual teachers. Both incarnation and re-incarnation are faulty expressions, if the lexicons be correct, as reference to any dictionary will tell you that *incarnate* means "made flesh": so we have it in the creed of the Church—"he was made flesh" (*incarnatus est*).

Now, spirit can never be made flesh, though it requires spirit to make flesh, as no flesh is eternal, and no material can exist except when and where spirit operates to produce it. The spirit never becomes material, though it derives perception of material things through a material organism. The soul and the body are always perfectly distinct, and in order that a spirit should produce, animate, and control a body, it is only necessary that there should be a vital union between the spirit and its organism. This is proved by psychological facts, and notably by theosophical experiments, which, instead of simply demonstrating the existence and power of elementary intelligences, prove absolutely the sovereign and supreme sway of human intelligence over all forms of matter and lower grades of spiritual being. Supposing Madame Blavatsky, or any other Theosophist, really does accomplish all that is done in the name of Theosophy, according to its organ in India and the testimony of its friends in Europe,—What can be shown more clearly than that the human mind, or will, or spirit, is capable of disintegrating and reuniting matter, and controlling weaker wills and lower spirits till they perfectly obey its domination? Spiritualists may plead for the agency of disembodied spirits, and pronounce Madame Blavatsky a physical medium, but what are disembodied human spirits but those who were once embodied, and what powers can there be exerted by the disembodied, which are not present, even though usually latent, in the embodied man?

The doctrine of Re-embodiment naturally leads the thinker to something like the following conclusions, if he only carefully follows out a logical train of deductive reasoning, which must inevitably lead him to that point where he acknowledges at length, with the understanding as with the sentiment of the spirit, the Divine Justice in all the affairs of life; the Universal Paternity of the Divine Mind, the universal fraternity of mankind, and the necessity of every conceivable human temptation and trial, to round the spirit out at length in the full glories of resplendent angelhood.

The angels,—What are they, and how do they differ from ordinary spirits? is a question repeatedly asked, but never answered till the soul understands the meaning of the command: Be ye perfect! and knows that the perfect way is the path of everlasting blessedness, because of perfect love to God, and love to all souls in the universe. Celestial life is quite distinct, in its rounded beauty, from that cherubic or seraphic life, which is associated with the idea of perfect innocence and purity, compatible with childish simplicity but not with mature spiritual development. Paradise has been forfeited, the fruit of the tree of the knowledge of good and evil has been partaken of at the instigation of the serpent, or man and woman would not be here struggling with sin, battling with temptation, shut out from a realization of heavenly things, as the dwellers on earth usually are.

The Christ-man is he who has been subjected to every human trial and sorrow, and yet has overcome them all. He has been in the wilderness with the wild beasts, and has known what it is to have the tempter appear to him as an angel of light, telling him, if he yields to sense and not to conscience, he shall be accounted worthy to take rank among the gods. "It is finished!" is the parting ejaculation of one who has braved every storm, completed every work, and at length has grown prepared for that supreme triumph over death, which makes the resurrection and ascension possible.

The narrative of Christ and his earth-experiences is utterly unintelligible to all save those who can read between the lines the history of the progress of the spirit, but when the real nature of the spirit is understood, then both a personal and a corporate, an ideal and an actual, Christ can be not only imagined, but actually perceived and inwardly realized. After the flesh we then know Christ no longer, but in the spirit he is with us always. We do not say that a knowledge of an historic Christ is needful to all, for were it needful it would be vouchsafed to all mankind, and there could not be, as there are, hundreds of millions of human beings destitute of all knowledge of his very existence. It is not needful to know anything of history to know Christ, neither need we use the terms Christ, or Christian, to signify our allegiance to the spirit of truth.

The Kingdom of Heaven is within, and when we pray, "Thy kingdom come, Thy will be done on earth, as it is in heaven"—What can we mean, if we pray devoutly and sincerely, but that we long to see the day, when in ourselves and all around us, the Will of God, which is essential Justice, Love, and Wisdom unclouded, shall be obeyed, and obeyed because it is beloved? Coercive measures may be necessary among ruffians and barbaric peoples, but they never tend to a love of law, only to a fear of it, and frequently to its hatred. The law of love and the love of law are inseparable, and who can intelligently love or obey a law he does not appreciate, because he does not understand it.) The rigour of the letter of Mosaism can never win the world to the simple Israelitish trust in Jehovah, as an Infinite Parent, which made the Psalmist exclaim, in a moment of filial trust and grateful recognition of God's bounty: "Like as a father pitieth his children, so the Lord pitieth them that fear him." "The Lord is good to all; and his tender mercies are over all his works." These, and many other beautiful passages from the rich treasury of ancient Hebrew literature, express not slavish fear nor servile submission, but are full of that fervour of love which is the essence of all true religion.

Can we have any ennobling idea of God, if we merely rest on sovereignty, and declare that all are not equal in God's sight, and that it is not for us to complain of inequalities, because God is a sovereign, and has a sovereign right to do as he pleases with his own; while all we receive is a free gift from him to us? We do not deny the sovereignty of Deity, nor man's entire dependence upon the Infinite Spirit for life, and breath, and all things; but upon the simple plea of sovereignty, you can justify the awful travesties of Calvin, when he taught the reprobation of some and the election of others. Calvinism, Fatalism, Mohammedanism, Secularism, and, alas! Judaism and Christianity only too often have this fearful blot upon their escutcheons. Neither the God of the Calvinist, nor the Mohammedan, nor the orthodox Jew, nor the narrow-minded Christian is impartial; while the "nature," at whose shrine the Secularist bows, is but a blind, remorseless tyrant. Struggle as you may to reconcile all human inequalities by the theory of Divine Sovereignty, or that of Secularism, which denies intelligence, affection, and consciousness to the Power that moulds our lives, brings us into being, and hurries us out of it, you will utterly fail to evolve a philosophy acceptable to the highest minds on earth. Man has thought out a wiser and a better God, and possesses a truer and more loving nature.

Where the philosophy of Re-embodiment chimes in so beautifully with the deepest and truest thought of man, is where it takes its stand upon the cardinal, primal, central, and ultimate affirmation of Divine Justice. This justice being the base of all the operations of nature, no one is preferred before another. God has no favourites, all are equal in his sight. His universe is the expression of his infinite benevolence, while those who have suffered most, have learnt most and enjoy most; while those who have suffered least, have learnt least and enjoy least. We do not care what your theories or hypotheses may be, if you grant the truth of this divine and central axiom, but we shall for ever refuse to bow before a God or Nature which substitutes caprice for justice, and partiality for equal love.

No one can fail to see in the best and brightest lives, lived out on earth by saint and seer, by prophet, martyr and reformer, an evidence of this most perfect justice at the centre of all being. The child is instinctively just, and it needs the sophisticating influence of earthly commerce and self-interest, to make foul play acceptable to any of your children. All men and women, wherever found, instinctively admire a truly just and absolutely impartial person; such an one can always influence a family, control an army, or a State; mutiny can never continue where he is in command, and if, from age to age, we see with increasing brightness this love and sense of perfect justice and impartial goodness developing in human life, surely no one in his senses can question the existence of Infinite Rectitude and Impartiality as the base and centre of all existence. If you can acknowledge and adore this Justice, and yet be opposed to the philosophy of Re-embodiment, we do not think on any moral grounds you can need to accept it, as you have learned the lesson it is ordained to teach; but to those who cannot otherwise perceive this loving justice in all the affairs of life, Re-embodiment offers such explanations of life, and such consolation in the midst of adversity, as nothing else can give.

The mystery of creation is insoluble to the modern Scientist, who can perceive nothing beyond mere law, or fate, governing all things. Among physical Scientists, no one, perhaps, stands higher than Darwin, the far-famed apostle of Evolution; but Evolution without Involution is inconceivable. Nothing can be unrolled which has not first been rolled up. The outer universe is like a scroll, gradually opened, revealing the mystic characters which Spirit has written upon it through all the ages. To the purely materialistic mind, the lesser is constantly evolving the greater, the lower producing the higher: blind force begets intelligence, and man, composed of primal atoms or of molecules, is supposed to possess powers and attributes which these atoms or molecules do not individually possess. But surely the merest tyro in science must be aware, that combinations and multiplications cannot create attributes foreign to the nature of substances multiplied or combined. Before anything can be evolved by multiplication or combination, the essential elements must exist in the primal atoms, and if it be possible to trace all life—organic and inorganic, mineral, vegetable, animal and human—to original atoms, then these must be self-intelligent, if they are really the basis of existence.)

To illustrate: a single atom may be so infinitesimal, that it is quite invisible, both to the naked eye and with the aid of the strongest microscopic power available, while a million atoms combined may be clearly visible. Would it be possible for the million (all alike, primarily or individually) to manifest size and form, unless each separate atom had size and form? The size and form in the one case may be so minute that it is beyond microscopic detection, in the other, so great that it is easily perceived by unassisted human vision. (If it be true, that size, form, colour, or any material attribute, must exist in the unit or it cannot be manifest in the bulk,—will not the same course of necessary reasoning lead us, by processes of logical deduction, to the inevitable conclusion that *will, mind, spirit, intelligence*, use what word you choose to express the governing force in nature, must lie at the root of all existence? Thus the spiritual man is the real man, the spiritual world the real world; while original cells, or primordial cellular tissues, or animalculæ, in the form of protoplasm, can be only the earliest and most rudimentary manifestation of Spirit in its primal contact with the earth.

The monad is the first; the duad, the second; the triad, the third registration of spiritual impulsions through matter; while every type of life registers further and further efforts of Spirit, till at length the human form is produced, and Spirit rests from the work of producing any further types of life on earth. This is what is meant by God "resting from his work on the seventh day" or first Sabbath of the world. God (or to speak correctly the *Elohim*, or divine emanation, *i.e.*, the Divine Soul) was engaged through countless æons, vaguely called days, in the creation of species. The evening and morning alluded to signify alternating states of impregnation and harvest: the night between the evening and the morning, the period of gestation or germination, which is always carried on in secrecy and darkness within the earth or womb.

No type produces its successor, but every type has been necessary to induce that condition of soil and atmosphere, which rendered the advent of the next higher type possible. We avow our faith in direct and specific acts of Spiritual Creation, and declare this truth not inconsistent with any demonstrable theory of evolution. The Darwinian order of the succession of types may be correct; the only error may be in supposing that there is no direct spiritual impulse, to produce each separate and successive type. The monkey did not develop into man, but the monkey was an earlier manifestation of Spirit than man. The spirit, who was yet to form a human body, first produced the organism of an ape; but no animal form contains or embodies the Divine Soul, but only gives expression to certain emanations from the Soul-unit, which is never embodied in any form below man. Therefore, the animals are not immortal; they have no persistent individuality, while the life that animates them is a derived and reflected life.

If this be true of animals, may it not, say some, be true also of savages and of all human beings who have not attained to the dignity of spiritual self-hood. The doctrine of Conditional Immortality is finding favour in many quarters to-day, because it appears from many passages in the New Testament that immortal life is a reward; and to those who are not New Testament Christians, the doctrine commends itself as consistent with earthly life as a state probation, and heaven as a state of felicity, never enjoyed until earned. There is no good ground, however, for supposing that the individuality of any being is ever lost. The only question is: Had that being ever a conscious and distinct individuality to lose? We never knew of a human being who had not some soul-life within him; and we cannot conceive of the human form except as the expression of the human soul directly, while the perfect man is the Christ-man or Messiah, who manifests not simply some of the life of the soul, dimly through the veil of flesh, but manifests the fulness of the Godhead bodily; and that fulness of the Godhead is naught else than the full display of the soul-life, which is one with the Divine, and is the direct link between man and the Infinite Spirit.

At first, when the soul approaches the earth, though it has all divine possibilities within it, these are but in embryo, and the embryonic emanation from the yet unembodied soul, produces upon earth the simple monad. Through all the succession of types on earth, the soul is labouring unseen, till at length it presents not a form derived from some of its attributes separately, but a form produced by all its attributes conjointly. As there is great difficulty in the way of realizing how the types first appeared in form upon the earth, we must call to your notice the fact of materialization, admitted alike by Spiritualists and Theosophists; though the Theosophist explains the phenomena differently from the Spiritualist. It is recorded by Spiritualists that in many *séances* flowers have been materialized, and then have as suddenly and mysteriously disappeared. It is also stated by many competent witnesses, that human forms have been gradually built up from the floor, apparently; at first appearing like thin columns of moving vapour, and at length assuming the full proportions of the human body. It is stated by those who have had experience with Hindoo Fakirs, that a perfect tree from the seed of a gourd has been developed, and has flowered and then dematerialized in less than half an hour. The friends of Madame Blavatsky declare, that in her presence they have seen a cobra formed and then as mysteriously vanish, simply by her placing her handkerchief on the table, and employing her occult powers. Whatever explanation may be given of these phenomena, they must command the attention of the scientific world, in the near future, to an extent they have not yet done; and whether the general conclusion be Theosophic or Spiritualistic, in either case, immense light will be thrown upon the problem of creation; *will* or intelligence, whether embodied or disembodied, being indispensable to the production of such marvellous phenomena.

Apply the fact of materialization to creation, or to evolution, and you can understand how the original types first sprang into existence. At certain epochs of the earth's history, a type pre-existent in spirit assumed a human form: and as the spiritual medium declares that he or she is under the control of higher spirits than his own; and as the Theosophist, the initiate, or the adept, declares he has elementary spirits under his control, so both statements may be correct. The higher ever controls the lower throughout all space. Rise high as you will, there will always be some power above you, and to that power you may stand as a medium or subject. While subject to the higher, the lower may be subject unto you; and so throughout the boundless realms of space, life may appear as a ladder, upon the rounds of which intelligences ever stand, each round controlling the one beneath it.

The first human beings who appeared on earth, may have entered life through the portal of Spirit-materialization: and in the coming days, when celestial life shall be ultimated below,—not the mere typal germ, not the lowest and crudest expression of life will be made manifest, but glorious souls will take upon themselves a form as they may please, and the Second Coming of Christ, in like manner as he ascended, may be interpreted spiritually, to signify his re-appearance on the earth, in all the glory of celestial presence.)

Not as a puling infant,
Not as a weakly child,
Not as a man of sorrows,
Will the Saviour at length appear;
But he who comes to gather
His sheep into his fold,
To number up his jewels,
And place them in the gold!
The radiant golden setting
Of heaven's immortal state:
Will take them to his Kingdom,
Through Purity's white gate,
Through pearls from sorrow formèd,
Through gems from pain grown bright,
Into his endless Kingdom,
With unspeakable delight.

IV.

SPIRITUALISM, AND ITS TRUE RELATIONS TO THEOSOPHY AND TO CHRISTIANITY.

(Delivered in Paris.)

Spiritualism and Theosophy, continued. Spiritualism and its True Relations to Esoteric Christianity, and to every Social and Political Reform. Who was Melchisedek? The Hermetic Philosophy. The Coming of the Kingdom of Harmony. Anno Dominæ. The Golden Age, and final Destiny of Earth.

IN our last Lecture, we were only able to vaguely touch upon a few of the most conspicuous ideas, which the four subjects suggested to us on that occasion, brought into prominence. Could we give, say twelve consecutive Lectures upon the esoteric side of Spiritualism and Theosophy, and then sum up our remarks by showing what practical influence for good spiritual teaching must necessarily exert upon the world in the transformation or transfiguration of earthly life, we might be able to present you with something like a systematic dissertation upon the various themes with which you have requested us to deal. As it is, we must leave it to yourselves at your own leisure, through private meditation and such inspiration as you can individually obtain, to supply the manifest deficiencies in the scheme of philosophy we are endeavouring to present to you; as we can at best do no more than just touch lightly here and there upon some of the sublimest truths and deepest principles of spiritual being, into which you are evidently such anxious and studious inquirers.

In our previous Discourse, we called your attention to the seeming conflict between Theosophy and Spiritualism, as no real conflict at all. Certainly, nominal Spiritualists and

Theosophists are often bitterly opposed to each other, and say unkind—and, we think, unjust—things, sometimes the one of the other. Such conduct ill becomes seekers after truth. We must credit all our fellow students with sincerity equal to our own, and in all docility and humbleness of mind, must allow that none of us have all the light, or are able to discover all there is of truth.

Students of spiritual things are like persons on a mountain-side: some are nearer the summit than others; some very near the base. Those who stand highest have the widest view of the gorgeous natural panorama spread out before them; those who have gained the summit, can look all round and view the scenery from all sides. Perhaps on one side there are hills; on another, water; on another, table land; on another, a deep declivity. Those who look only to the north, cannot see what is to the south; those whose eyes are turned westward, cannot see what is to the east; and is it surprising, while all are climbing on the various sides respectively, diametrically opposite views should be taken of the surroundings? Yet all these views are right, as relative or partial truths; all are wrong, as absolute or final conclusions.

Students of religion, of the spiritual nature of man, or indeed of any natural science, are like these mountain climbers: one sees one side of a truth, another sees from another standpoint; and like the men in the fable, who disputed over the colour of a chameleon, they all were right in declaring what they saw; till at length a wiser man than any one of them interposed, stepped in and told them how the white chameleon was also red, blue, yellow, green, purple, grey, or any other colour they had seen it—it looked different in different lights. Science points you to the perfect ray of white light, and tells you white is the sum of colour. There are three primary, and a much larger number of prismatic, hues, but altogether they form white. Some who only saw the blue ray, might declare light is blue; some who saw only the red or the yellow, might declare light to possess only the one colour they perceived.

So with the jarring sects, so with divided schools of thought, wherein many men have many minds. The Christian, the Theosophist, the Jew, the Buddhist, the Spiritualist, and the controlling spirits,—all are right and all are safe when they confine themselves to declarations of what they know; but just so soon as arrogant and negative assumptions are put forward as incontestable facts, and that is pronounced impossible or untrue that some particular individuals have not discovered, then the strife commences, the clash of weapons is heard, battle begins in darkness, and persons are often accused of bigotry and uncharitableness, or folly or guilt, merely because they refuse to put out their eyes because some of their neighbours are blind, or to shut their ears to all the voices of the Spirit because some of their companions are deaf.

Should you visit Brighton, or any other South Coast town in England, and look across the Channel with the naked eye, you could not possibly discover France, while from Dieppe you could not view Newhaven; and were it not for the traveller, who has crossed the water in a boat, or for the powerful field-glass which supplements your vision, those who had never seen across the waters, and had never crossed them, could not imagine what lay beyond. Facts are what we know; what we only guess at should be put forward most modestly and tentatively, while they who are assured of the truth of facts, no matter how stupendous, are always justified when questioned seriously upon them, to give direct affirmative answers to their interrogators. Still there has always been need of secret orders and occult brotherhoods, to give special training to those who were prepared beyond others, to understand and exercise supernal powers of spirit over matter; and as dangerous weapons and sharp tools are only safe in the hands of the wise and mature, while the ignorant and infants would soon wrest them to their own undoing and that of others, so there have ever been but few upon the earth, who have been capable of rending the veil and peering behind the screen of symbol into the inner mysteries of the Spirit. You are doubtless aware, that while Freemasonry acknowledges three necessary and common degrees of initiation, *viz.*, Entered Apprentice, Fellow Craftsman, and Master Mason; and while entrance into the blue lodge is needful to entitle to the advantages accruing from entrance into the brotherhood the world over, still there may be many higher degress taken than these three; while the Past Grand Master of an ordinary order, may not know anything of even the first principles of some higher and more secret brotherhoods beyond, the very existence of which may be unknown to the mass of mankind, ordinary Masons included.

Some years since, when a Theosophical Society was started in New York, it was declared that it was necessary to take nine degrees to qualify a member to enter into the full mysteries and powers of the order; that only three degrees could be taken in Europe or America, the remaining six could only be taken in the East. Since that time you have heard much of Koot Hoomi and the Himalayan Brothers, while "Isis Unveiled" and the "Theosophist," also, "Ghost Land" and "Art Magic" have familiarized the reading public with some of the mysteries of Occult Science and Brotherhoods; but all the orders which are made mention of to the public at large, are quite external compared with that most powerful and divine of all brotherhoods upon the earth, *viz.*, the Order of Melchisedek.

This Order is composed of the Sons of God, or, as they have also been called, Sons of Osiris, or Sons of the Sun. This Order never varies from age to age. Its immediate inspiration is from the Guardian Angel of the Planet, who never changes, and who is the God or presiding Deity of the world. Under the dominion of this Supreme Archangel are twelve angels, who manifest to the earth through twenty-four embodiments, twelve males and twelve females constituting this Order, the very existence of which is practically unknown to all but those in communion with it. The members of this surpassing Order, are the ruling spirits of the planet. The Order itself is in the spirit world, but there are always upon the earth the perfect circle of chosen representatives, and these are they who have attained to oneness with celestial spheres of life.

Predicting a Messiah, the prophets of old declared that he should belong to this Order, while in the Epistle to the Hebrews, Christ and Melchisedek are identified. Jesus was always regarded by the early Christians, who were Gnostics and esoteric Spiritualists, as the earthly manifestation of this Divine Circle, while the entire radius of the circle comprised the 144,000 redeemed out of all the nations of the earth, and styled the first-fruits of the Heavenly Kingdom, in the Apocalypse.

Tracing the progress of this Order through twelve dispensations of time, and allowing that 144,000 expresses the number of those ingathered in each successive dispensation, the number of souls who attain to oneness with this Order is 1,728,000 during the grand cycle of time, in which is accomplished the precession of the equinoxes, during which period of 25,840 years or thereabouts, the sun travels through all the zodiacal signs, and completes its journey around Alcyone, the far-distant star, or to speak correctly, the central sun of this universe, and often called the centre of the sidereal heavens.

It is to this sun that the apex of Egypt's greatest Pyramid was designed directly to point, and as Professor Piazza Smyth, the Astronomer Royal of Scotland, has suggested in his able and fascinating work, "Our Inheritance in the Great Pyramid," in the year 2,170 B.C., the polar star (*Alpha Draconis*) shone directly down the shaft of the Pyramid, while twice every year—once at the vernal and again at the autumnal equinox—the sun illuminated the entire disc of the stupendous fane, with golden rays of glory. Whatever may be the meaning of the lidless sarcophagus in the King's Chamber, to the student of weights and measures, —granting the perfect demonstration in the Pyramid of many a mathematical problem, and granting also its proof that the Egyptians of old possessed a system of weights and measures vastly superior to the French metric system, now almost universally regarded as the best extant,—the Pyramid of Gizeh was evidently intended as a Masonic Temple, a temple of science and religion, a temple to the sun externally, and to the Deity esoterically; as the sun was ever regarded as the manifested presence of the planetary Archangel, while Alcyone was revered as the home of God.

Modern scientists may turn a deaf ear to spiritual interpretations of ancient mysteries, if they will, but who is great in the scientific world to-day, who does not know that either the pryamidal form is a blank, or it is the expression of ancient spiritual and scientific knowledge. Professor Smyth sees in it a prophecy of Christ, and predicts his second coming and the end of the world shortly, as the Grand Gallery 1881½ inches in length, is by him understood to refer to the duration of the Christian era. This gallery then abruptly terminates, but following a tortuous passage through which it is extremely difficult to crawl along, what is the surprise of the explorer at finding himself in the magnificent

King's Chamber, where all is light and beauty, but in that chamber as in all other parts of the Pyramid, there are no hieroglyphics or inscriptions of any kind,—the Pyramid speaks only in form, in its simple expressive design, and to those who are altogether uninitiated it speaks not at all. It is the stone which the builders have rejected, and is destined to become the head stone of the corner in the temple of material science; while viewed spiritually, the truths it symbolizes and the spiritual facts it declares, are destined yet to be acknowledged as the keystone of the Arch, by all who in the coming era shall become Masons, in the true Lodge of the Spirit.

It has been said by some interpreters, that the Pyramid speaks no more after 1881 or 1882 A.D. True it is that about the middle of the year 1882, the 1881½ years symbolized by the Grand Gallery came to an end, but it is difficult to compute with precise accuracy the true year of the commencement of the Christian Dispensation, especially as there are those who have studied the records deeply, who declare that Jesus was born about 100 years earlier than Christian historians declare, while others make a distinction between the culmination of astronomical and spiritual cycles, the latter being said to culminate about 300 years later than the former. It is useless to try and prove spiritual truths merely by reference to external history, as that history is by no means infallible or indubitably correct, and spiritual facts do not in any sense depend upon the letter of history. No one really lives the "Christ-life" by simply believing that a star shone over Bethlehem 1884 years ago, and led the Persian Magi to a stable where they found a babe, in whom the predictions of Isaiah were fulfilled. Many there are who believe in the letter of sacred documents, who know nothing and care nothing for their spirit. These are not in communion with the Christ Sphere or Star Circle. These know nothing of vital union with celestial states. These have ideas about God and immortality accepted blindly upon authority or tradition, but being destitute of interior light, they are in gross internal darkness: the light that is in them is darkness, for it is only the letter which killeth; while they who have by celestial influx received the light of the Spirit, need not that any man should teach them, for the Spirit teaches them from within. The Holy of Holies, the Ark of the Covenant, the Mercy Seat, and the Shekinah are all within, and Solomon's true Temple of perpetual wisdom is enclosed within their shrine of outward life.

The religion of Jesus, considered esoterically, is the simple universal religion of the Spirit, which acknowledges one universal Deity, and the manifestation of that Deity to man through the medium of his own soul. Who can read the Sermon on the Mount, the Golden Rule, the two Great Commandments, upon which Jesus said all the Law and Prophets hang, without perceiving at a glance that Jesus insisted upon universal truths, and enforced the essential precepts of the Hebrews upon the minds of all his hearers.

What says the Sinaitic law? Nothing, but what your best social reformers of the present day can heartily endorse. The recognition of one spiritual Deity; and the paying of undivided homage to the Eternal mind alone; the prohibition of all profane language and impious oaths; the observance of one day out of seven as a day of rest from labour, that man and beast alike may be refreshed and reinvigorated for the next six day's toil; the utter overthrow of murder, adultery, theft, false witness against one's neighbours, covetousness and all uncharitableness and injustice; surely this will be regarded as good by every intelligent utilitarian, who simply seeks the physical and worldly good of the human family. The commandments of the Decalogue are all wise and true, while the rigour of their enforcement by imperfectly enlightened legislators, was completely set aside by Christ. He came not to destroy but to fulfil *the law;* but not to endorse or perpetuate human cruelty, aggressiveness and violence; though no doubt the sanctions and penalties common among mutinous Hebrew tribes at certain degenerate and idolatrous periods of their history, were necessary to the enforcement of law and the maintenance of order, and were really intended to protect society, at the expense of disturbers of the peace.

Though we heartily dissent from corporal punishment in all its forms, we know of parents and teachers who conscientiously employ it, believing it to be for the good of those under them and dear to them. "Spare the rod and spoil the child," they interpret literally, forgetting that the severest suffering any delinquent can undergo, comes to him from the upbraiding of his own conscience. There are judges who believe they are doing right when they sentence criminals to execution, but woe to those who believing such penalties to be sinful, pronounce such doom upon their fellow-men, to maintain their seats and salaries, or who strive to soothe their smarting consciences by applying that most abominable and treacherous of all infernal salves: "If I do not do it some one else will, and it might as well be myself as another." It might *not* as well be yourself as another: there may be others who are in similar positions to your own, who have not your light, and for them to sin in ignorance is not sin to them; for you to sin with your eyes open is sin to you.

The whole doctrine of the Gospel hinges upon individuality and individual accountability. "No man can deliver his brother, or make agreement unto God for him." "Every man shall bear his own burden." "Whatsoever a man soweth that shall he also reap." These and hosts of similar passages from the Old and New Testaments might be quoted to show how thoroughly the essential religion of all Bibles is in accord with man's intuitive sense of right, and how the really inspired "Christ of God" ever points man to his own indwelling soul, and teaches him there to find the Deity.

All foolish disputations about the personality of God are vain. God may be more than personal, he cannot be less. Every attribute we love and admire in man, as our spiritual being unfolds, must have its counterpart in the Eternal, whose offspring we are; and it will not be till spiritual culture is pursued with that assiduity with which physical and intellectual pursuits are followed, that there will arise upon earth a multitude who will unite in common brotherhood, to make practical the teaching of the Golden Rule.

The word Christianity is unimportant, so is the use of the name Christ, but the Gospel, called the gospel of Christ, is eternally true, and practically beneficial to all minds in every age. That nominal Christianity is not essential, we have only to turn to Matt., vii., to hear Jesus say: "*Not* every one that saith unto me, Lord, Lord, shall enter into the kingdom of heaven; but he that doeth the will of my Father which is in heaven." Jesus says that those who do his Father's will are truly his relations, "the same is my mother and sister and brother;" and when we enquire as to what that will truly is, do we not find it beautifully set forth in that inimitably touching and graphic description of the judgment, recorded in Matt., xxv., where Jesus says as plainly as tongue can speak, if words mean anything, that the doing of God's will is all summed up in a life of pure benevolence. He who never turns a deaf ear to the mourner's cry, who never refuses to extend the hand of sympathy to the down-trodden and oppressed; he who can call a Magdalen a sister and a prodigal a brother; going in and out among the destitute, the sinful and the sad; compelling even the libertine, the drunkard, and the blasphemer to feel the power of all-constraining love;—he who does these things, shall never fail. The fifteenth psalm and the Gospel of Jesus, describe the righteous man in precisely similar ways; and should you turn to the Vedic Hymns, the Precepts of Hermes, the Law of Buddha, the Maxims of Confucius, or the Teachings of Zoroaster, you would find that there is in all theologies a golden thread of love, which truly glorifies them, and which justifies the esoteric interpretation of the old Hebrew declaration: "The Lord is one, and his name one;" name being synonymous with outward expression or revelation. Surely it cannot be derogatory to the dignity of Jesus, to declare that he as a truth-teller revealed in many instances precisely what the ancient seers had taught; not the originality or newness, but the truthfulness of what is taught is the true touchstone by which we may try the spirits who communicate with us, and decide whether they are or are not of God. Truth, the same in every age, has appeared in many guises, been clad in many varying habiliments, but if we dig deeply enough we shall assuredly find a unitary basis for all the religions of the world, upon which they all rest secure for ever.

Can any one read the Gospels, and declare that Christianity must needs be founded upon what these say Jesus taught, and then identify the religion of Jesus with those accessories and excrescences, which, notably since the days of Constantine, have disfigured the simple Gospel of Truth? The accretions which are hiding truth are like the eclipsing vapours which, rising from the earth, obscure the sun; and unhappy indeed are they who worship the earthly miasma, and imagine they are paying homage to the divine light.

Christianity to-day is in precisely the same predicament that Judaism was in 2,000 years ago. The light of the Spirit had been quenched by sensuality, dominant tyranny, and the worship of Mammon, which is the grossest of all idolatries. The spiritual significance both of the Law and

Prophecy was hidden from the people. They engaged in empty forms; they prayed like parrots, heathenishly using vain repetitions; they made an ostentatious display of devotion in synagogues, and at corners of the streets, that they might be seen of men; and they had the only reward such mock religion can ever win: they were applauded by their fellow Pharisees, and had the satisfaction of recounting, avowedly to God, but really to be heard and admired of men, their many virtues, in the holy temple which they profaned by their self-laudation and idolatrous self-complacency, and wicked despising of their fellowmen who, though outwardly more sinful than they, by reason of humility and desire to improve, were nearer to the kingdom of heaven, even though publicans and harlots, than were these self-satisfied formalists.

These outwardly pious people condemned Jesus bitterly, and pronounced his mission from Beelzebub, because he cast out devils and worked miracles of healing on the Sabbath day, thereby transgressing in their eyes unpardonably the letter of the Decalogue. But Jesus says, "The Sabbath was made for man, and not man for the Sabbath." "It is lawful to do well on the Sabbath day." No outward observance which stands in the way of charity can ever be of divine appointment. There must ever be a misconception of the divine will whenever any command is considered divine, which does not always stimulate every pure and ennobling wish of the human heart. Jesus even justified his followers in plucking ears of corn on the Sabbath, to satisfy their hunger, though some would see in that act of theirs a breach of two commandments. He even justified the action of David and his companions, who ate the showbread, which none but priests might eat; and when discoursing on the law of love, he attributes every asperity of the olden law to the men of old, and not to the Eternal Parent.

True Christianity is therefore the religion of the Spirit. Compare it with esoteric Buddhism, or any other system of spirituality you may please, and it will be found in perfect agreement with the spirit and intention of every truly inspired teacher, through whose ministry the world has caught glimpses of the eternal right.

To return, for a moment, to the Pyramid and the mysteries of the ancient world, we must ask you to observe the very great difference which exists between the spiritual religion of Egypt, expressed mathematically and geometrically in solid masonry, and the animal worship which savours more of fetishism and idolatry. The grandest structures have no animal representations at all. The lotus flower, the cross, the ibis, the apis, the anubis, &c., &c., are all exoteric, and form no part of the symbolism of the Grand Pyramid. This is perfect unity in trinity, a perfect whole, a compact unit, and yet three-sided, resting upon a perfectly square base. The Square means Universal Brotherhood, and signifies the primal and ultimate unity and brotherhood of man. The Triangle represents Fatherhood, Motherhood and Childhood; esoterically, the Love, Wisdom and Power of the Eternal. The Father (Osiris), the Mother (Isis), the Child (Horus), signify respectively the Father-Love and Mother-Wisdom of the Eternal, as in the eighth chapter of Proverbs, Wisdom, personified, declares: "I was with *him* in the beginning." Wisdom is spoken of as *she*, while Love is the Word or *logos*, by whom all things were made. Love in man has unfortunately degenerated into lust and passion, but wisdom in woman has never become quite corrupt. But woman's wisdom is intuition: it is the hidden wisdom, the wisdom of the veiled Isis, but in the coming days, all over the civilized world, and eventually over the whole earth, will this hidden wisdom unite itself with love, and then there shall be a perfect birth of the Christ-child, or the Horus of the ancient days. Love originates, wisdom carries to perfection, all truths throughout the universe. The motive must be loving, the execution must be wise, and then the law is perfect and all-powerful. Then the children born on earth will not be born in sin nor conceived in iniquity. They will not need a baptismal font to cleanse them, they will not need to be born again of water (or matter), they will bask in the sunlight of the Spirit, and on the altars of their hearts will leap high the divine flames, the fires of the Holy Spirit, which will not only purify from dross but will enlighten and illuminate the inmost mind.

The most ancient philosophy of Hermes, upon which the old Egyptian rites and emblems are based, teaches these truths most explicitly, and they are symbolized in all the ceremonies of Egypt and of Greece; while in India, the Vedic or Vedantic philosophy inculcates precisely the same spiritual truths, and so closely do the books of Hermes and the Vedas correspond, that many scholars regard them as transcripts or probable copies of each other. The student who is searching for the cradle of man, and is wading through a mass of antique lore, assisted by the modern sciences, comparative theology and philology, cannot but think that either India gave birth to the Egyptian faith, or Egypt to the Indian. But it is not needful to arrive at any definite conclusion on a mere matter of history like this, to perceive the grand spiritual oneness of all ancient faiths; it is not needful to infer that one nation borrowed or copied from another, or that by means of immigration and emigration spiritual facts were made known to nation after nation: the Spirit speaks in every age and every tongue. The true *illuminati* have ever been led by the inner light and the guardian angels, who have been their inspirers; all alike have seen the sun, the stars, the constellations in the heavens above them; all alike have felt the breath and heard the voice of the Deity within; all alike have held communion with the angels, who visited them in their starlit towers or shaded retreats among the rocks, upon the mountain sides or in the valleys; all have been knit together in a fraternity of Spirit, which makes all members of the Star Circle. And these are they who can read in the heavens above them and in the earth beneath, the signs of the coming of a new Messiah; these can trace the King in humble guise, by the light of the Pentagram in one age, and the Sexagram in another; but all acknowledge the perfect Circle as the only absolute emblem of Deity, and that circle is Truth itself, the sum of all perfection.

Modern Spiritualism, with its physical phenomena and divers utterances (sometimes apparently conflicting), is only the harbinger of the New Era. Signs and wonders are envelopes: letter carriers, telegraphic messengers, rappings upon your doors, ringing of your bells to arrest your attention. Phenomena can never be the ultimate, and it is indeed entirely useless, unless it conveys a truth to your minds; and it is worse than useless, it is positively evil, when perverted to unholy ends.

And here we draw a very clear and well-marked line of demarcation between mere magic and genuine spiritual communion. Simple magic is not divine; it can, however, become so, if employed for holy ends. Jesus underwent the temptation in the wilderness, when he knew how fierce the struggle was which wages in the medium's or initiate's breast, if he is ever called upon to choose between devoting his powers to self-glorifying magic, and a work of pure self-sacrifice and devotion to the interests of his fellow-men. We are told that the devil requested Jesus to convert stones into bread, to satisfy his personal hunger in the desert, and that Jesus withstood the tempter, and replied to him in these words: "Man shall not live by bread alone, but by every word that proceedeth out of the mouth of God." Then we are told that Jesus did produce bread, and with it fed several thousands of hungry congregants who had assembled to hear him, and had travelled far without thinking of their material wants, and who were famished with hunger.

Taking these stories literally or figuratively, the careful student cannot fail to see the lesson which they teach. In the one case selfishness says, Work a miracle to gratify your own appetite; in the other, Love for suffering humanity prompts the exercise of miraculous power, to feed a starving throng.

The second temptation endured by Christ was somewhat like unto the first, though the first appealed to the flesh, and the second to the mind. When carnal appetite had been resisted and restrained, then the temptation was to vain-gloriousness, to love of display, to self-agrandisement in the eyes of the people. Imagine a man throwing himself down from a pinnacle or parapet, and, being sustained by invisible power, falling to the ground unhurt! How great would be the consternation among the people, how willingly would those who sought a sign, and could track the Messianic deliverer only in deeds of magical prowess, have come forward and crowned him as their king! But miracles performed for selfish ends, are only questionable magic. Angels do not stand by to protect those who rashly imperil their lives for no good end, whereas when one is on the path of duty and is obliged to encounter danger on some errand of mercy, he may rest assured that loving angels protect him on his way; and even though the earthly form should perish, the spirit would have conquered in life's fray, and be prepared for entrance upon purer and brighter fields of being in the life beyond.

The third temptation of Jesus was to the spirit. Worshipping the devil, literally means worshipping Mammon, sacrificing principle for policy; and should any magician or student of the occult undergo even such rigorous discipline as Jesus underwent in the desert; should he fast forty days and forty nights; should he succeed in completely subduing the flesh to the will; should he be able to work miracles innumerable, yet if he worked only for popularity and fame, for selfish interest and worldly gain, he would be but a Simon Magus withstanding the apostles of truth; a black magician, a wizard, a sorcerer, an enchanter or worker of spells, exercising an unholy, unhealthy, baneful influence upon mankind, and forming such alliances with spirits of darkness, as led people in the middle ages to believe that persons signed compacts with the evil one, selling themselves to the devil that they might win earthly conquests.

Goethe has illustrated the baneful effects of all such spurious courses in his "Faust and Mephistopheles." This learned poet and philosopher was no doubt acquainted with the Rosicrucian and other secret Orders, prevalent in Germany in the 17th and 18th centuries, and existent still, though of course veiled in the garb of secrecy from the intrusion of the vulgar. The fables of the Rosicrucians concerning the philosopher's stone and *elixir vitæ*, were not simply childish tales or imaginative dreams, as many persons imagine them. The transmutation of metals is scientifically possible. The crucible of the mystic foretells the triumph of chemistry in future years, while alchemy itself is a true science, when spiritually as well as physically understood. The philosopher's stone and the elixir of life will only be discovered in the moral world, however, when man has learned to govern will by spirit, as matter is governed by will. The Kingdom of God will not have fully come, the reign of the Prince of Peace will not in reality have begun, until man has passed beyond the magical departments of Theosophy, wherein the power of human will is made manifest, to that divine estate where the lower will says to the higher: Thou, not I, must rule! Theosophy in its modern Indian guise, and in its purely wonder-working phases, is but the exercise of human will over man, beast and matter; over elementary kingdoms of life here and in the unseen world; but the Divine Theosophy of Buddha, or the holiest of Lamas of Thibet,—of all who have truly followed in the wake of the most gifted of the world's true sages—is what the word Theosophy really means: the Wisdom of God, divine wisdom which will enable the devotees, at heavenly wisdom's pure and sacred shrine, to literally fulfil the predictions made by Christ concerning his followers: They shall heal the sick and cast out evil or obsessing spirits; they shall cure insanity, and relieve those oppressed by sin from its enslaving power; they shall take up serpents and drink of poisons, and yet shall remain unharmed, because they are filled with the Spirit's resistless might; and the soul having subdued every form of matter, by having perfectly controlled the human organism, which epitomizes all the forces of the three material kingdoms of nature, and having completely subdued the will of the mind to that of the Divine Soul, shall pass unscathed through every fiery ordeal of persecution and temptation; shall be able to demonstrate to a wondering and awe-struck people such supreme triumphs of the soul as Daniel made manifest in the lion's den, and Shadrach, Meschach and Abed-nego in the burning, fiery furnace, heated seven times beyond its ordinary heat, at Nebuchadnezzar's cruel command.

If any Materialist should cavil at such wonders, and pronounce them impossible, we can only say they are impossible to him, and to all on his plane of thought. But is not navigation impossible to many? Can every one steer ships across the ocean safely? Are not the feats accomplished in the chemist's laboratory impossible to many? But shall any deny them because they are exceptional, and can only be proven by men of special training? The lion-tamers of the East, the serpent-charmers, who toy with venomous creatures whose fangs have not been removed, can fascinate and control the lower life of nature, which corresponds to what they in themselves have overcome. No one can tame and control any beast or bird, insect or reptile, until he has first subdued that in himself to which that creature corresponds.

And when at length man shall be perfect on the earth, the planet shall be perfect also. Slaughter will be unknown, ravenous beasts and deadly plants will become extinct, as the earth no longer affords means for their development and subsistence. As the mammoth, mastodon, and other monsters, which roamed primeval forests, are now extinct, because conditions are no longer offered for their perpetuation, so will the earth at length outgrow all that is destructive and unsightly. The supreme will of mind over matter, and of soul over mind, will at length convert the whole earth into a paradise. Then will the Golden Age have come ; then will diseases and death itself be unknown ; then in place of death will there be peaceful and glad transition, and the soul no longer needing its earthly tabernacle, will dissolve it. Flesh and blood will never enter heaven, the material forms will never pass to spirit-life. Still, the ascension of Jesus into heaven, is typical of the translation which will at length be in place of death; for those whose earthly careers are ended, will glide painlessly and imperceptibly from their material forms; becoming invisible to mortal sight, it will appear as though their bodies went beyond the clouds, though every particle of material will gravitate to its place in the material kingdom, while the spirit, in a spiritual form, will ascend to its native element, and appear in outward guise upon an earth again, only if such reappearance be needed to demonstrate immortal life to the dwellers upon some outward orb. Death shall be swallowed up in victory ! There shall be no more death, and no more sea ; no more division, no more strife or wrong. The lamb of gentleness shall lie down with the lion of strength; the little child of peacefulness, docility, and love, shall be the guide ; and the coming rulers of the world shall be those who, in gentleness and childlikeness, are prepared to occupy supernal thrones and judge the tribes of Israel.

The predictions of Jesus with regard to the future glory of his followers, refer to that divine estate of angelhood when the twelve powers of the mind, called the twelve tribes of Israel, in Kabalistic phrase, shall be governed absolutely by the soul within ; and those in whom this soul-life is manifest, are more than adepts, initiates, or magicians,—they are numbered among those who, like the Christ of Galilee, or the Buddha of the East, used all their powers solely for conquest over wrong, disease and death ; and who. therefore, with every magician's power, have beyond all this the invincible might and majesty of the Divine Soul. This at length must conquer. Hells there may be, hells there must be, hells there are, till this divine result shall be accomplished. A spiritual gehenna must burn outside the gates of earth, and outside those of Paradise, till every weed is burned, every iota of alloy consumed, every scrap of chaff burned in the unquenchable fire. But Dives in the flame is there for correction, for the burning away of the sin of selfishness, which made him on the earth forgetful both of brethren and the poor. He must suffer, and all must suffer, until by spiritual effort they span the gulf, bridge the yawning chasm, and through love to the brethren become themselves the angels who will do what as yet Moses and the prophets have not done.

Every one who has done a wrong on earth, must return to rectify it; every spirit who has wronged another, must meet that other and make restitution. The fires are ever burning, the crucible grows never cold, the law is eternal, the means of purification everlasting, the fire which cleanses never goes out; and into the everlasting fire, not that they may everlastingly remain in it, God plunges all his jewels, and only takes them out when all their alloy has been burned away!

This is the truth taught alike by esoteric Christianity, by modern Spiritual Revealments, and by true Theosophy. Nirvana, the Kingdom of God, of Christ, or Heaven, means not extinction of being, loss of entity or individuality; it implies oneness with all in love. As the globules which form the ocean and the sand grains which make up the hills are all individual, as the crystal dew-drops never lose their entity, so the soul, individual once, is individual ever. The soul that says, I AM! will never be less than the self-conscious *ego* it now is. The outward frame may change, ever so often: the astral body or spiritual form may change, as does the material envelope, but these are neither immortal nor individual: they are but ever-changing agglomerations of moving forces, which the spirit attracts, dissipates and repels. Memory, affection, understanding, will,—these are of the Soul, the primal unit only; and this four-fold nature of man is immortal, while the purely earthly part may but appertain to the elementary kingdom of nature, and be transported through the universe to other worlds, as they require what the perfected earth has rejected.

This Golden Age, or epoch of perpetual harmony, has been heralded by Spiritualism. Already the knockings have been heard, and thirty-three years after 1848, there were those who told you that the purely initial stages of the Movement were passed through, and that from 1881, the calendar should recommence with Woman's Era, *Anno Dominæ* instead of *Anno Domini;* but the perfect era is that of the Divine Duality, when the Christ and the Madonna, the lady and the lord, must rule together. But as man has had his special period of dominion, woman may also have hers, and therefore through two little female children, the Rochester knockings were produced, in the self-same year when the first Woman's Rights Convention was held in the United States.

To-day the English Parliament is agitated with the ever-recurring question of Woman's Suffrage. Protests against taxation without representation, are growing more numerous and influential daily, and surely no one who can read the signs of the times, can fail to see that the next great event in all civilized lands, will be the acknowledgment before the law of woman's perfect equality with man. No longer veiled in the harem or even in the cloister, no longer compelled to sit tacitly by, and while taxed as heavily as her brother, have no voice with him in controlling affairs of State; no longer refused admission to the priestly or prophetic or ministerial office, compelled to bow in submission to the will of lords and masters, she will take her place on earth as queen of society, even as the Catholic Church has declared that Mary Immaculate is queen of heaven. But how anomalous is the spectacle of crowds bending low in fervent adoration at Mary's shrine, exalting womanhood by pronouncing a woman "mother of God and queen of heaven," while the priesthood declares that through woman's intercession, the Son of God receives the prayers of men, and through his mother answers their requests, while she is called the spouse of the Holy Spirit, the daughter of God the Father, and the bringer-forth of God made manifest in flesh. How anomalous, we say, is the spectacle of all this supreme devotion paid to woman, by Jews and Protestants styled idolatrous, while woman is still forbidden to approach the altar to offer the sacrifice on the people's behalf, or to enter the pulpit to exhort both men and women to repentance.

All over the world the cry is going up to-day, that men, and young men especially, do not and will not go to church. A moral *interregnum* is feared and predicted, by reason of the present wide-spread indifference to religion. Morality is at a discount, vice at a premium, in the highest places of State. The law sanctions woman's degradation, but even in polite circles the male delinquent forfeits no right or privilege, except for unusually dastardly conduct; while the female sinner is ostracized and condemned. Where is the justice of a man-made law, permitting man a liberty denied to woman? Where is the justice of condemning one sinner and altogether exculpating her *particeps criminis?* Where is the justice of a state of society, which underpays female labour and imposes in many parts of Europe the hardest labour upon woman, and compels young men to devote some of the best years of their early life to the indolent and demoralizing life of members of a standing army?

Is it not a fact that one of the loudest cries raised against woman's entrance into Halls of Legislation, arises from the plea that they are not fit for women, that woman should breathe a purer atmosphere than that of those fetid halls? But must legislation ever be carried on in impure places? Are legislative enactments necessarily so corrupt, that they can only be matured in centres of moral infection? If there be vice in Parliament or Congress; if the aggressive spirit rule and the voice of woman has not been heard there since their foundation; if to-day the nations are embroiled in warfare, and the best blood of the countries is shed on the battle-field; if civil service and other reforms be the great cries of the age; if present forms of government are so distasteful to the people that Nihilistic insurrection and Communal strife are the rule and not the exception all over Europe; if the cry of alarm goes up from England because of Fenian outbreaks and dynamite explosions, which neither the arm of the Civil Law nor the Church can quell; if the Russian Emperor is in hourly danger because of the detestation in which the office of Czar is held by the bulk of Russia's population; if Absolutism in Germany is threatening with forcible disruption, and England's policy with Egypt is more than questioned on every hand; if the French Republic be as yet insecure, and across the ocean America is fast becoming a prey to bribery and corruption, while only her immense size and her vigorous youth are her protection,—surely the time has come when, after 1,800 years, and more, of masculine monopoly—yielding so bitter a fruitage of crime, pauperism, vice, persecution, and war—the new era may be inaugurated with the voice of woman pleading for justice. And should a female Paul arise and forbid men to speak, telling husbands to keep silence in the church, and if they wish to know anything ask their wives at home, though the masculine half of the population would raise an indignant howl and pronounce the promoter of such a proposition an idiot, still the spirit of justice would approvingly witness the turning of the tables on man, that he for a while going out of office, should give to the other half of humanity the right to rule, at least, for a term in his stead.

We do not say that woman will be sole ruler in the New Dispensation, but we do pronounce this dawning age the age of woman's supremacy. That it would be, Henry Bulwer (Lord Lytton) foresaw, when he penned the "Coming Race," and portrayed the women among the Vril-Ya as superior to the men. *Anno Dominæ*, the year of the Lady, introduces to the world that female portion of the Spirit of Truth, which remained in spirit-life unknown to the earth, while the teacher Jesus expressed but one-half the Messianic angel to the world. But ultimately, and even now wherever the highest culture is to be found, men and women will rule and work together. For in the highest parts of the earth, the era of harmony, of true duality, is dawning, but where the single ministration is all that can be given, it will be woman's voice and woman's influence that will cause the wilderness to bloom and the arid waste to sing. It will be woman, who, by moral suasion and the power of right over might, will put down intemperance and fraud, abolish war throughout the earth, and lead the nations to a commonwealth of peace, while the governing body will be composed of persons from all the annexed nations, and there will be a Universal Parliament.

The dream of the near future for Europe, for America, for the Colonies—Australia, South Africa and British India—is the establishment of independent republics first, then the amalgamation of the various races and nationalities into one great united and pacific nation. As many streams may run into one great sea, and lose themselves in the vast body of water, though they take their rise in many sources and flow distinct until at length they empty themselves with many mouths into one great ocean, as the Amazon and its tributaries do, so to the prophetic eye of Spirit, the time e'en now draws nigh when all the most enlightened nations shall become one people, and the differences between races will be forgotten, as they were forgotten in old Rome, when she became the mistress of the world; because a Roman had in his veins the mingled stream, which bespoke for him an origin among long-disaffected and disunited tribes.

Even now the fusing process is in progress in the United States, even more than in England or Europe; and when this blending is complete, war will be impossible. You will have no enemies, and no people will be foreign to you. You will have opened all your ports to every nation. Absolute free trade will everywhere prevail. The rights and welfare of humanity, not of a single tribe, will be considered; and to be human will be enough, while patriotism will mean universal fraternity. The Crescent and the Cross will retire from Europe, and be no more the signs of civilization. The Circle will be the emblem of united life, while the Sexagram, (six-pointed star) will be the symbol of that actualized progression, which will give to half the globe, redeemed from strife, a foretaste of the yet far-distant age of *universal* peace.

Africa may yet be convulsed. The worship of Allah may lead the Fetish tribes to the acknowledgment of one God, while the earth, commencing its career through the second half of the Grand Cycle, at the middle point of which we now stand, will through the next six ages pass on into the embrace of those bright dual souls, who will yet perfect their form upon its surface. Then when every atom of the globe is harmonized; when human will controls matter utterly and absolutely, and the intellect, no longer proud and overbearing, bends before the Spirit, will God's Kingdom have come, and his *will* will be done on earth as it is in heaven.

And who are the workers, who, like John the Baptist, are preparing the way for this glorious consummation? Divers and singularly different are they. Carlyle and Garibaldi rebuking wrong, Gordon in Egypt fighting for justice and liberty, all who in any branch of science, art, literature, religion or reform are seeking to raise the human mind, even though it be by purely material means, all are among the heralds of the New Messiah. Those who know not of immortality even, as they also who are aware of it, are working for this glorious end. And most of all they who would emancipate Woman, and thereby unfetter the soul; give reign to intuition; let affection rule the earth; make the law loveable, and because beloved obeyed. Join in this work, and you, in your sphere, have entered upon the

GOLDEN AGE OF HARMONY.

IMPROMPTU POEM.

THE STAR CIRCLE.

FAR from the earth!
Beyond its atmosphere, where planets roll
Majestic through all space, where worlds of light,
Unseen by mortal eye, shine in their places bright:
There can our eyes behold, in shining sparkling gold,
A Circle of Bright Souls, whose music onward rolls,
Outward toward the earth, and inward toward the sun,
That distant orb, Alcyone, round which, their courses run,
The worlds uncounted, through eternal day,
Matchless and glorious on their heavenly way.

By what divinest power; in what supreme estate;
Can souls immortal live, who've entered heaven's gate?
What is the angel-throng; what the archangel hosts;
What the nine choirs of soul, who make but truth their boast?
Can they approach the earth; do they to earth draw nigh?
Yea! nearer than ye think, with all your phantasy!

Each planet guarded is by a Celestial Soul,
Who, taking charge of it, as though upon a scroll,
Writes all its history; and, by the potent will
That angels all possess, this angel, up the Hill
Of Progress,—howe'er long, with mingled wail and song,
With mingled peace and strife, through life and death, and life
Re-born, grown more divine through earth's experience,—
Leads up the Human Soul to Heaven's sweet recompense!

Ah! can ye count the Stars, which twinkle through the night?
Say! can ye e'er discern one tithe of their pure light?
Can any human art, or scientific skill,
Pierce through the ether vault, and through the spaces, still,
Where worlds majestic move, and tell what life is there,
Or limit worlds unseen, floating in ether air?

Science may touch the earth, as with a magic wand,
And straightway to her sight, may nature's law expand
And show how atoms move. as they select their place,
And prove how robes * are formed; and how at length the grace

---

* Material forms are here spoken of as "robes" of Spirit.

Of manhood, womanhood, from childhood, may adorn
What once was wilderness, an arid waste forlorn.
Art may with magic power portray earth, sea and sky
While music may take wings, and soar on ecstacy,
E'en as Beethoven delved into the heart's deep well,
Or Mendelssohn, on wings, to heavens ineffable,
Carried beyond the earth the pleadings of the soul,
And outwardly expressed somewhat of God's control.

The Sculptor takes the block of marble from the mine,
And, by most strange control, may from it best divine
Th' expression of a saint, or some pure little child,
Who as a goddess stands to man, all undefiled ;
While from the brow of Jove Minerva glorious springs,
To bear along heaven's road, on intellectual wings,
Her consort, who is known as Ruler, great and high,
The mightiest of gods, the Chief Divinity !

Then Angelo, in Rome, St Peter's dome thought out :
And Raphael made divine, through genius none can doubt,
The form of human life, transfigured e'en below ;
While Phidias, in Greece, at Atheus, dealt such blow
To marble, that it woke responsive to his touch,
As though his living breath impregnated so much
The solid bust of stone, that life shone in the eye !
In Art so great as this, perchance ye may descry
Some glimmerings of light from that perpetual star,
Which ever shines on earth, with radiance from afar.

When Dante spoke of heaven, beyond all shades of night,
And Beatrice found enrobed in dazzling light,
In pure and snowy sheen transfigured, perfect love
Awoke his trembling lyre, and praise to God above
From every string sent up its pure and sweet refrain,
Which Milton seemed to hear, above earth's cry of pain,
When "Paradise Regained" his chosen theme must be,
And o'er the warlike years, he, Paradise could see,
Not past, but yet to be.

When Homer wrote of gods and goddesses, who strove
In ancient Troy, he caught some of that living flame,
Which through the passing years the poets all declaim ;
Till Wordsworth, Shelley, find, in dreams of perfect peace,
The light of that pure Star, which bids all passion cease.

But 'twas in Bethlehem, when Orient Magi stood
Before a weakly babe, to offer treasures good ;
And 'twas on Indian plains, where pure Gautama found
The life of perfect rest, that heaven did most abound.
Confucius must point unto a Western Star,
Which shone in Buddha's eyes ; while Galilee afar
Must hear its valleys ring, and hill-tops sweetly sound
With that divinest voice, through which souls peace have found.

That Star, in ancient times, was unto Egypt known,
And kings and nobles bowed before its light alone,

While priest and prophet caught from heaven that living flame,
Which gave them the design their ancient structures claim;
Worship was offered to Osiris, God of Light,
And Isis counterpart, who ruled with mildest might
Of justice, bathed in love and wisdom, robed in peace.
There was the primal Star, whose light can never cease,
The matchless Central Sun, round which all planets run
Through Constellations Twelve, passing, while man must delve
On earth, through every state which leads to heaven's own gate.

The Circle of the Stars must needs a centre find,
An all-controlling force must all in union bind.
That centre is pure rest, where all is calm for aye,
Where peace and order rule in love eternally.
Though there is strife around, that centre is the same,
Past, present, and to be, it shines with steadfast flame.

There, at the centre, dwells the Angel of the matchless space,
In which Twelve Planets move in orbits of supernal grace.
Twelve Systems, each with twelve mysterious Orbs of light,
They shine in union pure, harmonious to the sight
Of angels evermore, while to their uttermost,
One hundred-forty-four bright children this Star must boast.

There are Twelve Systems, which revolve in ceaseless day
Around Alcyone, while on their earthly way
They surely must include the system where ye dwell,
And take in Planet Earth, to whom the tale they tell,
That she is but a part of that mysterious whole,
Which answers to the voice of the Great Central Soul!

In man, one central Orb—one Centre—must be found;
That Centre is the Soul, I see revolving round,
When man is perfect made, twelve Powers of the Mind;
Then, again, twelve Gifts of Sense, which bind
The Spirit to the clay, and clay to life of mind.

In this most glorious whole—the circuit of the sky,
In this interior grace of soul ye may descry
The bonds which knit ye all together in one race,
Assuring each and all of future dwelling place,
Among those orbs of light, among those stars so bright,
Ye gaze upon by night, scarce visible to sight!

Now ministering to earth, we watch a gracious Queen,
One who, in earthly form, has persecuted been;
One who, at Holyrood, must sorrow, strive, and turn
Only to God in need: to him whose love doth burn,
Bright as that central fire, though all else should expire.

She, and a mystic band of virgin souls most white,—
Clad in the purity which victors from the fight
Have won, through trials o'ercome, temptations dashed to earth,—
As the Vestal Virgins watched the temple fires of earth,
When Rome was Queen; so now, unseen by mortal eye,
The souls of many watch, and guide earth's destiny.

She, this illustrous Queen, is chosen at this day,
To give an outward form to truth's surpassing ray,
At one point of the Star; and there are many see
She holds her light to earth, in love and purity.

And there are other souls, who work in other ways.
The Star, the Sexagram, with undiminished rays,
Will be the typic Star, for this New Age to be.
The Star Circle in Heaven must shine eternally,
Twelve pointed; and when all earth's periods shall be run,
Then from the Tree of Life, twelve fruits, securely won,
Shall be the harvest growth, the yielding of the whole,
Which the Twelve Angels brought from the Region of the Soul

This Star shines with the light of every martyred soul,
Of every lowly life unrecognised below;
While every genius pure, and prophet's radiant light,
Give form unto this Star, as downward flows its light.
It is the Dual Star of Wisdom and of Love;
Its perfect name is TRUTH, high in the Heavens above.
Its outward shimmerings, near the confines of the earth,
Are breathings from those friends who wake, into new birth,
Whate're is pure within. Follow, ye all, this light;
To others be ye stars; then will life's path grow bright,
And heaven's immortal peace your spirits will infill,
And Truth, your amulet, will guard you from all ill!

BENEDICTION.

(May the Dual perfect Light of the Star of God's perfect Truth, ever wise and ever loving, be your constant Guide through Time and your Crown Eternally!)

V.

RESURRECTIONS:

THEIR SPIRIT AND THEIR LETTER.

(*Delivered on Easter Sunday, April* 13, 1884.)

THE Gospel Stories of the Resurrection, have been so often read and commented upon, that, perhaps, little fresh matter may be added in this Discourse, to what you have heard already. Nevertheless, as festival and holiday occasions bring many strangers to our gatherings, as well as our regular attendants, we feel that we may be speaking to some in the present audience, to whom what we have to say may place the matter of the Resurrection from the Dead in quite a new, and we hope a helpful, light.

(The doctrine of the resuscitation of the physical body at the last Great Day, the Day of Judgment or final account, looked forward to with trembling hopes and fears by all the nations of the world, from times immemorial, we need scarcely remind you is by no means new, *i.e.*, it did not originate with Christianity or any developments of Christianity, and few, indeed, if any, are the Christian dogmas, which in their traceable origin do not antedate the year 1 of the Christian era, by several thousands of years.

The BOOK OF THE DEAD, which conveys, perhaps, more definite information concerning the religious beliefs of the ancient Egyptians than any other accessible document, distinctly unfolds the idea of a physical resurrection in the future, very similar to that looked forward to by Christians. The Egyptians were all believers in the immortality of the soul, but differed among themselves, even as the Jews afterwards differed concerning the fate of the body.

Pharisean and Sadducean views of immortality, were at variance as regards the resurrection only. All the Jews, who accepted the Talmud as in any way authoritative, were believers in the immortality of the soul; and though Moses made the earth the centre of moral gravity for man, so long as he dwelt upon it, the best Rabbinical interpretations of the Hebrew Law coincided perfectly with the universal faith of Orientals, in the immortality of the Breath of God in man, as the Soul is ever called by the Hebrews.

No one, reading the Gospel narratives, can fail to be struck with the animosity existing between Pharisee and Sadducee, on this very question of the Resurrection. Some commentators have called the Sadducees sceptics, and even infidels, but they were as good Theists as were the Pharisees: they disagreed only in the peculiar views they took of the fate of the body after death.

Sadducean conceptions of immortality and a future state, are more spiritual than Pharisean ones, as the latter bow blindly before a shrine of dust, and look forward to a perpetuation throughout eternity of the limitations of time and sense; while the former contemplate the spirit as entirely distinct from the body, and see no need of a carnal resurrection from the dead.

The Egyptians, from whom the Pharisees, no doubt, originally derived their ideas, were those who considered the embalming of the body a work of the utmost importance. All distinguished persons were so embalmed, that they might last for thousands of years before their bodily assumption into heaven, were the judgment delayed so long. There are mummies now in the British Museum which go to prove to every Egyptologist, that this looking forward to a physical resurrection was one of the greatest hopes and most noteworthy peculiarities of the materialistic side of the Egyptian religion. Some there were indeed among the Egyptians, who so confounded the real man with his physical nature, that those were not lacking to teach the inseparability of existence from the outward frame. Three forms or degrees of embalming were devised; and it was supposed by some that immediately the body crumbled into dust, the individuality of its former occupant was destroyed also. No one can listen to some Christian sermons preached to-day, avowedly in defence of immortality, without tracing a close resemblance to the most materialistic thought of ancient Egypt, if he knows anything of the nature of that thought; while even spiritual communications concerning the future of man, can scarcely be said to transcend the sublimest and most interior thought of the enlightened Egyptians of old.

Regularly, at Easter-tide, the Church arrays herself in her brightest garb, sings her sweetest songs, decks her altars and her priests in sumptuous array, and calls all the world to worship at the feet of the Resurrected Jesus; while in the glad Spring-time all nature invites the world to witness those stupendous transformations of scenery, which by their annual and orderly occurrence point the worshipper at the shrines of nature only, to that Supreme, revivifying Force in being, which only allows death to prey for awhile upon the beauties of the world, soon resurrecting them by the power of the Spirit working through the agency of what is popularly called "natural law;" till with each succeeding spring-time, the world has advanced yet nearer to that glorious Golden Age, or millennial period, so long foretold and so eagerly sought for by poet, seer, and prophet, in every age and clime.

(It was Thomas Paine who said, that a contemplation of Nature led not to Atheism but to Deism; and in Deism this brave reformer found what he called a positive and absolute antidote to Atheism. On the one hand regarded as the champion of infidelity by many Materialists; on the other, execrated by theological bigots because of his determination to cut loose from all theological restraints, this man—great writer, fluent speaker, and able politician, though he was—has been perhaps more misunderstood and maligned than almost any writer or agitator of modern times. Read his voluminous articles, peruse them carefully, criticise them fairly, and you will find in the teachings of the author of "The Age of Reason," some of the soundest and most natural Theistic arguments ever presented to the world. We do not wish you to understand us to agree with every rabid criticism made by Paine; his language is often excessively severe, and his conclusions oftentimes faulty and extremely external. Nevertheless, with all his defects he has marked an era in the history of literature and government, and when styled the Author-hero of American Independence, by an eminent American Statesman and man of letters, his praises were not too loudly sung.)

Turn to France, and the France of to-day—nominally and enthusiastically republican, yet with many seeds of monarchy still remaining—is turning from the Church with its ceremonies and its priesthood, to the acknowledgment of no other Deity than the God revealed through nature; whose words are spoken in the roar of the ocean, in the peal of the thunder, in the murmuring streams, in the babbling brooks. in the voices of birds, and most of all in the intuitions of humanity. And if to crown the meed of Revelation accorded through these strictly natural messengers, there shall come a direct voice from the Realm of Spirit, speaking through the prophets and prophetesses of the approaching new Spiritual Dispensation, France is ready to lend the listening ear, and to receive the new angels gladly.

But the power of the Roman Hierarchy has waned, and waned for ever, across the Channel. The magnificent ritual and music at Notre Dame, and the hundred other magnificent churches, where the ceremonies vie with those of Rome itself, all fail to captivate the masses of the people, as of yore. The Church is as vigilant as ever, but the love of the people is surely drifting into other channels. What shall those channels be? Who shall carve them out? Who shall direct the spirit of the new nation into the grooves of harmony and purity? Liberty, Equality, Fraternity, are three great words, and these are the watchwords of the new French Republic; but who shall translate them into the language of daily life? Who shall give to the French nation a word signifying Home? Who shall so change the tide of religious and social life, that the country shall be born anew into more than its ancient glories? Neither the Army nor the Fleet can accomplish this new birth.

(Your standing regiments of idle men, here and abroad, are a standing disgrace, not an honour to the nation which supports them. And in Germany, where every boy must enter the army and be qualified to take up arms for his country in time of war, are the morals of the land any better than with your Gallic neighbours?) In Germany neither Catholicism, Lutheranism, Calvinism, nor Judaism can control the masses. Religion there is at a greater discount even than here. Kant, Strauss, Fichte, Goethe, and a hundred other illustrious minds, have taught the Teutonic race to think for themselves. (But to what does Free-thought lead? Is it a desideratum, if it leads only to scepticism and a denial of everything, save what can be apprehended by the five senses of the body?)

How is it with Italy? Garibaldi may have freed the country technically. The Papal Dominions have long since been ceded to the Crown, and the Pope is now little better than a prisoner in the Vatican, supported by donations from England and America, while the Church is in ill-odour with the multitude.

What of Russia, where Absolutism prevails, and Nihilism also; where the Czar is nominally supreme, and yet in peril every moment. The Russian Church is powerless to stem the tide of growing discontent; while here in England, dynamite outrages make the lives of many a daily terror; while Parliament dilly-dallies with the greatest questions of the day, and spends session after session in needless comment upon trifles.

The one word which every true prophet and reformer must emphasize to-day all over Europe is *Renaissance!* and that means New Birth. You have had Ruskin endeavouring to bring about a *renaissance* in Art; you have had an attempted æstheticism caricatured in "Punch," and represented by Oscar Wilde; but *renaissance* is more than a resuscitation of pre-Raphaelite eccentricities, or even excellencies. The world is not a crab, for ever completing series after series of retrospective movements, in order to make onward progress. Forward, not backward, is the cry of the prophet. Not with Ritualism to restore the Church to what it was before the Reformation; not with Æstheticism to restore the world to what it was in mediæval times; but with Modern Spiritualism, when divested of the puerilities and superstitions which are still unfortunately attached to it, will the true prophet ever throw in his lot, advancing boldly and bravely over the crumbling ruins of effete dynasties and exploded fallacies, over the wreck of Superstition's altars and those of dread, to where the angel in every household shall attest the fact of immortal being, and death shall be indeed robbed of all its sting, the grave despoiled of all its seeming victory.

O Death! *where* is thy sting? O Grave! *where* is thy victory? Surely in the worship of Mammon, which has blinded the eyes of mankind, that the spirit is as though it were not, and the future seems to hold nought but oblivion and silence forever. Why are the joy-bells pealing forth their clarion notes to-day? Why have multitudes of worshippers and sightseers assembled in all the great temples of religion throughout the Christian world to-day? Surely the occasion is one of great joy! What good news has the preacher to tell, as he mounts the pulpit stairs and addresses that vast concourse of human beings? Some in his audience have come from far, for words of comfort; some have but yesterday consigned all that was earthly of their best beloved to the tomb; some have come, like the women in the Gospels, to anoint the inanimate forms of their beloved dead, with the sweetest spices they can procure,—the heavy sigh, the scalding tear, the simple flower laid upon the grave, the heartfelt prayer uttered or unexpressed,—all are noted by the angels; and though the preachers shall tell you the angels who came to the women at the sepulchre of Jesus, nearyl nineteen centuries ago, have gone away into heaven, and from thence appear on earth no more,(still those brooding angels may smile, nay, perhaps, oftener weep, at the materiality of Christendom, as the preacher ignores or derides Modern Spiritual Communion; as they are still here to whisper in dulcet tones the heart-consoling message into the mourner's ear: "Your friends are not in the grave; they are arisen, and they go with you as perpetual companions, as abiding comforters following your footsteps where'er your journey lies."

The facts of physiology have demonstrated the fallacy of a corporeal resurrection, and no comfort whatever can the soul derive from the thought of perpetual imprisonment in a form of clay. Matter may not be evil, the earth may not be a hell, but the true place for matter is in its perfect subordination to Spirit. The true use of earth is as a school. Do you wish to remain in a preparatory school for ever. If you have graduated from the lower, you go to the higher seminary. You may return to school for a while, if you have not yet learned all the lessons taught in that school, and longer need its discipline; but once you have gained all the knowledge to be imparted there, you can never return to it except as a teacher. We do not say spirits will never be re-embodied on the earth, either as scholars or teachers. If the need shall ever arise for future embodiment, the need will undoubtedly be supplied. But possible re-embodiment, though scouted by some even in the ranks of Spiritualism, must surely be far less dreadful to contemplate than that awful resurrection on the last great day, depicted by Young in ghastly verse; and when to the ghastliness of the scene you add the blasphemy therewith associated by many in the orthodox church,—we mean the resurrection of the wicked to everlasting torment—the dogma becomes so heinous, that to advocate it is far worse than to proclaim oneself an Atheist. Better let the cold ashes lie for ever inanimate in the tomb, than raise them only to throw them to the devil; better, far better, think of your friends as living again in the flowers and grasses which adorn your burying-places, than believe that even one spirit shall have its body raised again by God, that it may endure eternal anguish.)

We do not wonder at prevailing hatred of religion, if such travesty of the divine character has been allied with religion as popularly presented for fifteen centuries. But what says the New Testament, from which these hateful dogmas are avowedly deduced: "As in Adam all die, even so in Christ shall all be made alive." "I, if I be lifted up, will draw all men unto me," These and many other texts need only to be quoted, they explain themselves. Redemption is as wide as the fall; if all fell in Adam then all will be raised in Christ. But there is no gospel which provides a resurrection or a saviour for a smaller number than the number which have fallen into sin. Take whatever view you will of Christ or Adam, literalize or spiritualize the legends of the Old, and the gospels and epistles of the New, Testament as you please, the fact remains, no more are lost than are restored, no more die than will be raised again; and surely no person, with one spark of humanity within him, can sing the Easter Anthem, praising God in his heart that half the human race will rise to everlasting shame and sorrow.

Great interest is manifested by many in the purely literal resurrection of Jesus, while to us the spiritual triumph is all that seems really important. Literally, there can be no identical resurrection of the body, the body being so mutable that it changes completely in an average period of seven years, and somewhat every moment. Waste and recuperation remodel your structures so often, that you really have no individuality apart from your spirit, which holds all there is of your real being. The body of Jesus, we are told, even by the most conservative in matters pertaining to religion, was a perfect human body. He assumed man's flesh, and was subject for thirty-three years to human limitations. Even the Athanasian Creed teaches this. How then can there be a physical resurrection of the identical body worn by

Jesus during earthly life? His body as a man was not his body as an infant. He lived long enough to accumulate between four and five distinct bodies, and if a physical resurrection of the entire earthly body of Jesus were to take place, would it not be necessary to raise every particle of matter which had ever formed his body? If he ate, drank, slept and discharged all the natural functions common to human life, this resurrection was impossible; and, as an earnest of our own, were it possible, it would be worthless, as every tyro in science knows that the very food employed in upbuilding the physical structure, may be derived from the resurrected bodies of defunct ancestors.

If the body which is to rise at the judgment, is the identical body in which the spirit passed from earth, how sad the prospect of a resurrection which in many cases must be the resuscitation of an impaired and unlovely structure, from which the burdened spirit was only too happy to effect a hasty exit, at the hour of its dissolution.

If the raising of Lazarus, of the Widow's Son at Nain, or of the boy restored to life by Elijah, be cited as examples of resurrection, then immortality would be disproved rather than proved by such a doctrine, as we are nowhere led to infer that these resurrected bodies were immortalized. It may be said of them, as Frederick Robertson, the eminent incumbent of Trinity Chapel, Brighton, said of the resurrections of inanimate nature every spring-time: "They all die again." Only the spirit is immortal; only the soul lives for ever; and whensoever you predicate immortality upon what is mutable, you embark upon a sea of difficulty and doubt, which can logically carry you nowhere but into the howling wilderness of blank denial of all, save what is transitory and perishing.

(The instances of resurrection from the dead, to which we have already alluded, are not parallel with anything other than the accounts often rendered of similar wonders having taken place in various Oriental countries, where interment often takes place almost immediately after the patient is thought to be dead, especially when he has been suffering from a contagious disorder, or plague is rife in a district. In the South of Italy, it is quite common for less than 24 hours to elapse between death and burial. In the Orient this space of time is considered ample, and it is needless to remind you, that not so far away from home, where interment is usually deferred much longer, persons have been buried in trances, and even robbers going to plunder new-made graves, have awakened the supposed corpses by cutting the jewellery from the persons of the apparently dead. In the case of Lazarus, who it is said had been dead four days, we are only told the bystanders said so. The remark, he has become offensive, was not made by Jesus. Utterly unconscious of all outward things he may have been; utterly beyond restoration by any ordinary means that could have been applied; dead to all but the voice and will of Jesus, who—endowed with almost superhuman affection and will, a personal friend of Lazarus and his family, one at whose feet the family was wont to sit, as the disciples of the Greek philosophers might have sat before Socrates or Plato—may have alone possessed the power to call him back to life; and remembering that the life of Jesus was was that of a rigid ascetic oftentimes; that he had undergone forty days in the wilderness, alone with wild beasts and evil spirits, and had conquered temptation in its three-fold forms before entering upon his public ministry as a teacher and a healer;—one who knows anything of the records of what is now popularly designated Theosophy, will have no difficulty in finding an explanation of wonderful phenomena, so soon as he compares it with the goal towards which all true Theosophists are striving, and the accredited testimony of those who have made Oriental Mysticism and Magic a life study.

To the Adept, or Initiate, the Gospel is not paradoxical. It simply illustrates in the person of the Evangelists' hero, the practical carrying out of the laws and principles laid down by the sages of the Orient. It is quite beside our subject this morning to institute comparisons between Buddhism, or any strictly Oriental system, and Christianity. To our minds Christianity is only a later development of older systems, a more recent flowering out of the tree of religions in the world. Constantinian Christianity, which has equalled Mohammedanism in its devotion to the sword as a means of propagandism, is certainly no part of the religion of the Nazarene.

The assumptions of orthodoxy, on the subject of the resurrection of Jesus, are nowhere supported by Matthew, Mark, Luke or John, who simply content themselves with recording, each in his own way, that Jesus appeared to his disciples after his death and burial, and satisfied them that it was he himself who communed with them; all agree that the body of Jesus was not in the tomb when the women went to seek it on the resurrection morn, and all alike speak of the difficulty, even his most intimate friends encountered, in recognising him when he appeared to them. He had been dead only since Friday afternoon; they had possibly seen him on Saturday, when he was interred; all his disciples had sat with him at supper on Thursday evening, and yet though he rose before daybreak on Sunday morning, they mistook him for the gardener; and even Mary had a long conversation with him before she knew him, and she was last at the cross and first at the tomb. Would you forget the appearance of a friend in one, two, or three days? Would you need your friend to speak your name in some peculiar way, that you might know him, if he stood before you in the identical body in which he died so recently? It was only after Jesus had called Mary by her name, in the old familiar way, that she turned to him and said, Rabboni. Then, on the same day at evening, when two disciples were journeying to Emmaus, we are told Jesus met them on the way, and expounded Moses and the Prophets to them, and yet they did not know him till they had persuaded him to sup with them, and then he made himself known in the breaking of bread. True, we are told he made himself so visible to Thomas that the doubting apostle thrust his hands into the wound-prints, and believed, when he had material evidence that a solid body stood before him. But such occurrences as these, coupled with the statement often made, "he vanished out of their sight," show these manifestations to have been far more closely akin to modern Spiritual Phenomena than to any alleged corporeal resurrection, as taught by the orthodox.

Materialization has been the means of convincing hundreds, not to say thousands, of the precious fact that their beloved, miscalled dead, are yet alive. The triumphant spirit of Jesus may have disintegrated the material form, and thereby rendered it invisible. When on the cross, he exclaimed: "It is finished!" may he not have alluded to the completion of his earth experiences, and the final victory over matter he had won? The disintegration of a material body offers no insuperable obstacle to the chemist, who discourses glibly enough upon volatilization and etherealization of substance, by processes known to chemistry. Who is there of note in the scientific world, who refuses to call man's body an agglomeration of molecules? Who is there who dissents from the atomic theory? All scientific discoveries prove that it is within the power of man, under given conditions, to render visible things invisible, and invisible visible. The conversion of solids and fluids into gases, is a triumph of human intelligence. The consolidation of atmospheric particles into solid form, and the dematerialization of forms so constructed in the chemist's laboratory, is a simple triumph of mind over matter. And where shall these triumphs end? Who shall say to the human will: "Thus far thou canst go, but no further!" As well might Canute's flatterers attempt to persuade him he could control the ocean tides, as for modern Agnostics to persuade the rational Spiritualist that materialization is impossible. The philosophy of the subject is natural and scientific. Its applicability to individual phenomena must, of course, be decided by the amount of evidence granted at a specified time, and in a certain place. The Acts of the Apostles tell us, Jesus was seen by about 500 brethren at once, and inform us also that Saul saw Jesus on his way to Damascus; and yet Paul says after the flesh he has not seen Christ, but in the spirit only. He it is who declares there is a natural (animal) and there is a spiritual body; that flesh and blood cannot enter the Kingdom of Heaven; though Jesus was seen in heaven by the martyr Stephen, and Paul was caught up to the third heaven by power divine.

The Resurrection is surely the complete and final victory of the soul over sense; and whensoever and wheresoever your own lower nature is entirely the servant of your spirit, you will have the freedom to come and go in ways at present utterly beyond your ken. The risen life, we are all implored to live, is not a life in which the animal body clogs the spirit for eternity; but life's conflict ended, the battle fought, the victory won, the soul governs matter where once it was ruled by it, and when a needed manifestation is vouchsafed, immortality is demonstrated by the power of Spirit over all material things.

No soul can die; no thought can perish; no good become extinct. Immortal is every pure desire; immortal the results of every noble effort. Only the outward form may perish; only the vesture change; while the soul, without beginning, knows no end, and at length arrives at its true Home, where life is a pæan of praise to the Infinite; a psalm of joy; a constant well-spring of happiness and bliss to all the universe.

Conquer Sense by your own Spirit, and the Resurrection, with all its glories, is yours for aye!

IMPROMPTU POEM.

THE TWIN ANGELS.

BEHOLD! How all things die!
Death's cold and icy hand upon the flowers is laid—
They perish in their very bloom: Are they of death afraid?
Perchance they may be; still it seems to spirit's watchful eyes,
They only fall asleep to wake again at glad sunrise.

Behold, how forest glories fade! The trees grow sad and bare,
The cold wind whistles where the leaves once so abundant, fair,
Clothed the drear bark with verdant hue, thro' all the summer time;
But winter's cold and icy breath shears all in northern clime.

Somewhere, far off across the seas, the trees are always green,
The flowers never fade away, all things are decked in sheen,
Impervious to the hand of death, it seems to him who strays
Thro' orange groves, on isles of spice; but there the savage lays
In wait, and the tiger and serpent are there,
So of those fair groves ye must needs beware.

But 'tis in those fair tropic lands, the withering power of death
Is felt more quickly, than where your cheeks are fanned with the icy breath
Of the North-East winds from the Baltic Seas, and the frozen zone afar,
Where ye think ye can find the brain of the earth, and the mystic Polar Star.

Life feeds on death, and wheresoe'er life's table is thickest spread
With daintiest viands and beverage, whereon gods might be fed,
It is there Transition's Angel takes the fullest, broadest rule,
And this veiled angel—Oh! what is she, but a Teacher in Nature's School.

In the far-off ages, so long ago that ye needs must turn to the rocks,
And hear them tell of the direful storms and terrific earthquake shocks,
Which rent the crust of the planet of yore, before man his place could take,
As head of creation; 'twas then and there, in some dark and distant place,
That the Spirit of God in the storm-wind moaned, and in thunder's awful din,
Prepared the way for the Age of Gold, which e'en now doth but scarce begin!

O beautiful Angel! whom men most dread: Why should we turn from thee,
And veil our faces with trembling hands, when thou offerest liberty,
To the captive spirit imprisoned here,
That sighs and prays for a brighter sphere?

But, mystical Angel! thou'rt not alone, or we might be afraid of thee;
Thou hast a fair Sister, arrayed with flowers, and with all the springtide's glee,
And her name is not Death, but Renewal of Life! she the Resurrection brings,
Fair Goddess of Spring, of the opening flowers, of the bird that most sweetly sings.
Were it not for thy veiled handmaid, Death, thine herald, we ne'er could know thee;
The sweets of reunion were never felt, if bereavements could not be.

O beautiful Angel of Life Renewed! by the sepulchre sit to-day;
To the weeping mourners, who come to grieve, and over their dead to pray,
Reveal, as thou didst in the olden time, the life which the Spirit doth know,
Say softly to every sorrowing heart: "Not dead but arisen!" Then go
And point to the Life, which all may share,
When Love conquers Strife and Sin everywhere!

BENEDICTION.

May the Angels of the Resurrection bring you all glad tidings of Life Immortal, and reveal to you the Father's boundless Love to all His Children.

VI.

RELIGIOUS TRUTHS AND CONTROVERSIAL THEOLOGIES.

THE attention of the World has perhaps never been more extensively called to the study of Comparative Theology than at the present moment, when this somewhat new science, with its kindred science, also a novelty, Comparative Philology, is arresting the serious attention of all classes of minds, scholars especially.

Until within the past half century the prevailing thought in Christendom was that all the inhabitants of the world, excepting Christians and Jews, were idolaters, bowing down to images of wood and stone, and believing these poor idols to be the supreme powers who governed and guided the universe. When occasionally a Unitarian, or an extremely Broad Churchman within the pale of the Establishment, undertook to say a kind word for the great religions of the world, far more ancient and widely spread than Christianity, he was denounced as a heresiarch or a blasphemer; as it has ever been the policy of professing Christians to claim for their own system a monopoly of truth, and for Christian countries a monopoly of civilization. Christians, it is true, are not singular in this, as it is customary for all partisans to exaggerate the excellence of their favourite institutions, while they persistently decry all others. But party feeling is not an element of true religion, neither has it any foundation in what is popularly termed the Gospel of Christ.

Let us spend a few moments to-day in considering the true origin and nature of Religion, and its relation to controversial theologies, always remembering that Theology is or ought to be a true science; as the word means the Science of God, or divine things; as Geology means the science of the earth, and Philology the science of language.

Many of the fiercest disputes between theologians have hinged upon the interpretation given to the *logos*, or Word, introduced to our notice not only by the author of the fourth

Gospel, at its commencement, but earlier by Plato, who discourses frequently and sublimely upon it. It is noticeable to even the most cursory student of language, that the termination only varies when the *logos* is changed into "logy"; and that these "ologies," about which we hear so much to-day, all spring from the identification of science, knowledge, treatise, word, &c., with the *logos* of the philosophers.

It is needless to state that "science" means knowledge, and that without definite and demonstrable information concerning a certain subject, there can be no science of that subject. If Geology and Philology are sciences, must not Theology also be regarded as a science, and must it not be the province of all true theologians to speculate no longer, but to commence with the demonstration of spiritual truth to the comprehension of their pupils, as far as may be? We beg you to bear in mind, however, that no abstruse mathematical problem, for instance, can ever be demonstrated to those who have no knowledge of mathematics, and no capabilities for succeeding in a study of mathematical laws and principles. Not every brain is a mathematical brain, as not every brain is adapted to classical studies. It is frequently remarked, the best Classic is the poorest Mathematician, and *vice versa*. University men usually excel either in one branch of study or the other, but not usually in both, and this not because of any opposition between Classics and Mathematics, but rather by reason of the fact that excessive cultivation of certain organs of the brain, has a natural tendency to induce depression in other directions.

No one who devotes himself to Pugilism is likely to become a great intellectual luminary. No one who follows warfare as a profession, and loves cruel sport, is apt to be a great expert at the peaceful arts, because of the inflammation of certain propensities, tending naturally to attract the forces of the brain to particular points, as centres which absorb more than their due allowance of the universal energy, which becomes focalized at these points, and from them rather than from other points in the organism, it is most extensively thrown out to the world.

No one in his right mind endeavours to limit knowledge by his personal attainment; no one but an idiot will be found to deny the existence of every thing which is not included within the narrow compass of what he has individually realized. The realm of sound is an unknown and utterly untrodden realm to the man who was born deaf, and if you ask him to give a definition of sound, as he fancies sound to exist, he must compare it to something he can approach through one of the four avenues of sense which are not closed to him; but you cannot accurately describe a noise by comparing it to anything which can be tasted, felt, seen, or smelt, and yet the deaf man who sees, tastes, feels, and smells, but does not hear, is obliged to compare sound in imagination with something his own perceptions have enabled him to apprehend; while the blind man, who compares scarlet in his own mind with a very loud noise, is equally at sea so far as correct apprehension goes, though in another direction.

The spiritual nature of man, to those destitute of spiritual perception, is necessarily an algebraic *x*, an unknown quantity: yea, it is to some more, or rather less than this: it is an unthinkable condition of being, as much so as Zöllner's Fourth Dimension in space is to a majority who have read his decidedly clever work, "Transcendental Physics."

Can there not be a fourth dimension in space? Certainly there can, says the eminent Leipzic Professor; but we, as three dimensional beings, cannot realize it, and had we only two dimensions ourselves, the thought of a third would be equally impracticable.

We all measure the universe by such measuring rods as we can devise and handle. We can sound no ocean without a plummet line, and thus the facts of existence by the majority of writers and speakers, are so superficially and impertinently dealt with, that a minimum of human knowledge is nearly always at a premium, and a maximum at a decided discount. Nothing can be more puerile and contradictory than materialistic negation. When those who are studying the facts of nature from their material side, bring us facts, we gladly accept them, and are willing to bow before any teacher, even though the sum of his knowledge be expressed in a treatise upon the habits of earth-worms, provided his knowledge of these lowly creatures is greater than our own. But should any professor of science undertake to blot out all the facts of nature, with which he is personally unacquainted, just because there are limits to his knowledge and powers of discovery, we should decline to regard him as any authority at all on matters concerning which he had at first the good sense to confess himself ignorant.

There can be no science of Agnosticism, no philosophy of ignorance, no text-books to explain to students the nature of non-existence. All scientific declarations are strictly affirmative. We could never *know* that 2×2 were not 5, unless we did know that they made 4. The knowledge that something is what it is, precludes all possibility of our thinking it may be what it is not. But where knowledge ceases and ignorance begins, science is necessarily cut short in her career.

From the earliest times there have been those on earth who admitted Theology into the category of their studies, and perhaps the most ancient Religion known to men, was that which is popularly termed Astro-Theology. The Astro-Theological system of Hindostan, Egypt, and other ancient Oriental climes, was so stupendous, and moreover so deeply spiritual, so intensely esoteric, that very few modern Egyptologists have done any more than just touch the outer fringe of the garment worn by religious truth in the olden days.)

Recently, a long series of consecutive papers have been published in the MEDIUM AND DAYBREAK, a London Spiritualistic Journal, the substance of which their author, Wm. Oxley, has just brought out in book form. Associated with these papers there has waged what has been termed a "Theological Conflict," in the same paper, extending over many weeks. In this conflict an attempt has been made to show, on the one hand, that Christianity is only a later development of the religion of Egypt, and on the other, that Jesus of Nazareth was a veritable personage, a great historical character, and the real as well as the alleged founder of the Christian religion. (The conflict has been on the whole well conducted, though in our opinion personal feelings mar almost every controversy most seriously, and because of this conviction we usually decline to enter into discussion or debate with any one, either by lip or pen.

In a debate each party has a client, each takes a position he feels bound to sustain, and the result usually is a pitched battle between two opponents, or two diametericallv opposite classes of ideas, which are defended on both sides with heated partisan effrontery. In the presentation of what you feel to be truth to the world, it is better never to act and speak as though you had an enemy to attack or an opponent to silence Those lectures which give one the idea of having been given simply to answer somebody, are not as a rule most effective spiritually. Clear, impersonal argument, free from all suggestion that your audience necessarily disagrees with you, is far more likely to reach the intellect and sympathies of your auditors than any amount of aggressive reasoning, however logical.

We were once present at a banquet, where a number of distinguished orators had collected. One among the number was a man of fine commanding presence, bold eagle eye, lofty brow, possessed of an unusually large amount both of brain power and psychologic influence. His voice was loud and stirring, and could be heard at the farthest corner of a larger building than the Metropolitan Tabernacle. This fine, imperious, noble-looking fellow, with an immense amount of self-satisfaction, said: "I always go to battle, to fight the foe, when I ascend the platform. My auditors are my enemies, my tongue is my arrow, with which I pierce them to the quick. They fear me, they know they cannot resist my words, for I speak as one having authority. I never permit myself to address an assembly until my quiver is full of the sharpest arrows. I fortify myself with unanswerable reasons for all I advance, and I challenge the dissentient from my conclusions, to establish the fallacy of a single point in my argument."

When this celebrated orator had resumed his seat, an old, trembling man rose to his feet. With feeble voice, and snow-white locks, and tottering limbs he faltered forth his tribute to the power of speech. With winning smile and in kindly tones, utterly destitute of pride or *hauteur*, he said: "My friends,—I know you are such, and whenever I address a company, large or small, savage or civilized, I address my friends, and those whom I address know that I wish to be a friend to every one present. I have been in many lands, and spoken to many singular assemblies, but never to a hostile one. I have no enemies, as I feel no animosity toward any. I know I am not highly gifted, but God has used me—poor, imperfect creature though I am—to comfort some of his sorrowing children, and that is my mission to humanity, to try and be a comforter."

While the venerable man was speaking, tears were in many

eyes. No heart in the room could have been untouched by his few simple words. Out of the abundance of his kindly heart, his mouth spake words of tender sympathy, and every one who heard him, knew he spoke from his own pure soul, and so he reached the souls of all whom he addressed. The eloquent orator, the erudite scholar, the haughty priest, the crafty barrister,—all may wield an influence, but the influence of love is the only sovereign antidote to the innumerable ills which afflict society.

How was it with these two speakers? The former had twenty times the learning of the latter; the latter had a hundred times more feeling than the former; the one hammered away at dry statistics, read genealogical tables from beginning to end, consulted authorities innumerable to fortify his position, and when he had established it, all he could prove was some unimportant fact of literal history. The aged man could never have competed successfully with the younger in scholarly attainments, and yet all who listened to them both said of the one: "He is a great orator, a smart, clever, well-read man; he pleads his cause finely, but after all we can't decide until we've heard what can be said by his opponent." Those who had listened to the saintly veteran, exclaimed: "We know he tells the truth, for we have the witness in ourselves; he heals our wounds, he ends our doubts, he dislodges our fears, he shows us light on the darkest pathway, and therefore we are assured he is sent by God, for he opens up our understandings, he silences our fears, and he makes us loathe our sins and deal justly by our neighbours."

We have cited this narrative, culled from our own experience, to illustrate our theme, as we feel it needs illustration in this day. When everything is being shaken, even to its foundations, it behoves all to see to the foundations, whether they be secure or insecure. Controversy may wage till everything historical is disputed; and there are those who declare that Christianity, Judaism, Buddhism, and all the great systems of the world, are built on sand, and are themselves mere mythologies. The personality of Jesus is denied, so is that of Buddha. The Old and New Testaments are discounted as fabrications of the priesthood, or regarded as Kabalistic treatises upon the Solar Mythos. Osiris and Jesus are said to be the same, and both are said to be the material sun. The disciples of Christ are said to be the twelve Zodiacal signs, while the Holy Spirit can be only solar light or heat.

The glowing symbolism of the East undoubtedly points to astronomical and astrological principles and facts. Mathematics and Geometry unquestionably must be called in to solve the problem of the Pyramid, and decipher the riddle of the Sphinx; while it is self-evident to us, that material science in the olden time was in the keeping of a learned and initiated minority, while the multitude were destitute of all such information as the priests possessed. As Egypt is the centre around which present controversies revolve, and as it is to Egypt that the thought of all Europe is turned to-day, politically and religiously, by reason of the present war, and the appearance of the Mahdi, it may be well for us to offer a few remarks upon that land and its antiquities, in so far as they throw light upon the subject immediately before us.

How old the Great Pyramid may be, is not decided. Professor Smyth, Astronomer Royal of Scotland, long ago fixed the date of its construction at 2,170 B.C., and by many ingenious interpretations endeavoured to foretell the second coming of Christ, as probable soon after 1881 A.D. It is true that Professor Smyth's predictions have not yet failed, because he takes into consideration, the narrow passage-way connecting the Grand Gallery with the King's Chamber, and as this measures at the least something over fifty inches in length, and each inch is said to represent a year, there is yet, even now, ample time for the fulfilment of the Professor's expectations, and even now may be the time of war and danger, prefigured by the narrow passage already mentioned. But as those of the school of Dupuis are too external on the one hand, so are Christian apologists apt to be too literal also, though in another direction, in that, while the Materialist sees only the letter of the allegory, the Christian often loses sight of principles in personalities, and limits all manifestations of truth to a single outpouring of the Spirit, once for all, in Palestine, through Jesus of Nazareth, at the commencement of the Christian era.

Professor Smyth has very forcibly called the attention of the reading world, to the suggestive fact of the site of the Grand Pyramid being truly central. It is stated that this is on middle ground absolutely, and that such central position (the very centre of all the land upon the globe) could not have been chosen accidentally, especially at a time when knowledge was not ripe as to-day. It is further stated that this Pyramid pointed, at the time of its construction, directly to Alcyone, the far-distant star or sun around which the sun of this system accomplishes a period of revolution once in every Grand Cycle, and that the star *alpha draconis* (the polar star 4,000 years ago) shone directly down the shaft of the Pyramid, at the time of its erection.

Ignoring the celebrated wisdom of the Ancients, the Christian apologist traces the facts just referred to. directly to deific inspiration, claiming that God himself must have been the architect and inspirer of this temple to his honour, in the land of Egypt; and as this Pyramid is frequently alluded to (though vaguely to the uninitiated) in the Old Testament, proof positive is supposed to be forthcoming of the authenticity and prophetic, as well as historic, accuracy of the Scriptures, when the mystery of the Pyramid shall be fully comprehended.

(Without denying the prophetic character of the several books of the Old Testament, or derogating one iota from the dignity of Jesus as a Messiah, and a fulfiller of prophecy, it is quite possible to interpret the central wonder of ancient and modern Egypt, more universally than above; but to do so requires an amount of knowledge not ordinarily within the grasp of the Christian minister, who is taught to bend every fact concerning the ancient world, until it serves to establish the miraculous origin of Judaism and Christianity, and the purely human origin of all other systems.

What the Christian and the Jew are wont to say of Brahmanism and Buddhism, that the Brahman and Buddhist are equally apt to say of Judaism and Christianity, the view taken of Mohammed by Christians, is substantially the view taken of Jesus by Mohammedans and Jews; and where, we ask, is the logic or evidence to prove the divinity of one or two systems of religion, and the purely human character of all the rest? If God spoke to Moses, to Abraham, and to Melchisedek, why should he not have spoken to others not mentioned on the Hebrew scroll, but regarded with veneration as divine messengers by hundreds of millions of Orientals? Christianity and Judaism together do not embrace one quarter of the inhabitants of the globe, while the Oriental faith is shared by a much larger number. The spread of Mohammedanism has been quite as wonderful as that of Christianity, and proselytism has been carried on by Mohammedan missionaries in many instances quite as fairly as by Christian embassies.

Mohammedanism is spurned by many, and rightly, because it debases woman, keeping her veiled and in subjection to her lord throughout her lifetime, while it substitutes the harem for the home, and esteems voluptuousness as compatible with the loftiest spiritual exaltation. But, in Christian lands, has not woman been abased? Is she not to-day shut out from public offices, though taxed equally with man for all property she has earned or may have inherited? Has not woman been denied access to your halls of learning and your pulpits, until very recently, when she has been admitted to equality with man under protest; and has it not been that very church which adores woman in the person of the "Immaculate mother of God, the Virgin Mary," which has banished woman utterly from the priesthood, and declared that Paul's severest words on feminine subjection are none too strong? Though all over Europe in Christian lands the Virgin is adored, sometimes it appears to the exclusion of her Son, still outside the gates of all ecclesiastical and civil places of power, woman must stand knocking vainly for admittance, until the liberating hand of Republicanism, Free-thought, or Spiritualism shall open the long-closed doors to her, and admit her equally with her brothers to every place of rank and power and glory.)

The most ancient symbol of Egypt is the Circle, expressive of the absolute unity of the Divine Mind, and of all Nature. The spherical form is that of worlds perfected, and is the one form presented to you as symbolizing the perfection of unitary life in the Heavens. This form, most perfectly portrayed to the gaze of the ancient *savans*, in the sun Alcyone, was the accepted symbol of Deity, over all the land of Egypt, while the emblems of immortality were all closely allied. Among these, the serpent with its tail in its mouth was not infrequent. The most distant sphere known to be a sun was considered the highest expression of divine life discernible by man, and it was to the spiritual life there made manifest, and not to the matter of which the outer form of worlds is composed, that the ancients paid their homage. The ineffable centre of life was regarded as a central sun, while to this system of worlds the sun, which is the centre of this system, symbolled and expressed the ruler of the system spiritually.

(Believing, as did the ancient astrologers and astronomers, in the inhabited condition of all worlds in space at some period of their history, much maligned and misrepresented though astrology has been and still is, the original astrological theory was in effect, that worlds all came into existence in the same way, were all governed by the same laws, all existed for the same purpose, all were intended to afford scope for the development of spiritual power, the ultimate attainment of the spirit being its exercise of complete dominion over all forms and forces of matter.

The angel who dwelt in the sun (Osiris) was not regarded as the Eternal Being, but as the angel or guardian of the solar system. This archangelic guardian of the earth, with Isis, his consort, was worshipped as the highest expression of Deity the human mind could directly contemplate, while under the direction of this supernal potentate, twelve angels were said to move, each having for his Kingdom one of the Signs of the Zodiac. It was further believed by the Egyptians, that the earth regularly passed from one spiritual dispensation to another, in an average period of from 2,150 to 2,200 years, and the completed cycle of the earth occupied a period of 25,840 years, or very nearly that space of time, it being universally conceded that the journey of the sun (the home of Osiris and Isis) around Alcyone, was accomplished in precisely the same amount of time required by the earth to complete the grand cycle of twelve Messianic Periods. At the culmination and commencement of each special spiritual period, it was always declared that some special angelic ministrations were vouchsafed to the earth, and from this recognition of periods (spiritual periods of seed-time and harvest), arose the doctrine of Avatars, Messiahs, and Incarnate Deities.

The Adam of the second chapter of Genesis, is considered by some as identical with Osiris, and also with Melchisedek, as he evidently refers to the most ancient Spiritual Messenger. of whom mention is made in the Jewish Kabala; and surely no one familiar with the story of the Exodus, can be surprised to hear that Judaism, considered religiously, is largely a derivation from the older Egyptian religion. The ornaments borrowed from the Egyptians by the Israelites, refer no doubt to ornaments and ceremonies, symbols and metaphors, which afterwards formed part of the Jewish forms of government and worship.

The oldest form of government known to man is Theocracy. All the governments of ancient Egypt were theocratic, as spiritual power was looked up to as the supreme qualification of rulers for the tenure of office. The civil rulers were always in subordination to the ecclesiastical. The prophets were the most highly esteemed of all, next in order came the priests, who were often members of royal families, royal personages being generally ordained priests. Sacerdotalism, in its darker aspects, was a far later development. and arose from the corruption of the prophetic and priestly office, when filled by selfish, designing men, who sought their own personal aggrandisement rather than the welfare of the people, on whose behalf they were expected to perform all their functions.

Free-masonry and Religion are so nearly allied, that the history of the one cannot be written without also writing the history of the other. Free-masonry, in its most modern form in Christian lands, has added many ornamental and external lodges, which appear to confine it to an advocacy of the Christian religion; but the Mason who regards his lodge as a kind of club or benefit society, who makes use of Masonry as a passport to favour at home and abroad, but who does not care for it except for financial reasons, social prestige, and its many collateral advantages, does not comprehend anything of the original scope of Masonry, which included a complete study of the occult sciences, and the practice of spiritual power.

The same terms may be employed in England to-day as in Egypt 6,000 years ago. The square may still form the base, the triangle may still be supported upon it; the three primal degrees of Masonry—Entered Apprentice, Fellow Craftsman, and Master Mason—may still be taken by all who enter the Blue Lodge, and are thenceforth regarded brother Masons by the fraternity in all parts of the globe. But it has been stated, and that truly, that there are not simply three, but nine, degrees which may be taken, and six of these degrees are beyond any height attained by the ordinary Past Grand Master. These degrees include the study and practice of Magic, and are acknowledged, even verbally, by none in modern society, save those who call themselves Theosophists, or profess to take extraordinary interest in the spiritual side of occult brotherhoods.

What does the ordinary man of the world, who is an external Mason, know more than others of Rosicrucian mysteries, of Eleusinian and Bacchic rites, and of the far-famed mysteries of Egypt and Asia? To him Magic is imposition, even Spiritualism is but an imposture, while the book of Daniel, the Apocalypse, and the Kabala are incomprehensible fables or absurdities. He is either a member of a Christian church or Jewish synagogue, dealing with the letter of Scripture only, or he is a sceptic, regarding all spiritual matters as superstition. But ancient Masonry, while it included all the external and collateral advantages attaching to modern Masonry, and was far more necessary then than now, was far wider in its scope and deeper in its purpose; as it constituted the brotherhood, which held together the learned and the inspired in all quarters of the globe.

The *literati* and *illuminati*, however, never disclosed the meaning of their secret rites and ceremonies to any outside their Orders, neither did the most ancient and powerful lodge of all, ever inscribe its secrets in hieroglyphics, all of which penetrate no deeper than the surface of the true wisdom of the ancients. Every so-called *lost* art, every science called modern, was known to the ancients. Plato speaking figuratively to the uninitiated, nevertheless, even to them discloses the fact of his acquaintance with the circulation of the blood; yet modern scientists attribute the discovery of this fact of human life to Harvey. Far away in Egypt, the builders of the Pyramid were fully conversant with the rotundity of the earth, and its spherical motions, though in modern times Galileo was condemned for divulging a tithe of this most ancient knowledge. Socrates quaffing the hemlock at Athens; the early Christians, who were Essenes and Gnostics, persecuted by fire and sword because they inveighed against heathen idolatries and attempted to unfold the "*mystery* of Godliness" to the world, are alike instances of the frantic endeavours made by interested parties, in times of corruption, to hold knowledge away from the people.

The modern priesthood includes those, whose knowledge is so superficial that they really know nothing of the "hidden wisdom" mentioned in the Epistles, and those also who know more than they think it wise or safe to divulge. The Pope's Encyclical against Free-masonry, is only a proof of the natural horror with which an arrogant hierarchy must always regard a rival secret power. The Church of Rome has its milk for babes and its strong meat for full-grown men. The Church never admits the laity into its inmost mysteries. but proclaims to them the Infallibility dogma, threatening them with excommunication in this world and everlasting punishment in the future state, if they heed not the voice of Peter's successor, who speaks with authority from heaven. But to-day this authority is questioned all over Europe, and that Protestant supremacy which has so long held sway, both in England and America, is also being rapidly set aside. The Church no longer has a monopoly of learning, therefore its influence is waning with the learned, while the working people are daily becoming more impatient of all restraint, and prefer even violent and suicidal revolutionary movements, to stagnation under the dominion of aggressive rulers.

The *Logos* or Divine Word, proclaimed as the Breath of God by Plato as well as by John, is that divine Spirit of Truth which the Hebrews traced to the time of Adam, the Messianic Messenger whose advent to the earth inaugurated the Dispensation prior to the Hebraic; that period of history in which Egypt passed through one of her exceptionally glorious cycles of dominion. Then the tide of inspiration flowed from the banks of the Nile to the Jordan; at the same time there arose in Asia, both Confucius,—the Chinese philosopher, whose mission was to the intellect of man more particularly,—and Sakya Muni Gautama, the Indian Prince, whose mission was to the spirit of mankind. These two great lights shone together, the influence of the philosopher blending with and merging into that tidal wave of thought, which gave to Greece its halcyon days of philosophic splendour, when Pythagoras, Socrates, Plato, Aristotle, marked the full blossoming of the flowers of intellect, on the borders of the Hellenic seas.

Then came Jesus, not in the might and pride of intellect, but as Buddha came, with self-renunciation, humility, charity, the weapons of the Spirit only. His mission was to unfold the *logos* in every human breast, to glorify God's image in the human soul, not to maintain the rigour of Mosaism nor the intellectual speculations of philosophy, but to tell all mankind to worship the Father by deeds of loving-kindness to their brethren. In his Gospel, Love is the fulfilment of the Law. He asks not for your worship, he craves not your laudation, he asks only that you cultivate God's image in your heart. Thus controversy ends, and the practice of religion supplants all dogma; for he who loveth not his brother, whom he hath seen, can never love the Eternal, who is invisible, and who asks nought at our hands but that we fulfil the royal law, and frame our lives after the pattern of the Golden Rule. Not Christ as a person, but Love as the ruling principle of life, *must* be accepted, or the world remains unsaved and unredeemed.

When standing armies are abolished, when vice and pauperism no longer abound, when the fallen are upraised by the hand of love, and the whole Race of Man is the object of your care, then, but not till then, will God's Kingdom have come on Earth; then, but not till then, will His Will be done on Earth as it is in Heaven!

IMPROMPTU POEM.

WHO AND WHAT IS CHRIST?

FAR off, in distant lands, in ages long gone by,
The Ancients thought they saw th' Eternal riding by
In solemn state, through heaven, whene'er the sun shone bright;
They worshipped at His shrine, and called it their delight
To build rich temples fair, in every Orient land,
Which might, through ceaseless years, in hoary grandeur stand,
To point the mystic road,
To Light's supreme abode.

On the banks of the mystic Nile, an ancient altar stands,
Built to the Solar God, with swift and dext'rous hands,
Pointing the way to heaven, when its apex, crowned with light,
Is twice a-year adorned, when there's equal day and night.

To the Angel of the Sun, Osiris, who doth hide
Half of his heavenly form in Isis, his veiled bride:
And to Horus, the Child Divine, the Egyptians honour paid,
While their costliest works of art, were on such altars laid.

'Twas in depth of winter time, when the days had shortest grown,
When the breath of summer flowers and singing birds had flown,
They appointed a solemn feast, on the birth of a glad New Year,
To celebrate deliverance from cold and death and fear.

It was then that the Ancients traced the Saviour of Man, who, laid
Three days in the cold, dark tomb, was then re-born, arrayed
In the resurrection robes of the lengthening light of day,
While the spirits who ruled the night, were conquered and fled away.

'Twas then that *Virgo* appeared with *Bootes* at her side,
Standing as though far off, watching his radiant bride;
While *Capricornus*, the Goat, was the Zodiacal Sign
'Neath which, in the *stable* of earth, must be laid the new Child Divine.

It was afterwards, far, far away from the haunts of the men of old,
There appeared on the earth the sign which the Ancients had long foretold:
The five-pointed Star, whose light led the Magi from Persia, to where
Mary, the Jewish maid, must a child in virginity bear.

But the virgin need only be pure, free from guile, full of wisdom and love,
For motherhood may be divine, when sanctioned by light from above;
And the Teacher, who came to the West, was the Star which Confucius foretold,
When he spake of its bright Western beams, its radiance of heavenly gold.

But was one form on earth *all* God's Sons? Has the Father in Heaven one child—
But one only? who spoke to the earth, in Judea, with tones so mild
Yet so thrilling, that multitudes heard and acknowledged his spiritual sway,
Though the rulers and priests hound to death, he who revealeth the *perfect way*.

The Christ must be ever within, a Sun of Righteousness to shine,
God's image within the Soul, pronouncing man's life divine,
As the *Logos*, the breathing Word, the *Will*, and the *Light*, and the *Way*,
And the *Truth*, that must lead you to God at length, howe'er widely ye stray.

Whensoever the Spirit of Truth, Loving-kindness, or Charity sweet,
Shall pervade all your hearts and your minds, then the *Christ* in your hearts will ye greet;
And it matters not where be the shrine, or what be the phrase ye employ,
In fellowship, loving mankind, ye find Christ, and God's Kingdom of joy.

BENEDICTION.

May the Light of God's Perfect Truth so illume your minds while here ye rove, that Heavenly Peace may fill your hearts, and give you some blessed foretaste of Eternal Joy.—Amen.

VII.

THE PHILOSOPHY OF RE-EMBODIMENT.

BY special request of a gentleman here present, and also in compliance with the urgent and often-expressed wishes of other friends, we have taken for our subject this afternoon, "THE PHILOSOPHY OF RE-INCARNATION," or, to speak more correctly, we must say RE-EMBODIMENT, as incarnation and re-incarnation are words scarcely fitted to express the thoughts we wish to convey concerning the human spirit and its manifestations through earthly organisms. (Incarnation means to be made flesh, re-incarnation to be made flesh over again; but as the soul never becomes material, as the spirit is never converted into matter, there can be really no incarnations and no re-incarnations, though embodiments of spirit may be numerous and successive, so long as an earthly form is calculated to afford the spirit means for the unfoldment and exercise of its latent talents.

We know there are some persons who are so averse to the theory of a plurality of terrestrial existences for the same spirit, that they become angry and abusive if the question of re-embodiment is only mooted in their hearing.) For all such we are sorry, but it is not our province to blame them nor to call them by the hard names they apply to others. Truth is its own apology for being, it cannot be obliterated in support of any theory whatsoever, it refuses to bend at the shrine of any idol, no matter how venerable. If it is unpalatable to certain minds, the minds must grow eventually to embrace it and glory in it; but truth can never change, because the laws of being are not in harmony with certain people's ideas of what they ought to be.

(If there be one cry more earnest than all others in the world of thought to-day, it is the cry for justice. Nothing short of the strictest and most absolute justice will satisfy the irrepressible cravings of the human mind. Every cry for liberty, for freedom, for emancipation, is but the expression of some deep-seated yearning for equity. Even the dynamite explosions are evidence of the tremendous outcry of the human mind against tyranny, usurpation, and partiality. Whether Irishmen are right or wrong in the opinion of your Government, they feel themselves to be unfairly treated. Whether their grievances are as real as they say they are or not, still the protest against injustice is the inspiration of every struggle and outrage. Once let a people feel themselves unjustly treated, and you have aroused the implacable hatred of that people against you. Once let a child or a person in your employ feel that you have favourites, and that he is not one of them, that others, for no merit of their own, are preferred before him, to gratify your whim or arbitrary caprice, and over that child or adult you can gain no power, unless he fears you and renders you an unwilling obedience, perforce or through cowardice.

The entire religious world is agitated, nay, convulsed at this very hour, because of the failure of theologies to account for the government of the universe consistent with the justice of the Eternal. No doctrines have driven so many persons into Atheism as those of Calvin. Election and Reprobation are so horrifying to the lover of impartiality, that the very name of God is blasphemed wherever Calvinism has held sway. It is not against the idea of Supreme Goodness that men turn with disgust to Agnosticism or infidelity; wherever Atheism is most rampant, is where the name of Deity has been defiled by its association with measures reprehensible among men, wherever civilization has made any progress. Some there are, indeed, who so confound illimitable nature with their puny knowledge of a fragment of the universe, that they imagine everything to be absolutely irreconcilable that they cannot themselves reconcile, but surely it must be admitted that the supreme and sovereign hope of the world is directed toward the advent of an era of unsullied equity, when all the bewildering inconsistencies of the present shall be lost sight of for ever in the realization of humanity's most ardent dream, a dream which, whether embodied in Eden, Arcadia, Utopia or any other Oriental or classic form in the past, is the hope of the world of working men to-day, who, though less poetical in the clothing of their mental images, have still in view the realization of the self same dream which caused Plato to write his "Republic," and gave to all the Athenian Sages their divine gift of prophecy.

No one studying the classic authors can fail to discover, that the primal basis of life, according to all of them, is Spirit. No one penetrating even but a little way into the spirit of the Eleusinian and Bacchic mysteries, can fail to trace in the splendid and voluptuous ritual of the Greeks, an attempt to illustrate the career of the Soul through many stages of material existence, ultimating in the perfected bliss of angelhood. It is impossible to consult the pages of the celebrated Hermetic writings, without discovering ere long that the old Egyptians in their very dramatic representation of the movement of astral bodies, set forth in glowing imagery the transit of the Soul. Take whatever view you may of Greek and Asiatic Mythology; interpret the religions of India, Persia, China, and Assyria, as you please; consult the pages of the Jewish or any other Kabala, and the burden of every portrayal will be found to be none other than an attempt of the human mind to answer the stupendous questions of every age: Whence am I? What am I? Whither am I bound?

We are quite well aware that some Jews and some Christians are sufficiently conceited to make it their boast, that only through Moses or through Christ was the will of God revealed to man, while outside the pale of Judaism and Christianity there are to be found none who have enjoyed a clear and direct revelation from the Infinite. It is certainly not our purpose to enter upon a wordy war with any sectaries regarding the superior excellence of some particular theology or philosophy over all others; sectarian strife is sufficiently rife at present to excuse us from the charge of a neglect of duty if we decline to enter the ranks of controversialists, and match our strength with that of others in defence of some peculiar form in which truth has been or now is embodied. We claim that revelations are incessant, that the Soul is ever the discoverer, while Reason may be the analyst and exponent of truth; and that to no age more than to others, to no people more than to others, has God vouchsafed a special revelation.

But may it not be that as some material substances are diaphanous or transparent, while others are light-resisting, that in the realm of mind some mental states may correspond to windows of clear, white glass, while others may best be compared to flint or brickwork? It is not the fault of the sun, if the light streams in through open windows, but does not enter through the medium of solid masonry; it is not the fault of this same sun, if Jupiter afar off responds to its every radiation, and glories in space as a brilliant lighted world. while Mercury anear the Solar Orb is immured as yet in chaotic vapours, like unto those which doubtless once surrounded Jupiter. In the history of the progress of worlds we discover them slowly emerging, through vast cycles of time, from the gloomy darkness of their primeval state; so that while geologists may utterly discard the notion that the sun was created on the fourth day of this earth's development, it may still be admitted that prior to the close of the tertiary period, the earth was not responsive to solar light and heat as afterwards. Not the nearness of a world to the central orb of the system, nor its remoteness from that centre. determines the heat or luminosity of the planet. The planet's own growth regulates its own condition, and not until it has passed beyond chaotic and transition periods, can it rejoice as a reflector and assimilator of the light and heat which are ever flowing toward it from the central globe.

When in ancient times Solar-worship was instituted, the sun was the sacred emblem both of the Divine Soul and of the human soul. What the Eternal Spirit is to universal nature, that the human spirit must be to human nature. Every impulsion of life is from the Deity, and vibrates outward from the centre toward the circumference of being. Every form evolved upon an earth, is due to spiritual operations working from within, till at length these impulsions are embodied in the forms of matter you behold around you. First the inorganic, then the organic, must appear: first the mineral deposits are formed, then the vegetable and animal kingdoms appear, till nature's types cease with man, in whom is the culmination of nature's evolutionary line.

Charles Darwin, studying the origin of man, was one of the ablest and devoutest students of the ascent of forms of life, the world has ever seen. Neither bigoted nor sceptical, neither impetuous nor superstitious, neither iconoclastic nor foolishly conservative, he was indeed an epoch-making man. His greatness consisted largely in his sound judgment, cool deliberation, and steadfast adherence to proven facts. Hypotheses and theories were to him of minor value. He discovered first, and theorized afterwards. He endeavoured to subject all theories to nature's revelations, and never believed in the policy adopted by some, of paring down facts till they were small enough to enter the narrow grooves of antiquated theory. Better break every skin in Israel and have new wine, than deny a truth, because only old wine can be contained in venerable bottles. This was the teaching of the great Galilean teacher, and this was the policy of Darwin, and for this, though ostracised at first, his name, even before his passage from material life, became as a household word, to be mentioned with reverence instead of scorn; while from St. Paul's and Westminster, and many humbler temples in the land, arose eulogy, not execration, over his remains when these were committed to their resting place in earth.

(For what Darwin has done, the scientific world owes him unfaltering loyalty. Eternal gratitude is due to such as he, for the discoveries they make regarding man's corporeal envelope, even though that envelope be but a thing of dust and clay, a school house, and a preparatory one at best, for its immortal occupant, the Soul. But if material researches may thus be valuable, if he who investigates the development of the outward is truly called a hero—What shall be the rightful honours paid to those who draw back the mystic curtain which screens the Spirit from your view, rend the obscuring vail in the midst of the temple, where humanity blindly worships while it dreads the Unknown, and let in such light concerning man's immortal origin and destiny as shall flood the page of human history with light derived from spheres of ageless and eternal Spirit?

Immortality is the faith and hope of the world; annihilation is alike inconceivable and intolerable to any sane or healthy person. Morbid sorrow, incurable disease, and a host of kindred afflictions may generate in the minds of men an apparent desire for absolute extinction of being, but where is the ordinarily happy or healthy woman, man or child, who does not shrink from death, and recoil with horror from the prospect of annihilation? But who can realize what it can be not to be? Think of yourselves as mouldering in the grave, or suffering torment in a world of future punishment! You may, but you cannot realize being nothing: no one, and nowhere. Instinctively the thought of man turns to immortality, and let the idea of extinction be broached ever so remotely—by Theosophists, Occultists, or others who pretend to find in the Buddhistic records a teaching of the ultimate loss of the soul's individuality,—and a perfect storm of angry indignation is aroused against the advocates of such a doctrine, even though the event of individual annihilation be postponed to a period so remote, that no human arithmetic can compute the æons which must elapse ere the fatal hour arrives. Instinctively the soul within you says—I AM! I always have been: I shall ever be. No changing forms of dust can e'er destroy my entity. I from eternity exist, and to eternity my pathway lies, hedged in though I may be with mortal sorrows, afflicted with many cares, weighted down with burdens grievous to be borne, I yet can see the future glory which awaits me, when after all my earthly trials are o'er, I reach the land of peace ineffable, where ample compensation will be assuredly afforded me for all the labours and the trials incident to time and sense.

We say, the Soul of man says this, because it has ever said it, in all the various theories which men have framed concerning the purpose and end of life. The soul spake thus upon the banks of the sacred, mystic Nile, whose waters, forever ebbing and flowing, suggested human experiences and change; while the lotus flowers, which bloomed always upon its banks, were symbols of the Soul's eternity. It spoke thus when Buddha, meditating upon eternal things, saw as in a crystal mirror every changing scene of life pass before him, while he himself remained unshaken by the lapse of ages. It spoke thus when Jesus, questioned by his critics on the Spirit's duration, pronounced those memorable words: "Before Abraham was, I am!" The Soul says—I AM! It lives in an eternal present. Abraham, the type of human change and sacrificial institutions, must be recent, when his brief span of influence is contrasted with the soul's eternity. Not only forward into the future but backward into the past, the Spirit's vision stretches, and the Soul can say—I am! I was! I shall be!—Past, Present, Future, all rolled into one consciousness of life. Simple being and the realization of being, this is all that can be predicated concerning spiritual life itself.

We know there are many who profess to believe in prospective, though not in past immortality. We fail, however, to discover by what processes of logical reasoning they can deduce the dogma of the endlessness of life one way if not the other. Whatsoever is born may die, all that begins may end. Worlds, if they began, may cease to be: only that which had no beginning can have no ending. This fact is clearly kept in view by scientists, who declare, and that most logically and consistently, that only atoms are eternal. Primaries, say they, have always existed, and will therefore never cease to be. But no scientist ever claims to have discovered primaries: they elude the grasp of every sense. They are strictly and obstinately invisible. No amount of toil or diligence has succeeded in wresting them from that invisible state in which eternally they dwell. All that the scientific world can know, by actual experiments concerning matter, is that it is destructible.* The indestructible has never been discovered, and yet its existence is a necessary inference of science. If spiritual teachers shall come to you with definitions of these essential primaries, is it not discreet that you should listen with all diligent attention to what they have to say? If every material research has failed, and they are still beyond you, then if they be described to you as souls, as conscious, self-existing entities, preserving their indentity intact for ever,—Why rebel because your relentless and barbaric divinities—Chance, Luck, Destiny, Fate, Law, Necessity—are dethroned, when by their displacement you behold in regal splendour, in robes of spotless beauty, one only God revealed, whose completeness forms the sphere of Justice, the hemispheres of which are Love and Wisdom, the outgoings, Power almighty.

Sooner or later you will all find yourselves obliged to vacate untenantable premises. If you endeavour to force a dogma on the human mind, unsanctioned by right or reason, your dogmatism may suffice (especially if you accompany it with sufficient arrogant intolerance of all other opinions than your own) for minds who are prepared to take your dictum instead of the findings of their own reason and moral sense. We emphatically declare that ordinary views of human immortality are little better than Atheistic negations, because they utterly fail at the crucial point, when asked to demonstrate the Justice of the Eternal. What says the materialistic thinker of to-day? I believe in no Eternal Justice;

---

* It is a dogma of the Materialists, that *Matter* is indestructible, eternal, but merely a dogma, which resolves itself into the logical conclusion that *something* must be eternal; and what is eternal must be absolute and primal, as no composition can be ultimate; thence the theory of atoms.

and this after nineteen centuries or thereabout of nominal Christianity, after centuries of preaching and the expenditure of millions of pounds annually in Home and Foreign Missions. Not the Archbishop of Canterbury but Charles Bradlaugh is the hero of the hour. The Pope's Encyclical against Free-masonry arouses contempt, scarcely indignation. Bishops are threatened with expulsion from Parliament, while the very name of religion is the synonym of hypocrisy or exploded fallacy with many. Why is this? Surely not because God and immortality are the fevered fancies of a disordered brain; surely not because all the hopes of the world for eternal life are built on sand, and will not bear the force of the surging billows of modern enquiry. The answer is in this and in this only: that popular and prevalent theological ideas have not demonstrated the problem of Eternal Justice.

Pythagoras, the sage of Samos, Plato, Aristotle, Socrates, Confucius, Buddha, Jesus, these taught no other gospel than that which in France, quite recently, the Spirit-world endeavoured to revive through the faithful labours of that devoted seeker after truth, who bore the *nom de plume* of Allan Kardec. His writings are not faultless, no human compositions are, even though dictated from the Realm of Spirit. The mediums with whom he sat were not perfectly transparent mirrors, in which every thought and sentiment from spirit life could be accurately or mistakelessly portrayed. Imperfections in style, incompleteness in statement, failure to grasp entirely the drift of thought,—these mistakes and such as these are common in the works which emanated from Kardec's facile and prolific pen; but these mistakes aside, and these imperfections discounted, *The Spirit's Book*, *The Medium's Book*, *Heaven and Hell*, *Genesis*, all of which are now easily accessible in the English tongue, besides other works not yet translated from the French, contain a fund of information and constitute a compendium of spiritual philosophy unrivalled in modern literature. We are not apologists for Kardec or his system, we are not prepared to endorse his every statement or to concur at all times in the views expressed by the revelating spirits; all we would say to the reading public concerning these remarkable volumes is, in them you will find food for years of thought, texts for thousands of discourses, while you will be confronted with the results of many years assiduous toil performed by a man who freely gave his time, his means, his strength, to collecting and diffusing information calculated to exonerate the laws of being from the charges brought against them, by those who know nothing of his inspired philosophy, and to vindicate the ways of God to man, as no other system than his has ever attempted to do, with anything like the same success.

The cardinal affirmations of Kardec's philosophy are these. God is absolutely just, strictly impartial in all his undertakings, no favourites has he, none whom he fancies, and elects to bliss while others are the objects of his unreasoning displeasure. No human soul is ever embodied on this or any other earth, except to learn a needed lesson or undergo a salutary discipline. Every soul begins at one point, and all progress towards one goal. The starting point is innocence disconnected from wisdom, the goal is innocence and wisdom fully joined. The experiences needful for some are needful for all. There are no short cuts to heaven; happiness must be earned, it can never be bestowed arbitrarily or vicariously. There are no hells in this or any other life, which are not schools and do not serve purposes of needful education. No crosses, cares, afflictions nor temptations are needlessly presented to or undergone by any, but every discipline of life, glorious or humiliating, pleasant or painful, is a needed part of the education of the spirit, and has for object the bringing forth of some latent power and excellence within. Surely such premises as these must be acceptable to all, whose boast it is that they acknowledge the universal Fatherhood of God, and Brotherhood of Man, while it must be clear to all thinkers, that there is but one alternative,—either there is a God or a Devil. If there be no law of perfect justice in the universe, which metes out to all their just deserts, then there is certainly a devil of injustice, even though it be, as the Materialists assert, unconscious and non-intelligent.

If there be any power in nature, which brings children into the world without consulting them and then loads them down with unmerited disease and sorrow, only to snuff them out of all conscious being, after they have suffered for a few years, with no reward; if some—born in affluence, fêted and caressed throughout their lives, knowing scarcely anything of pain, difficulty or temptation—shall be received into heavenly glory immediately upon the death of the body, while others. whose lot has been hard and who have fallen by reason of divers and mighty temptations they were not strong enough to resist, are doomed to long-continued if not everlasting punishment in the life to come,—then, we say, where such injustice prevails there is the devil. Teach every child and scholar to regard justice as synonymous with divinity, and injustice with devilry; hold up in all your homes and seminaries the idea of simple, absolute justice as the supreme good, and you need not feel any alarm concerning the future morality of the race. Say whatever you will against it, the doctrine of the successive embodiments of the human spirit in the material form, is illustrative of the Supreme Justice in the universe, to an extent unparalleled by any other philosophy.

Perhaps there may be carping critics still, who object to the phraseology of re-embodiment, and who pride themselves upon their ability to detect flaws in a system they utterly fail to comprehend. So far all objections to the theory of re-embodiment have been purely rhapsodic and extremely superficial, or they have been couched in such spiteful or flippant language as to render them utterly valueless as additions to genuine controversy; but as there may be persons here to-day who have hitherto failed to grasp the teaching on this subject, which has up to this time been given to the world, and as there are seeming discrepancies and discords in the teaching itself, we will endeavour to reply to a few of the more general and salient objections constantly brought forward by opponents, with such pride and vigour as though their arguments were unanswerable. Enthusiasm is not spite, nervousness is not vulgarity, and it is a pity when the one is mistaken for the other. We do not undertake to answer slander, but to the nervous and enthusiastic opponent of the re-embodiment idea, we will offer a few replies to his oft-reiterated statements, that re-embodiment implies retrogression, while, in truth, it implies always and only the perpetual advancement or progress of the spirit. accomplished by means of alternate existences in material and spiritual states of being.

Re-embodiment is not akin to the old idea of the transmigration of souls, with which it is often confounded by the ignorant. Transmigration, of course, implies a going back to a lower state than the one you leave, when you take on a fresh embodiment. Were one of you to become an animal, after having been a human being, you would have to descend the ladder of life, and place yourself on a lower round than that on which you now stand. It is a well-attested fact in physiology, that the human body includes all the elements required to form every structure comprising the three kingdoms of nature below man, mental science proving also that human intelligence embraces all the intelligence of the animal world, and superadded attainments. If transmigration have a foundation in fact, then transmigration must antedate human life. The soul not yet embodied in a structural organism, through which it can manifest its own individuality, may through the lapse of ages produce inferior forms, which manifest attributes of Spirit, but have no means of expressing the Soul itself, but only impulsions or vibrations from the soul.

The Theosophists, with their elementary spirits or fragmentary souls not yet human, have clumsily and imperfectly translated the spiritual significance of the occult science of the ancients. Gnomes, Sylphs, Undines, and Salamanders; Spirits of earth, air, fire, and water; Divinities of the four elements, and all the troops of Elves and Fairies mentioned in legendary lore, have not been simply fictions of the imagination. There are in spirit many types which have now no form on earth, but there can be no form on earth which has not a prototype in spirit. Some spiritual impulsions gain no outward expression, others are being embodied around you every moment.

The kingdoms of nature below man, visible and invisible, are preparatory expressions of that soul-life which is struggling to express itself through matter. Transmigration may be related to your past, but not to your future. Your soul having become sufficiently skilful to build the human, when it next assumes a body will assume a higher not a lower form than the one it now animates or occupies, and on passing into spirit-life will not descend into kingdoms of elementaries nor be borne aloft to supernal states of angelhood, for which it is not prepared. Spiritual spheres impinge upon the earth, they revolve with your planet, unseen through space, the seven spheres of which, you have been often told, mean seven distinct and appreciable gradations in spirit-life, surrounding and intimately connected with the earth; while beyond the earthly atmosphere, dissevered from all material bondage, are the homes of those who need not any longer to be associated with cruder forms of life.

Are all children equal from the moment of their birth? Can all learn with equal rapidity and ease? Have all equal genius or spiritual insight? Ask any parent, ask any tutor, and who is there among those who educate the young, who will not inform you of the aptitudes of one and the obtuseness of another? It is often stated by the opponents of re-embodiment, that spiritual influence or inspiration has everything to do with the presence of genius in one and the absence of it in others, but this view is erroneous at its foundation, though often true in its outward statements. The question naturally arises: Why is one inspired and not another? If God be impartial, this cannot be so. In the light of the philosophy we are endeavouring to make clear, this difficulty vanishes. Those who can most readily respond to spiritual influx, are the recipients of it and benefit by it. There is no calling one and passing of another by. The call is to all. The few only are chosen, because the few only are qualified. If, therefore, you can catch glimpses of those anterior existences which have prepared some minds for response to spiritual light, as some planets are responsive to solar heat and light through development of conditions to receive it, then the enigma is solved, discrepancies vanish. God's methods are justified to man, and the human spirit realizes equity not favouritism, strict justice not partiality, in all the economy of nature.

Have you never stood by the death-bed of a darling friend, and heard him whisper with faltering tongue: "Oh! that I could live my life over again." He goes out into eternity with that prayer upon his lips, and an answer to that petition is not denied him. After a period of rest, refreshment, and such experience as equips the soul for its new journey, he is again attracted toward an earthly form, again he plunges into the mystic river, and is again landed on the shores of time. This new experience endows him with new powers, and enables him to win new victories. If the old lessons have not been fully learned, then they must be freshly studied, and more completely mastered. If there be new lessons to be studied, then the infancy is but the period when the alphabet of a new language, the rudiments of a new science, have to be acquired. You do not call it retrogression, if having mastered French, and wishing to learn Italian, you have to begin with alphabet and grammar. If, having studied astronomy, you wish to learn music, even though you be a gray-haired professor of science, you must begin with scales and finger-exercises. The knowledge acquired at other times, on other subjects, is not lost; it is stored away in your inner being, and when you need it, it can be brought forth and utilized. But when engrossed in some especial work, your every energy bent in one direction, you are temporarily oblivious to all but what immediately engrosses you.

Earthly lives express the efforts of a spirit in certain specific directions. The child, who learns his letters with very great difficulty, has probably never seen them before, while he who picks them up readily, has only to be reminded of what he has previously known. Genius is due to past experiences uniting you with minds who can now easily assist you in the externalizing of what is within. No favourites has God, no child of earth will forever be denied the experience needed to unfold the spirit; and what sense is there in that reasoning which, professing to prize life highly, denies the necessity of earthly experience for some, while it admits it for others?

Children, according to the Church, who die in their baptismal innocence, are saved forever from earthly stain and conflict, are pure as driven snow in heaven, and yet are not so high as are the martyrs who have won their crowns. Why should these pure spirits never have the martyr's chance to win the martyr's crown? Why should your boys and girls who are kept at home safe from all pollution, be rewarded for their virtue, when they have never been tempted in the world? "Count it all joy," says James, in his epistle, "when ye fall into divers temptations," knowing that these temptations work your good. Every temptation of life must sooner or later be presented to every mind, and every mind must overcome it. How would you feel in heaven, among the saints in light, if you discovered either that you were occupying a place you had not merited, or that forever you must fill a lower place than others, because of a lack of equity in the divine distributions? To those who believe in spiritual temptation, apart from earthly embodiments, to those who believe in mediumship affording all the means necessary for the spiritual unfoldment of departed spirits, we have only to say: if you grasp and enforce the primal truth of justice in all the divine appointments, we can afford to differ on a question of ways and means whereby experience is gained; but if any shall hope to receive prizes they do not deserve, to wear laurels for which they have not fought, then they will be disappointed, for God has no favourites. Automatic or negative virtue does not pass current in heaven. If you have always told the truth and been honest and chaste, because temptations to intemperance, impurity, dishonour and falsehood, have never assailed you, then those temptations await you in future lives. When you have overcome them, but not till then, can you know the joy and rest of heaven.

But what of relationships in the spirit spheres. Not as sister, brother, cousin, niece, or aunt will you know each other there, and not by earthly names will you be called. Affection is eternal, love can never die, but merely earthly bonds are dissolved at death. During the sleep of your body, your soul is oft in sweet communion with the loved ones who are yours for ever. When the mysteries of sleep and double consciousness are solved, then will you realize, as you do not now, your relationships in eternity. The body is no more the individual, than the dress is the body, or the house its occupant. A glove conceals a hand: remove it, and the hand is there. The body is the raiment of the spirit; change it as you will, but the spirit's individuality remains intact. Every seven years your bodies may completely change, and if these gradual changes do not destroy the individuality of your real selves, neither will any number of embodiments. At length, when angelhood is reached, your memory will awaken from its lethargy, and you will fully perceive how through an unbroken series of existences, you have passed from primeval innocence to that angelic height, where, with purity restored, you have united wisdom hitherto ungained.)

In another lecture, we shall hope to enter yet more fully into the question of memory. This Discourse has but touched the fringe of an infinite subject. What has been said, however, will prepare you for what is to follow.

IMPROMPTU POEM.

THE HOME OF THE SOUL.

(CANTO I.)

THE Poets have sung of the Home of the Soul,
 In fair regions, forever at rest;
Have told of its glories, and sung in its praise,
 With its beautiful mansions, so blest!

They have said, that man's spirit, before it came down
 To labour and toil on the earth,
Was with God in His Paradise, perfectly pure,
 And in heaven the Soul found its birth.

The legends of old time, all over the world,
 Have stated this truth, in a dream
Of some far-famed Eden, where man was at rest,
 By the side of life's clear, flowing stream.

In Eden, the Spirit had but to enjoy
 Each fruit and sweet flower so fair,
While the mind every moment itself might employ,
 Contemplating God's bounties so rare.

Man and Woman, together in Love's sweetest bond,
 In affection celestial did prove
How the sweets of pure union forever were theirs,
 If obedient to God they would move.

While, in midst of the garden, life's fair, blooming tree
 Was their solace, and shelter, and food,
While all creatures obeyed them, and came at their call,
 For God smiled, and pronounced them "all good."

But a Serpent came in at the wide-open gate,
 Which led to that Paradise land,
And tempted the woman to eat of such fruit
 As developed her self-will, and caused her to stand
Abashed and affrighted, and conscious of ill,—
God's law she had broken, was breaking it still.
With tears, lamentations, and bitterest cry,
She said to her husband, "Oh! where can we fly?
"God's voice is upbraiding, I cannot abide
"The anguish his anger brings close to my side!"

O poor, foolish Adam! to eat of the fruit
 Which Eve, serpent-tempted, pressed close to thy mouth;
For this thou wast driven to cold Northern clime,
 No longer to bask in the sweet, sunny South.

This legend is only a story, of how
  The Spirit of Man doth descend
From the regions immortal, where spirits have birth,
  To earth's wilderness, where they must spend
A time of probation, in sorrow and pain,
Until they a Paradise New shall attain.

The Serpent, beguiling, is Matter, whose sway
  O'er the Spirit exerted must be,
Until it grows strong through sharp conflict and pain,
  'Mong the blessed in heaven to be;
The Woman (Affection) whene'er led astray,
  Leads the Reason (the Man) into night,
While God's frown is the sorrow and anguish ye feel,
  When your consciences say you're not right.

The Spirit, through earth-life, sighs ever and aye
  For a Paradise yet in store,
As Milton declared there was one to regain,
  And a brighter we knew not before;
The Paradise future is innocent, too,
  But in wisdom possession ye'll take
Of those bright realms immortal, when freed from all stain
  Of the fruit of Life's tree ye'll partake.

(CANTO 2.)

In allegories strange and old, in mythologic guise,
The poets and philosophers have lifted up their eyes
Telling of fair Hesperides, or of Olympus' heights,
Or of Parnassus' sacred hill, or of the pure delight
Which over all Arcadia reigns, or of Utopia blest,
Or of the lyre of Orpheus, by which gods lull to rest
The pains and griefs of mortal man,
But heaven's full glories none may scan,
Until, from all earth's stains set free,
They rise as angels bright to be,
Among the hosts of shining light,
Who always love and choose the right.

If heaven is home, then surely there,
All ties of friendship will the closer bind,
Than when on earth ye scarcely knew your friends,
Because the veil of flesh did hide
Much of that radiant loveliness of soul,
Which once inspired your love and did your hearts control.

When Jesus said, "My mother and my brethren—who are they?
And answer gave, "My brethren are all of those who tread life's chequered way,
Obedient to my Father's will," he spake a truth divine,
That true affection of the soul, if once it shall be thine,
Directed toward another soul, your union is for aye,
The bonds of flesh ne'er sunder ye, Death cannot take away
Or e'en obscure the Spirit's sight,
Or chill its sunbeams of delight.

(CANTO 3.)

Oh ! where is the Home of the Soul ? for which every spirit prays :
Oh ! where are the Mansions of Love ? of which the great teacher says :
I go to prepare a place for my friends,
That they may be with me, world without end !

The Home of the Soul is the Paradise state, your spirits of old did know,
Ere yet in the battle of life they fought, back to this beauteous state they'll go.
When life's battle is over, its conflict done,
Then bright as the noonday sun,
With innocence regained, wisdom attained,
Ye will forever walk in white,
For the knowledge of truth, and the love of good,
Make Heaven's celestial light !

BENEDICTION.

To the Infinite Love and Wisdom of the Eternal Father and Mother of all souls, we commit you with this prayer in our hearts for you all : That life's multiple experiences may land you when earthly life is o'er, where all is rest and joy forever ! AMEN.

VIII.

REASON AND INTUITION.

WE frequently hear it remarked, that this is an Age of Reason; and those who make that claim for the present century, are often accustomed to despise Intuition, as though it were but a mere phantasy or figment of the imagination, forgetting that Reason is often blind while Intuition sees clearly; as true Intuition is, after all, the reception of knowledge by the mind from other sources than those of outward observation.

Our subject to-day brings us directly to that point where we shall be obliged to discuss the theory of Inspiration, and endeavour to account for the facts of Mediumship. Hitherto, in this Course of Lectures, we have been principally occupied in demonstrating spiritual propositions and solving spiritual problems, without entering directly into the subject of individual mediumship, except in the case of those exceptional personages, who have been quoted as the representative lights of the world, the special saviours and benefactors of humanity. However interesting and instructive dissertations on ancient history and general principles of spiritual government may be, a peculiar interest is always attached to that which is neither ancient nor foreign, but forms part of the private as well as the public life of humanity to-day. It is interesting to study the progress of the human family through ages of development, and everyone likes to know something of his ancestors, their habits and conditions, but the live questions of the hour must ever occupy the most prominent place in all practical instructions; the past being referred to only by way of illustration, and as a means of explaining, as far as may be, the mysteries of the present.

The Age of Reason is upon you, as Thomas Paine declared in the last century, when he gave to the world his justly celebrated work bearing that title. But the Age of Reason is an incomplete age; it is of the intellect only: it makes no provision for the Intuitions of woman, while it deifies the reasoning powers of man. Therefore in France it was ushered in with strife and bloodshed. Its work was purely iconoclastic; its weapons were carnal; it provoked strivings innumerable, and desolated many homes in the endeavour to promote liberty.

No one reading the History of the French Revolution, can fail to perceive that the goddesses Reason and Liberty utterly failed to usher in an age of genuine freedom or solid advancement. The Republic of the last century only gave way, after a very short reign, to another monarchy, to the establishment of what has been commonly called the Second Empire. Voltaire, Volney, Paine, Robespierre, and all the great intellects of the 18th century, simply paved the way for Buonaparte and his matchless conquests, a few years later; while the first Napoleon, himself an exile in the closing years of his earthly life, handed down to his successors no other legacy than that of thirst for material conquest, resulting in the overthrow of the Buonapartist dynasty by means of a teriffic war between France and Germany. It is true, that the influence of Paine, and indeed of almost all who took part in the French Revolution intellectually, was great in America; and so highly is Paine esteemed by many of your transatlantic brethren, that he has been placed on a pedestal nearly if not quite as high as that on which a devoted country has placed George Washington; (" The Author Hero of the American Revolution" being a title often applied by his friends to Paine; while the strictly orthodox in the Christian fold join in pronouncing eulogies upon the soldier, Washington, but consign the author, Paine, to everlasting condemnation in the world to come, while on earth his name is cast out as evil, and his books proscribed as full of blasphemy and pestilential heresy. However, the feeling against Paine is now rapidly diminishing, and while everyone must regard him as an iconoclast, and something less than a direct revealer of spiritual truth, it is manifestly unjust to pronounce him either an Atheist or an infidel. He was in all his writings a firm supporter of Deism, and allowed himself to be elected president of a society of Theo-philanthropists, in Paris, who were not only believers in a Supreme Spirit, but also in human immortality; though Paine himself seems to have doubted whether *all* men were immortal.)

Proceeding upon lines of intellectual argument only, he

admitted the existence of a God, and it is but justice to admit that Paine's idea of Deity was vastly superior to prevailing orthodox notions. He believed in a revelation from God, through the medium of Nature, but rejected the inspiration as well as the infallibility of scripture records. He really stood far nearer to the Theists than to the Atheists of to-day, though the latter often seem to claim him, because he was at war with the churches, criticised the character of Jesus, and overthrew dogmatic theology completely in his essays. Thomas Paine came to inevitable conclusions, relying upon such means for solving the problem of the universe as were at his disposal, and all credit be to him for so valiantly risking all things in a worldly sense, in the interests of what he believed to be the truth. Such a man merits honour, not execration, and it is truly lamentable to witness the spiteful and unreasoning hostility, which avowed advocates of the religion of Jesus manifest towards one who had doubtless many shortcomings, but to off-set these many sterling good qualities.

The tales told of his death-bed agony and recantation at the last, are wholly unreliable, and are about on a par with many of the sensational tales told by fanatical religionists. to frighten those who are on the verge of free-thought, back again into the orthodox fold.

Some years ago the story was freely circulated, that here in London, in the neighbourhood of Regent Street, great consternation had prevailed in a Unitarian chapel, because a member of the congregation had suddenly got up during the service, and proclaimed himself a believer in the absolute deity of Jesus Christ, at the same time urging upon the congregation the necessity of instant conversion to the true faith (his own). The same paper which published that account, went on further to state, that a great many persons recognised the hand of God in the frenzied ejaculations of this suddenly-converted and heaven-inspired disturber of the sinful peace, in which a congregation of heretics were wrapped on the borders of the lake of eternal fire, and that many from that moment withdrew from the congregation and severed their connection with Unitarianism, indentifying themselves at once with orthodoxy, while only the minister and a few others remained obdurate. As there is only one Unitarian chapel in the neighbourhood of Regent Street, that in Little Portland Street, where Dr. Martineau ministered for many years previous to the pastorate of the Rev. Philip Wicksteed, the present minister, and no such scene has ever occurred to the knowledge of anyone in that chapel, it was soon decided that the story was a "pious fraud." It is just possible that the person who wrote it believed it to be true, having gathered it from hearsay. It is also possible that some insane person, or someone under the influence of violent excitement, once behaved in an unseemly manner in a Unitarian chapel somewhere, causing a disturbance and a panic, but invariably such tales as these are pure fabrications, so far as their import and local application are concerned, and it is impossible to be too cautious ere we lend credence to any story circulated to the detriment of any person or body of persons holding generally unpopular views.

Enthusiasts are so numerous in the orthodox camp, and sensational preaching works such havoc among the intellects of sensitive and emotional people who listen to it, while partisan journalists and biographers are so anxious to bend history to support orthodoxy, that you will do well to regard, as simply beneath contempt, all the excited and scandalous stories which have been and still are in circulation concerning the awful effects of heresy upon heretics, and especially are death-bed scenes concocted to render more thrilling and ghastly than they otherwise could be made, the consequences of departing even in the slightest degree from the accepted orthodox standards.

In the face of such facts as these, it is not to be wondered at that immense capital has been made out of the dying agonies and awful despair of heretics in their last moments upon earth, while nothing whatever is said of the hopelessness of some Christian believers in the hour of their last extremity. Many of those who thus die seemingly in despair, however, are only suffering from the effects of some distressing malady, like that which caused the celebrated and saintly incumbent of Trinity Chapel, Brighton, the Reverend Frederick Robertson, to declare that when very ill he often saw everything through a thick, black crape veil. (Frames and feelings, even at the hour of earthly dissolution, are no criterion of wickedness or virtue, but are very frequently the result of despondency occasioned by physical ailments solely.) Let this physiological truth be once accepted by the multitude, and it will be, and that shortly, if education continues to advance during the next half century as it has done during the past fifty years, and one of the very strongest and cruelest weapons ever employed by the believers in an angry God and everlasting damnation, against those who differed from them in opinion, will be dashed from their grasp, or rendered powerless in their hands.

It has always been accounted a sin, in orthodox circles, for persons to think for themselves. According to Orthodoxy, God has evidently given brains to a very few, coupled with permission to employ them on religious matters, while to the great mass of mankind, reason must be employed on secular matters only, and then only within a circumscribed area, defined by the ruling powers; as kingcraft has ever been allied with priestcraft. and freedom of thought and speech on matters political, has, till very recently, been considered blasphemy, meriting imprisonment, and in extreme cases even death itself.

One of the most prominent signs of the present times, is the practical, if not the actual, disestablishment of Church and State alike. in all civilized lands. This disestablishment is, unfortunately, too often brought about by violent, aggressive, and altogether reprehensible means, as tyranny in a new form often usurps the place of the old tyrant, who has been compelled by the masses to abdicate the throne. There are laws on England's statute book to-day, which, if enforced, would imprison or fine every religious freethinker and every political dissenter throughout the land; and it is only because of the powerful *vox populi*, which cannot be silenced, that heresy in any form is permitted. But while we sympathize heartily with all who having wrongs seek redress; while we can side with the friends of Charles Bradlaugh and Mrs. Besant, in their agitation for the repeal of the Blasphemy Laws; while we have hearts to feel with the oppressed sons and daughters of Erin, who for centuries have been downtrodden, and afflicted with an unjust yoke; while we pity, from the bottom of our hearts, the poor Russians, who have been exiled to Siberia on the merest pretext, and can behold in the foundations of Nihilism itself a rude, savage clamour for simple justice, and the recognition of the rights of mankind universally, we cannot but deprecate and utterly disown the aggressive policy of those who seek by the assassin's hand, secretly or openly, to do evil that good may come.

War itself is an evil, and there is some justification for dynamite, on the plea that it is the poor man's substitute for gunpowder. But the secret foe, lurking in street corners, ready to stab one in the dark, must ever be held in greater detestation than he who openly declares himself your enemy, and challenges you to mortal combat in the daylight. But are the manœuvres of armies all upright, and can any one reading the history of ancient warfare, and then studying the annals of these days, fail to regard with contempt, if he has any honour in him, the detestable intrigue always resorted to, when war is undertaken for ambition more than to vindicate the oppressed.

Warfare is justified by Reason, but never by the Spirit. Intuition has ever discountenanced it, and when John Bright severed his connection with the English Cabinet, because of England's aggressive foreign policy, especially in relation to Egypt, he proved himself to be upon a spiritual eminence, vastly higher than that on which Gladstone, or any other of England's greatest statesmen, stand. We do not wish to be misunderstood, as implying that warfare has neven been justifiable, from the standpoint of those who engaged in it: therefore, your martial heroes, Nelson, Washington, and others deserve the tribute you pay to their bravery, and the monuments you rear to their honour, and yet it is Buddha in Asia and Christ in Europe and America, at whose shrine the civilized world instinctively bows, not because of the intellectual greatness, but by reason of the spiritual superiority of these ideal characters.

Intuition or Spiritual Insight is the Higher Reason. It is Angelic Wisdom, it is the knowledge of the Soul; and knowledge gained in celestial spheres communicated intuitively to man on earth, constitutes human intuition in its purest and highest forms. Instinct is the attribute of the animal creation. Throughout the animal kingdom instinct reigns supreme, and this voice of instinct is unerring and unfaltering in its tone: it never leads astray. It is instinct which leads the animal to search for such roots, herbs and grasses as will heal it of its wounds, and restore it to health when in sickness. Instinct leads the animal, the bird, the insect to make provision for every material want; but millions of living creatures appear to have no higher instincts than those which guide them to make adequate provision for material wants. Many there are who appear completely destitute of any higher love than clannish or the lowest type of family devotion. Cruelty is rampant in the lower world, as animality governs, and the instinct of self-preservation is the dominant and inspiring sentiment of being.

Reason in man is higher than instinct in animals, but Reason is far inferior to Intuition, and often even to Instinct, as a guide in the present stage of man's development, though in angelic life Reason, or the power of intellect, will be so completely blended with intuitive perception, or the clear and direct apprehensions of Spirit, that in the perfect dual life of angelhood, yet to be expressed in perfected human forms on earth, Reason, as analyst, and Intuition, as discoverer, will walk hand in hand: Reason explaining the why and wherefore of whatever Intuition realizes or perceives.

Reason can never discover the primal cause or fount of life: it knows simply nothing of the origin of being, and is therefore utterly agnostic on all spiritual matters. The idea of God is not irrational, but it is more than rational; so is the idea of spirit-life and that of human immortality. Thomas Paine, though avowedly a rationalist of the extremest type, was not devoid of intuition or spiritual perception, and thus his recognition of Deity is not in accordance with the views of Rationalists at large. All spiritual questions must be referred to the spiritual side of human nature, as reason unaided can only deal with the outermost covering or envelope of life.

Why should it be preposterous to declare in the teeth of modern scepticism and open denial of all spiritual realities, that man has spiritual faculties in addition to his intellectual powers and means of sensuous observation? Science, though silent on the question of the spirit world, cannot and does not attempt to deny its existence. Huxley is an agnostic, so are Spencer and Tyndall, and other luminaries in the world of scientific research, who rely solely on the power of intellect. A spiritual revelation is granted to man through the avenues of spiritual perception, even as the eye is needed to distinguish colour, the ear to detect sound, while each one of the senses has its own peculiar work to do. If every bodily sense has its own place and function, and the avocations of one faculty are not those of others, surely to the rationalistic mind it need not appear absurd to state that man has other faculties than the intellectual, other perceptions than the sensuous, and that these other and higher perceptions, *viz*, the spiritual or intuitive faculties, are the primal source whence man derives all his absolute knowledge concerning spiritual existence.

It has usually been observed that woman is more intuitive than man, while man is more intellectual than woman, and for this reason, woman has been denied admission into Parliament, and has not been permitted to take equal part with man in the various trades, industries and professions, many of which are equally adapted to both sexes. It is just because intuition, in the person of woman, has been kept outside the Council and the Senate, that war has raged so terrifically in all parts of the civilized world, as well as among barbaric peoples. It is on this account that the history of Christianity has often been written in blood, and tyranny has reigned instead of meekness and gentleness of spirit which is commended in the Gospel, and is usually called Christian, no matter how harsh and vengeful the action of professing Christendom may be. Intuition in the human race is as unerring as instinct is unerring in the animal, but intuition in man far transcends animal instinct, for while instinct only makes provision for material wants, intuition discovers a moral code, realizes the existence of a spiritual world and a spiritual life, and, in a word, reveals God to the Soul, which can alone behold him.

It is not with the intellect or outer mind that spiritual truths are grasped. All that reason can do is to admit their probability, after Intuition has presented them to Reason, that reason may decide whether to accept them or reject them. Intuition does not contradict reason, but it always transcends it; and surely the transcendent and the contradictory are widely different the one from the other. You are all acquainted with the facts of the multiplication table: you have learnt it in your childhood, and are convinced that the propositions it lays down are axiomatic or self-evident. Should anyone, therefore, come to you and say: "It has been revealed to me by intuition, or by inspiration, that the multiplication table is incorrect," you would give no credence to such a statement, for the simple reason that you *know* of the truth of that which your opponent assails.

No religious truth can ever be opposed to any fact in science, and it cannot possibly be any part of true religion to believe that the world was formed in six periods of twenty-four hours each; neither can religion be affected by the credibility or incredibility of such stories as Jonah and the whale, Balaam and the ass, and other fables or allegories introduced into the Hebrew Scriptures, to set forth spiritual truths, but no more miraculously inspired than were Æsop's fables or Bunyan's allegories.

Thomas Paine, in his "Age of Reason," confines himself almost entirely to a criticism of the letter of the Bible; into the spiritual meanings of ancient fables he does not and cannot enter. So when Swedenborg appears, with the key of Correspondences to unlock the mysteries of the ancient records, he does not attempt to underrate any scientific discovery, nor to persuade anyone to believe in a pretended revelation from heaven, which falsifies the discoverable facts of nature, constantly being revealed with ever-increasing distinctness to the delvers for wisdom in the mines of the external universe.

Whatever may be the fallacy of some of Swedenborg's conclusions, his idea of Correspondence is in the main undoubtedly correct, as it simply implies that there is an inner as well as an outer world, and that that inner realm has its own language, its own signs, and makes its own appeal, in its own way, to the spiritual senses of humanity, employing all outward things as coverings simply for the esoteric truth concealed below the surface, and under the guise of literal external history.

When Swedenborg said, there are three senses in which the Divine Word or truth itself may be understood, he certainly need not have confined himself to the Old and New Testaments, for there are many other sacred books in the world which contain truth as well as the books pronounced divine by Swedenborg. It is very easy, however, to perceive the individual limitations of the great Swedish seer, when he personally accepted as divine only such books of the Bible as appeared to him to contain the inward or spiritual sense. Not finding the spiritual sense in the Chronicles, for instance, he refuses to include them in the sacred canon. He also rejects all the Epistles, reducing the New Testament to five books only: the four Gospels and the

Apocalypse, which latter work seems to have been his peculiar study.

Now, it is evident to all observing minds, that all teachers claiming inspiration have accepted such manuscripts as divinely inspired as appealed to their own sense of right, and awoke answering echoes within their own consciences. Luther rejected the Epistle of James, because it did not harmonize with his peculiar views of justification by faith alone; he also ignored the Revelation, because of its extremely mystic character, and the extreme value which in his opinion the author put upon his work. It seems evident, that every individual reformer or teacher finds it his own especial province to discover the precious ore which, though mixed with alloy, is undoubtedly buried beneath the letter of all the world has ever held sacred, and in so far as the reformer is a revelator, adding something to the stock of human knowledge, his work is a valuable addition to human literature; as the world depends entirely upon well-proven affirmatives for its progression.

No error can be greater than to limit nature by our knowledge of it, to the rejection of all facts which we individually have not perceived. How is it in all departments of scientific research? Are there not intuitive or prophetic minds, who declare that there are more planets than have yet been discovered? Then, at length, when Reason has acted upon the suggestion of Intuition, the telescope reveals that which hitherto was only supposed to exist. Do not all discoveries simply fulfil the dream of some poet, the prophecy of some seer, while the romancist, or writer of what is often called the wildest fiction, is simply the anticipator of coming facts in outward life? Jules Verne, Cervantes, Lord Lytton, and other writers of a highly romantic or visionary type, have stated nothing impossible in perspective. Even "20,000 leagues under the Sea" has been pronounced by the French Academy, which body has recognised intuition as a sixth sense, as a prediction of the future attainments of mankind; while the Vril-Ya of Lytton are not more wonderful people than the progress of society from barbarism to the present day leads us to expect as the future inhabitants of earth.

What is Intuition? Reason, cold, calculating, dealing only with what reaches the senses, may evolve a system of religion which deals with abstractions, but the abstract is never lovable, and never awakens the sentiment of affection in its worshippers. An abstract Deity may be inferred by reason, a vast reservoir of intelligence, governing all things by immutable, inexorable laws. But such a God is king simply, there is nothing of the fatherhood or motherhood of the Infinite Spirit in such a conception.) Such a being may inspire you with awe but not with love. The worshippers of such a being are usually fatalists or stoics, and it is to be noted that whenever the thought of God is of a masculine entity only, and wherever the priesthood is composed exclusively of men, that there vengeance is mistaken for justice, and human anger is considered to have its counterpart in the wrath of the Eternal.

Universalism and Unitarianism have instinctively worked for the emancipation and elevation of woman. These denominations have opened their pulpits to women as well as men, and there is no law governing the churches of these denominations, forbidding such inspiration as may flow through human minds and lips to-day, even though it should not accord with the prevailing sentiments of Christendom. Truly the masculine element of reason is not as yet sufficiently blended with intuition in the Unitarian body, and therefore there is a complaint, that Unitarian services are too cold and simply intellectual, to satisfy the emotional side of human nature, and emotion has always played a prominent part in the history of the spiritual experiences of the race.

(Emotion is as natural as intellect. The heart which feels is quite as important as the brain which thinks or the mind that reasons; and when the wise man of old penned the salutary injunction, "Keep thy heart, for out of it are the issues of life," he invented a precept which the world can never afford to despise or forget. The heart physically is as important as the brain. Rupture of the heart will produce instant dissolution. Heart affections frequently carry persons off in a moment, who are outwardly robust and likely to live for many years, judging by external indications; but outward indications are frequently deceitful, as we cannot judge of a person's bodily health, at all times, by superficial appearances, so we often err most wofully when we rely entirely upon the observations of the senses and the calculations of the reason, in forming estimates of character.

A new era is dawning in the science of medicine. The

old, clumsy, imperfect methods of diagnosis are being supperceded by clairvoyant or psychometric delineations. In America, to a much larger extent than in England, Clairvoyantes and Psychometrists are employed to assist physicians. These sensitive persons are always mediumistic, and though they may have powers of discernment of their own, peculiar to their extremely sensitive condition of mind and body, no one, sensitive enough to be clairvoyant in his normal state, is other than highly mediumistic, for mediumship is after all due to sensitiveness of brain and body, more than to all other causes combined.

Spirits are not called up by mediums "from the vasty deep"; the medium is not an evoker of spirits, by means of charms or spells, but when the clairvoyant describes a friend of yours, beside you in spirit, that friend is not brought thither by the medium, for he does not follow the medium about. You perhaps are not so organized as to be able to see the spirit form or hear the spirit voice, while the medium's peculiarly susceptible condition enables him to see and hear sights and sounds produced by vibrations on the atmosphere, impossible for you to detect.

Science declares that as man has progressed, he has come into a condition enabling him to see many colours and hear many sounds, of whose existence previously he had never even dreamed. Perhaps there are new colours, perhaps there are new sounds, some one suggests. There may be sounds and colours new to earth and its inhabitants, but wherever the faculties of man are at their lowest, he realizes the least, while wherever they are at their highest, he realizes most.

The spiritual world is not far distant, as some suppose; it is the very life and soul of the material earth. Just as spirit must pervade the material organism of man, or vitality would cease, so the spirit-world must penetrate the outer world, or there could be no animation or objective life on earth.

Intuition does not argue or reflect, does not calculate or measure, it simply realizes. Is it wonderful that the spiritual nature of man should possess such realistic powers, when man's outward frame has similar susceptibilities? If you have open eyes, and are not colour-blind, when light streams in upon you, you discover of what colours it is composed. You need no one to teach you that light is warm, if, touching your cheek, it makes your face burn. No one needs to asseverate that ice is cold, if once you have handled it. All knowledge is gained experimentally, and without experimental knowledge there can be but supposition or blind belief. But how much there is accepted in the material world daily, merely on hearsay, and how many there are who have had no opportunities to personally verify what they have been told! It is optional with these, whether they accept or reject the testimony of others, but witness of an impartial character is universally accepted as authoritative throughout the world, in all departments of life.

Intuition is the action of the soul, independently of mind and body, and therefore it is often far more reliable than any information gained in outward ways can possibly be. We have known not only one but numberless instances of intuitive knowledge putting to flight the most feasible and well-considered conclusions of eminent scholars, which were nevertheless erroneous, because they had built upon false data, therefore their hypotheses, no matter how logical, were foundationless. You often hear it said of a fallacious system,—grant the premises upon which the theory is built, and the theory itself is incontrovertible. The reformers of the world deny the premises of old theology, they deny many of what are falsely called the cardinal verities of religion, as the light of the Spirit reveals the error of those pessimistic views of life upon which all such doctrines as the total depravity of man, God's unabating wrath, and everlasting torment, find support.

Intuition does not confine itself to general and great questions; it enters into every detail of material life; it often speaks through dreams, warnings, and presentiments, but quite as frequently through the vision of the spirit directly, during the waking hours of the body's life.

Recently a lady of our acquaintance hired a servant, who had no one to say a kind word for her. She had no character, no reputation, no references to produce, and she generally bore a very bad name. The lady to whom she applied for a situation, after having met with constant rebuffs in other places, said, "I know you have no testimonials with you, I know you have few friends and many enemies, I know I shall be thought foolish for engaging you, and perhaps even my husband may scold me for my imprudence in taking a servant into the house without a character; but I *know* you are an injured woman, I *know* you are honest, and have been cruelly maligned, and I feel it only an act of justice to do what I can to give you a comfortable home, and make such amends to you as are in my power, for the injuries you have sustained through the false reports maliciously circulated against you." The lady's husband did upbraid her, acquaintances did comment upon what they called her insane folly, her unaccountable madness; but the servant proved a treasure, and was the means of doing her employers a most important service. Reason would have said, Have nothing whatever to do with her; but reason could not see through the falsehood, it could only argue from it as though it were a truth.

When Jesus said to his disciples, "Whosoever's sins ye remit they are remitted, and whosoever's sins ye retain they are retained," he spoke concerning the intuitive heart-reading, soul-discerning power, which the truly spiritual ever possess. He endowed them with no sacerdotal authority, such as Romanists and Ritualists lay claim to; he never placed the destiny of human souls for eternity in the hands of frail and feeble man, but he declared that those who are truly developed in their interior being, have powers of spiritual discernment the rest of the world do not possess.

When the age of Intuition shall have fully come, then deception will be impossible, as it is in the brighter spheres of spirit-life. Imposture cannot bear the searching scrutiny of spiritual investigation. Words may be false, actions treacherous, reputations forged, but if coming into living contact with another mind, you can analyse it, then brass can no longer pass for gold, hypocrisy will be unmasked, wrongs righted, and deceitfulness abandoned, when the earth produces a race of men and women, who can see beneath the surface, and judge with the unerring judgment of the Spirit.

See that ye despise not these interior Voices, which, to supplement, not to supplant, human reason, are God's revelation to Man through the medium of the Soul within.

IMPROMPTU POEM.

THE IDOL-BREAKER.

THE world has many idols, false deities, who stand
Before the Lord Almighty, e'en in this Christian land!
But the grossest of the idols, of all 'fore which ye bow,
Is the false god, named Mammon, with gold upon its brow!

Gold is the powerful idol, for which ye all forsake:
Ambition, the besetting sin, whose thirst ye strive to slake,
Even with blood outpoured upon the battle field,
Thirst for some new possession, for this your lives ye yield.

Who shall go out to battle—invincible in might,—
And, by the power of Spirit, put ancient wrongs to flight?
Who shall express in Council, that human love, whose might
Shall overrule the Senate, till all obey the right?

Who will be the Crusader, engaged in holy war,
To carry Heaven's own banner, to lands both near and far;
And, through the force of kindness, subdue the ancient frown
Of haughty, grasping nobles, and elevate the clown?

Ye build your massive temples, and rear them to the sky,—
Your steeple-houses lofty, that all who're passing by,
May hear your choirs sing anthems: "God is a man of war,
Mighty is he in battle," while, o'er in Egypt far,
Your troops subdue th' Egyptians, not by the power of love,
But by cold steel, gunpowder,—these come not from above!

Ye claim as teacher, Jesus, that saviour of mankind,
Who strove by cords of mercy, his sheep to him to bind;
Ye call his name more sacred than any name that's heard,—
Then why not pay obedience to his most loving word?

'Tis true, he said his spirit, with wings of peace o'erspread,
The dove of loving-kindness would not rest on every head,
Until the sword had gone forth to scatter death, dismay.
But they who used the sword, he said, must perish in the fray.

> "It must be that offences come:
> But, woe to him by whom they come!"

Are there offences here, against the law of right;
Are there not discords now, warring against the light?
    Baal, as God, still enthroned will be,
    Till all obey the law of Charity.

Elijah, in the ancient time, with visage stern and bold,
Calls Baal's worshippers to meet their God: on him to call, they're told.

With knives and lancets they afflict their bodies, for his ire
Demands such brutal sacrifice, while Elijah says, "By fire
Shall the true God answer ye this day;
So to your rites of worship speed ye on your way."

For hours and hours the people cry:
"O Baal! answer." But no reply
In answer comes to their earnest prayer;
Their cries and sobs may rend the air,
But Baal sleeps or hunts that day,
And hears not when his people pray.

Ah! in your hours of need, false deities will ye forsake:
Trust, then, alone in the living God, and for your portion take,
That Light which inly he reveals,
The Love which every sorrow heals!

'Tis told of an Idol-Breaker, that, journeying forth one day
On a holy expedition, he found upon his way
One idol, than all more beauteous, and he would stay his hand,
And save that precious relic, which did so lovely stand.
But the Spirit urged him on to strike, and, with one fatal blow,
The idol fell low at his feet, while in his sight did glow,
Gems, rubies, sapphires, diamonds rare,
With countless treasures beyond compare!

The idol, which was broken, yielded up this goodly store;
The idol kept the treasures from the people, as of yore.
So, at this moment, idols,—the Love of Place and Power,
Selfishness, Vain Ambition,—defraud ye, at this hour,
Of universal treasures. When freemen strike the blow,
And level the fairest idol, till on earth it lieth low,
Then, in surpassing beauty, will the treasures it conceals,
Lie open to your vision, for your use, your woes to heal!

Break! break! the massive Idol: the thirst for rank and power!
Remember, all are brethren; look forward to the hour,
When Love's triumphant conquest shall bid all wars to cease,
And labour, as ye may, to bring the Age of Universal Peace!

BENEDICTION.

May the Light of Love and Wisdom, blended into one perfect ray of Heavenly Light, so guide you in all your undertakings, that in your hearts and homes the Demon of Strife shall perish, and the Angel of Peace sit enthroned triumphant. Then from your happy homes, and peaceful lives, may influences go forth to banish Strife among the Nations, till dawns the Reign of Universal Peace, by Prophets long foretold. AMEN.

IX.

TRUE PRAYER:

ITS NATURE AND EFFICACY.

"Prayer is the Soul's sincere desire."

SO sang that truly inspired and sweetly devotional poet, MONTGOMERY, whose charming sacred lays form a very choice and important part of Christian hymnology. Montgomery has, perhaps, contributed no finer gem to the diadem of the world's religious fervour than the poem or hymn which contains the text or motto of our Discourse this morning. (Here in a single sentence the entire significance of Prayer is stated; here we have a compendium of the choicest theology, a definition capable of eternal unfoldment, at once logical, terse, brief, spiritual, and while sufficiently simple to be intelligible to the youngest child, at the same time deep, profound, scientific and didactic enough for the most erudite scholar, and the most sceptical philosopher.)

We are quite well enough aware, however, of the agnostic tendencies of to-day, not to expect that Materialism will concede anything to Spiritualism without a hard struggle; and far from blaming or deriding the scepticism of the hour, we regard it as a healthy indication of the world's progress, because wherever there is doubt there must be thought to engender that doubt. Belief is very easy to some minds, if you can justly call gullibility or superstition belief. Unbelief is also easy to many, as nothing can well be easier than to deny, or, at least, ignore everything with which you are personally unacquainted. The fool, in the time of David, said positively in his heart, "There is no God." The fool says the same thing to-day: "There is no God, because I have not seen God; no future life for man, because it has not been satisfactorily demonstrated to me personally." While the sceptic—who is not a fool but often a very earnest and truth-loving man, seeking for the highest wisdom—may often be found to exclaim: "I cannot feel sure that thereis a Supreme Spirit governing all things. I cannot feel sure that man is immortal; there may or there may not be a God, a heaven, a resurrection." And in this attitude of hazy doubt many of your great minds are at this moment.

This doubt is, however, not the gloaming which heralds the approach of night, it is the twilight which precedes the dawn of a new day. The stars may have become invisible, the moon may have set, the sun may not yet have arisen for these minds, and they are groping their way amid the shadows; the darkling mists encircle them, the cold wet dews are falling, but out in the cold, out in the shadow, they are but awaiting the sunrise, even though they know not that there be a sun. The attitude of the thoughtful world to-day is that of eager expectancy. Every one seems on the *qui vive*, on the tiptoe of expectancy, awaiting nobody knows what, but certainly a tangible something whose approach is felt mysteriously in the darkness, but whose form is yet concealed from the eyes of the waiting throng. Imagine a man, born blind, just receiving sight, and can you not picture to yourselves a vision before his opening eyelids, of a confused mass of moving substance, in which no form is clearly outlined, where men and trees seem fused together as though they were one incongruous existence? Can you not picture to yourselves one of Lord Lytton's heroes or heroines coming up from the nether world, and standing one morning upon an Alp, awaiting the sunrise and marvelling as to what possible thing the sun can be like in appearance, never having seen it. It is as though the world's thinkers, who are just redeemed from the slavery of ecclesiastical bondage, were for the first time admitted into the open field, and allowed to await the sunrise. The stars have retired, the moon has set, powers temporal and ecclesiastical no longer act for them as luminaries, and they are left in the chill, bleak dawn of a new oncoming day, to await the sunrise.

The world has just completed its passage through one astronomical cycle, and you are now in a period of expectancy, awaiting the culmination of the spiritual era which ensues later. The premonitory knockings have been heard, the initial steps to welcome the new angel have been taken, but yet the Lord delays his coming, and the virgins with lighted lamps must awhile yet stand outside the door of the palace, awaiting its opening from within, that they may be admitted to take their seats around the King's table, at the marriage supper of the Lamb. Purely astronomical interpretations of spiritual truth are in a strictly literal sense, perhaps, correct, but when the true inner wisdom of the Ancients shall be brought to light, then shall every symbol glow with radiant spiritual light, and the pathway of the Soul, from the dust to the celestial heavens, shall be seen clearly outlined in the symbols which record the passage of the sun in the heavens, and the journeyings of Sol with his companions around the more distant Alcyone.

(Supposing the purely physical science of astronomy explains to you the letter of the Greek Mythos acceptably: supposing you become converts to the learned though erratic Frenchman, Dupuis, whose "Christianity and Solar Worship" has created quite a sensation in some circles; supposing Gerald Massey's "Natural Genesis" shall so revolutionize the thought of Christendom, that to the eyes of many Jesus becomes a type of the sun of this system, and his disciples are the twelve signs of the Zodiac; supposing the development theory of the great German sceptical author, Strauss, be accepted alike by the Church and the world ;—Will spiritual aspiration directed to Christ and his apostles avail nothing? Will it be proved that all the prayers of Christendom are vain, mere idle breath, because they have been addressed to imaginary instead of real personages? Our answer is—Let our quotation from Montgomery supply you with an emphatic denial to your fears: "Prayer is the soul's sincere desire, uttered or unexpressed; the motion of a hidden fire, that trembles in the breast."

Thus prayer owes its efficacy to the nature and efforts of your own spirit. True prayer is the work of the soul, and by it you can reap spiritual harvests, just as by manual labour you can avail yourselves of the resources of the ground. We are all dependent upon at least two classes of influences in the accomplishment of all we undertake. No one can live either to or by himself alone. Crusoe on his lonely island, before Friday visited him, was not alone, and his consciousness of unseen companionship led him to suspect the presence of the devil on the island, when a mysterious footstep on the sand could be traced by him to no human agency. The sensitive child who dreads the darkness, who cannot go upstairs alone, because of an overwhelming timidity which paralyzes every sense, is a medium who as yet has not had the laws of spirit communion explained to him. The reason why spirits so often seem to be devils, is because of false early training partly, and partly by reason of the inner consciousness of mankind, that human life, as it now is, is not sufficiently pure to always attract the angels. However much we may differ from Madame Blavatsky, Colonel Olcott, and the Theosophists generally, on some points, we gladly refer you to the pages of the "Theosophist" for learned and spiritual expositions of prayer. Nothing can be finer than the Editor's ideas of invocation: nothing truer than his mode of distinguishing between the attractive potencies of thought, and the reality or unreality of personages addressed by name, or otherwise, in verbal or even inaudible petitions.

The spirit aspires after some plane of spiritual being, and allies itself with existence on that plane, by fervent spiritual effort, which is desire, and desire is supplication, therefore, according to our desires are our prayers effectual or non-efficacious.) The Roman Catholic will invoke Vincent-de-Paul, Francis Xavier, Philip Neri, and a host of other personages who cannot be omnipresent nor even ubiquitous. Now, do Catholics imagine that these saints, who on earth were only men, and many of whom were canonized because of the service they rendered to the Church while on earth, can hear every litany which mentions their names, and can respond to every petition addressed to them? It seems incredible that such views can been entertained by an educated priesthood, though the Irish peasantry cannot be expected to reflect very deeply on such matters. Moreover, different people form very different ideas of the beings whom they address, and thus it is spiritually impossible that all can be praying to the same individual, even though all are using the same name to personify the spiritual state, into league with which they desire to come.

(Shallow iconoclasts, who can tear down easily enough, but have few abilities or propensities for building up, ridicule Prayer because its form is often grotesque and its methods ignorant, but any child can destroy what has taken years to fashion; but can the child give you a better substitute for the thing he has destroyed? That is the vital question. Prayer is an unspeakable comfort to millions of tired, weary and desponding hearts. Relief found in prayer has prevented death by suicide, in many instances. Prayer has lifted many a burdened heart from under the heavy burden of woe, which would otherwise have crushed it; has rescued many a broken-hearted one from the grave: has restored many a shattered mind and body to health and reason; and has done more for the real salvation of the world from disease, crime, and manifold distresses than all other agencies put together. It behoves us, therefore, to consider its nature and methods of operation most carefully, before we dare to discountenance so powerful an aid to human well-being.

Prayers for rain and fine weather are amongst those most frequently ridiculed. These we will consider first, passing on ere we close to a consideration of those prayers which heal the sick and work so-called miracles.

Now we need not remind this audience that we are as earnest sticklers for the immutability of the laws of nature as any Materialist can possibly be. He differs from us, or we differ from him, not concerning the impossibility of setting aside the laws of nature—upon this point we are fully agreed—but upon the nature of the laws themselves. It is one thing to agree to the proposition, that nature's laws are immutable, and quite another to be satisfied with a definition given by a man, or party, of those laws. To us, we may as well say plainly—first as last—to our *positive knowledge*, law is the result of spirit action. There is no blind force in nature, no such thing as a destiny which is not planned by Intelligence. If people prefer to think that they are swayed by blind laws, if it consoles them to be resigned to the inevitable feeling that the inevitable is traceable neither to love, wisdom, nor justice, but to inexorable fate or unconscious being, they are at liberty to enjoy their frozen philosophy, so long as they do not endeavour to wrest from us our spiritual certainties. Let these certainties be attacked, so highly do we prize them, that we will leave no stone unturned in their defence, their exposition and their reconciliation with the facts of material science, as far as possible.

With the barbarous anthropomorphism of many Jews and Gentiles we have no sympathy whatever, and thus we shall offer no attempt at reconciliation with such conceptions of God as make him man's slave and puppet. Some people worship a god who might be one of the "elementaries" of the Occultists, so obedient do they expect him to be to all their requests. A great deal of so-called prayer is insolent dictation to the Supreme Being. Prayers are often offered at prayer meetings which tell God exactly what he ought to do and what to leave undone. Many changes are suggested by his creatures, who cannot understand why he does not profit by them. Now we do not wonder that persons who read the Bible indiscriminatingly and believe every word of it to be literal truth, should act as they do, because we are informed that Moses often persuaded the Lord to change his mind, and that *whatsoever* is asked of God in the name of Christ, believingly, shall be received.

Now, it becomes the duty of every rational student of Scripture, to throw such light as modern revelation enables him to throw upon obscure and misleading statements.) Setting aside, this morning, all views of correspondences, we will deal critically with the texts in dispute. In a previous Discourse delivered in this hall, upon the "God and the Lords of the Bible," we stated, as you will remember, that the Ancients universally believed in planetary angels, in the tutelary or guardian spirits of nations, tribes, families and individuals, and thus the tribal dieties of the Hittites, Amalakites and others may have been at variance with the tribal or tutelary ruler of the Jewish clan. We are told in the Psalms that all Gods must bow to the one true God. *Adonai*, the Jewish name for God Jehovah, signifies the Eternal One, he who always was, *i.e.*, he who is self-existent, and thus can have had no beginning. But it is not the Eternal One (Adonai) with whom the patriarchs interceded, but only his angel or representative. We are told that Abraham, on the plains of Mamre, encountered three angels or men, *i.e.*, spirits in human form, who prophesied concerning the destruction of the wicked city, Sodom, whither two of them went at eventide to accomplish its overthrow. The one to whom Abraham paid the greatest deference is styled the Lord. (It was quite common for the Ancients to address spiritual visitors as "my lord," and quite common for them to say, "thus saith the lord," when they spoke of the commands or instructions they had received from the spirit directors of human affairs, with whom they may have conversed by means of clairaudient and clairvoyant powers, or through the very ancient phenomenon of materialization or form manifestation, which was once far more common and triumphant in Oriental climes than it is now in England and America.

Now, is it not eminently rational to believe, that the Ancients used the word "lord" just as we use it to-day? A member of the Upper House of Parliament is a lord. Is he, therefore, the Almighty (*Shadai*)? Is he, therefore, a celestial being, one whose thoughts and intents are always pure? Is it not conceivable that lords may be cruel, capricious, tyrannical, unjust, while other lords are humane, charitable, wise, and sticklers for equity? No one who knows anything of ancient history can be unaware of the fact, that earthly rulers were frequently styled lords and gods, even while on earth, and that after their entrance into spirit life, many who had not been particularly virtuous while on earth were worshipped with divine honours.) Read the story of the deification of Romulus, in Roman history, for example. Read words attributed to Jesus by the Evangelist, who declares that he reminds those who criticize his authority, that those were called gods upon whom the spirit came. Turn to the account given in the Acts of the Apostles, of the desire of the multitude to worship Paul and Barnabas, as Mars and Jupiter respectively, because of the wondrous healing powers these mediums for the Spirit had exercised, and you will see in a moment that between the Eternal One, the Infinite God, whom no man hath seen at any time, and these innumerable lords, the Jewish law itself forbade any comparison to be drawn. Does not the Decalogue forbid you to liken God to any thing in heaven above or in the earth beneath? Is it, then, just to infer, that crude anthropomorphism or a degraded creature or hero worship is that original and pure Monotheism, which is and always has been Israel's pride and glory? God is a spirit, invisible, incomprehensible, without parts and passions, unchanging, ever just and kind and wise, according to the best rational commentators upon the Law and the Prophets. (The lords were only human spirits, many of them near the earth, not yet having outgrown earthly pride and prejudice. They were fallible and changeable, and were in many instances only the familiars of a priesthood, which was not always above sacrificing spirituality for worldly considerations.

Now, that you can invoke such spirits as these, that you

can really order about spirits, who, if not your inferiors, are certainly not more than your equals, is very reasonable to infer. Without resorting to the "elementaries" of the Theosophists, we may find many dwellers upon the threshold of earth, who are quite ready to do all in their power to further the worldly interests of those who summon them. Very earth-bound spirits, when left to themselvers, are poor, forlorn, miserable beings, blind, deaf, and altogether impotent in the world of spirits. Devoid of spiritual perception, they are miserable out of the flesh, having lost every means of enjoyment. As their pleasures are purely sensuous, if they can control any of you, if they can borrow your organisms to work through, if you will supply them with animal magnetism which they can manipulate, they will often gladly follow you about, and look after your temporal interests as best they can. But they are very fallible, because wisdom belongs only to exalted states of spiritual being.

At the expense of this digression, which we have found necessary to amplify our subject and make plain to you our philosophy, we will return to the topic, prayers for rain, &c., and request you to discriminate closely between an effective and a useless petition, independent of the form of speech in which the desire of the mind is clothed. It is of course impossible even for the Almighty to answer all prayers addressed to him in the letter, as one person who is a devout believer in the efficiency of prayer may be praying for rain at the instant when some one equally devout is praying for fair weather; and it is incredible that God should favour one petition and reject the other, and yet remain no respecter of persons. But when prayer for rain is steady, continuous, and united, when large congregations of earnest people, all over the land, are uniting their wills and desires at a given time for a given result, we are not bold enough to say that no result follows upon this concentration of mind and united direction of will. Not that there can, in any case, be any possible change in the laws of nature, but these laws of nature are found to be, by spiritual students, only the exercise of will, and then it must be borne in mind that the weather is, after all, to a great extent, under man's control. Man has the power to plant trees and also to uproot them. Where trees have been planted rain has been brought to districts where no rain has been known to fall within the memory of man; and where trees have been uprooted, there rain has ceased falling and the land has become barren. Thus the command of rain is not physically or scientifically anything like an impossibility, and who shall say to what extent united mind may influence the material world?

But the spiritual aspects of the question leave these physical points to be decided by human experience. The spiritual nature of Prayer is altogether independent of any physical result. You may, perhaps, have prayed for rain thousands of times, and never have succeeded in getting a single drop; but if you prayed for rain because you saw the flocks dying and the harvest shrivelling, and your heart was touched at the thought of the multitudes who would suffer starvation unless rain came, and thinking in that plight rain was the only saviour, you prayed for it, meaning all the while that you longed to succeed in inducing the higher powers to bless the sufferers of earth, the spirit of your prayer ascended to celestial abodes. your own spirit was enlarged and refreshed; you received spiritual rain upon your own heart, and while the higher wisdom you invoked may have given only a spiritual answer to your prayers, the response came spiritually to the spiritual craving and effort of your mind. Prayer, then, is mental effort. It is nothing physical. It can afford to do without words, or it may externalize itself through them. But its efficacy is due to its nature, and in any case it places you in communion with spirits whom you summon by encouraging and expressing thoughts which are, to them, attractive and agreeable. Pray unselfishly for another's benefit, and you can never pray in vain. Pray for self only, and you form no alliances with pure and unselfish spirits.

It is not claimed by us, as we have before stated, that the laws of being are changed to suit our needs, or in obedience to our requests. If the Author of all being be infinitely good. and if the laws of being are the regular and orderly manifestations of his nature and will, then if we could change them or their Author in the slightest degree, we should be cursing and not blessing the universe. It is utterly incompatible with reason to suppose that an angel more far-seeing than yourself would humour you to your injury, because you asked for something ignorantly which it would be your destruction to receive. In human ignorance man prays for many things which would destroy him if he received them. A child may look upon a beautiful bottle, filled with clear, transparent, sparkling liquid, and cry for it, urge the parent to let him just taste of it if no more, because it looks so bright and delicious. The parent, knowing it is poison, steadily refuses it. The child cries bitterly, thinks his mother very cruel, because she has denied his request. It grieved her to refuse her little one, and make him cry, but could she poison him to gratify his whim? and, had she granted his request, would she not have been taking a dastardly advantage of his ignorance? The letter of the child's cry was for poison, but the spirit of it was for some cooling, delicious beverage. Angels cannot heed the letter of your cries. You are so blind you often ask for poisons; they, knowing what you really need, give you a bitter draught of purging medicine when you petition them for unwholesome sweetmeats. But in the depths of your hearts, when you are not quite bereft of reason, you must feel thankful if you can only realize the blessing of a withholding as well as of a conferring Providence.

On earth you often hate to suffer. You cannot see any use in sorrow and pain, and so long as you look upon suffering as the arbitrary result of the wrath of God, we do not wonder at your resistance. If you cannot see beyond the grave, we are not surprised that you bemoan earthly inequalities. But when you shall have attained to angelic states, and shall have become endowed with the angel's wonderful power of retrospection as well as prophecy, for nothing will you be more thankful than for life's cares and crosses, for without them all the beauty and sweetness of celestial life would be lost upon you. No heart is strong in loving, that has not suffered. No soul can sympathize, who has felt no grief, and thus in place of the cherubic and seraphic throng of pure and happy souls, who in their unfallen splendour have never known earthly trial and sorrow, Spiritualism reveals to you angels who are of your own race, who have suffered on this or some other earth, as you are suffering, and who now enjoy what you will never enjoy, unless you bear the cross, and thereby earn the crown.

If Spiritualism demonstrates anything it is the law of equity; if it destroys anything it is the idea of substitutionary suffering, earning for you unmerited bliss; if it declares any truth more vividly than another it is that pain is disciplinary, educational, remedial, but never punitive in the vindictive sense in which the word "punishment" is too often employed; and because of its close alliance with the teachings of that Christ, who condemned retaliative measures in no measured accents, it is the target at which abuse is ever levelled by those divines and their followers who boast of the Christian name; who make profession of discipleship to Jesus, and yet not only countenance but positively advocate capital punishment, the vilest forms of human pollution, and a thousand-and-one kindred abuses utterly at variance with the sublime spirituality of that "Sermon on the Mount," which they verbally acknowledge as infallible truth, the direct word of the incarnate Deity, but which they resolutely set aside in every law court in the land. So long as capital punishment is allowed to stain the British escutcheon, the Gospel of Jesus will be a dead letter in England, and Christianity a spurious imitation of gospel teachings. So long as spiritual methods of healing are not only tabooed but even legislated against in Christian lands, the acknowledgment of the Bible as a divine book will make the Church and Nation a laughing-stock. So long as cures by faith and prayer are repudiated, and the plain teachings of Jesus are laughed to scorn in the popular magazine and newspaper. and even in the pulpit, infidelity will have its own way, and the latest theological hobby, "conditional immortality," will be ere long exchanged for no immortality at all. If the spiritual medium, who heals by laying on of hands, is a quack or an impostor because he does not use drugs and minerals, or exhibit a diploma or carry surgical instruments and bandages about with him, then Jesus is the founder of a school of quackery and imposture, because he declared concerning his followers—"They shall lay their hands on the sick and they shall recover." Then were all the apostles quacks and impostors; then were all the early Christians either poor, deluded fanatics, or in league with quackery and imposture, because they applied magnetized handkerchiefs and aprons to the bodies of those suffering from physical ailments, and cured mental disorders by spiritual power, not by the incarceration of victims of medical tyranny in lunatic asylums, where the poor, crazy sufferers are made ten times worse by the harsh treatment they often receive, and the cruel isolation from all their friends consequent upon their captivity.

Spiritualists are accused of not building hospitals, not

doing practical work by employing organized agencies, to remove crime, disease and insanity. Perhaps it will be found on closer inspection, that institutionalism does far more to aggravate crime and misery than to relieve these evils. The Roman Catholic Church is far more entitled to respect than are the Protestant organizations, because this Church has never repudiated spiritual gifts, though it has oftentimes greatly erred and abused its power, by attributing to satanic agency every manifestation which resisted the control of the Church. The manifestations at Lourdes, at Knock, Ireland, in various parts of France and elsewhere, are genuine beyond doubt. Chronic cases of palsy, epilepsy, &c., &c., have been permanently cured through spirit agency, with the assistance of priests who are strong magnetizers and spirit mediums. But this power of healing is not locked up in the bosom of the Romish Church. The Virgin Mary and the many saints canonized by Rome, have not the exclusive power and right to heal men's minds and bodies. The unlettered country girl, who is sent for to see her dying mother, and who reaches home just when her mother's life is despaired of by the physician, throwing herself down in a paroxysm of grief, tears and supplication at her mother's bedside, brings back to life the beloved parent whom no medical skill can save. She is praying frantically to God to save her mother, and all the while she is answering her own prayers. Every pore in her skin is open; she is violently agitated, and parting with her life-force copiously—her love, her sympathy, her intense desires for her mother's recovery ally her with kind, gentle, and powerful healing spirits. She who knows nothing of magnetism, psychology, or Spiritualism; she who has not the faintest idea of the power of will, and knows not the first thing about directing her magnetism to the healing of disease, is having it directed for her by unseen hosts, and her prayer is answered in harmony with these wonderful psychological laws which are to-day being studied alike by scientist and peasant.

Ask and ye *shall* receive, seek and ye *shall* find, Nature says to all her children. Open your windows, and the light and air are yours. Close them, and you may suffocate in darkness. Fathom the laws of being, and understand prayer as spiritual effort simply, and you will know that when the soul works, it may accomplish the end it seeks, while, if it be idle, the field wherein the treasure lies is all uncultivated.

Prayer is not to supplant, but to supplement and crown exertion. Muller, of Bristol, who relied on prayer for many years to support his orphanages, was a most industrious man, an indefatigable worker. Dr. Cullis, of Boston, U. S. A., who keeps open his Consumptives' Home by prayer, is very energetic. Do not, we beg of you, run away with the idea that you may pray instead of working. Prayer is work in itself, and no one who wishes to shirk labour and pray in idleness will receive any blessing therefrom.

Prayer is the desire of the Soul, and according to the nature of your aspirations will be the character of the respondents to your petitions, and the likelihood of your blessing humanity through their agency.)

IMPROMPTU POEM.

THE WAY TO GOD.

A CHILD kneels at his mother's knee, and lisps his little prayer:
"O God! O Father! high in heaven, o'er me exert Thy care;
Send down some blest angelic guard, to watch me while I sleep,
And bless my father, far away, sailing across the deep!
Bless mother, bless my sisters dear, my little brothers, too,
And help me in my daily life, to be to duty true!"

A sailor, wandering o'er the main, sees the pale moon at night,
Shine softly, as in bygone years it shed its mellow light
Over his old, beloved home, in country lanes so far;
He gazes toward the silent heavens, and sees the evening star,
And straightway all his heart goes back, across the briny sea,
And he remembers, when a child beside his mother's knee,
He prayed that God would make him good, and make his life sublime,
And now, in manhood's riper way, he prays the same old rhyme,
But slightly altered, e'er he sleeps: "Our Father!" he repeats,
Then hears no more until the storm against his cabin beats,
And he, old seaman though he be, crouches in fear and dread.—
A storm has risen o'er all the main, by it the ship is led
Over the rocks, where quicksands lie, and e'er he draws a breath,
A fearful cry goes up from those who dread an awful death!

"Oh, save me!" screams, in accents wild, a mother; at her breast
A little infant sleeping lies, as bird in soft, warm nest.
The child hears not the awful storm, knows not of danger nigh,
But suddenly awakes to hear his mother's startled cry;
And then, with tiny arms outspread and eyes distent with fear,
He looks into his mother's eyes, and sees her bitter tear.

"Oh, save my child!" the mother shrieks, in accents piercing, wild.
"If you have known a mother's love, Oh, save my darling child
And save me, also, lest so lone and desolate he be,
That even should I pass to heaven, and know his misery,
My crown, and harp, and palm would be a weight I could not bear:
I only ask to live for him—O Father! hear my prayer!"

Straightway the gallant seaman flies to rescue, swift to save;
A lifeboat speedily he brings, and from their watery grave,
Parent and child are rescued both, and safely reach the land,
While the brave seaman struggles on, to save the rest who stand.
Timid and faltering, on the wreck, till, lo! his strength gives way,
And quickly he falls overboard, swept by the waves away!

"Our Father!" is his dying prayer: "Father! I come to Thee!
Oh, gather me among Thy sheep, unworthy though I be!"
Scarcely the words have left his lips, when, lo! his eyes grow dim,
They see not the retreating earth, he hears a heavenly hymn,
A tender voice sings in his ear: "My son! I wait for thee;
Now earthly storms no more can tear my darling child from me!"

Oh! say, what mortal tongue can speak the glories of that state,
Where angel spirits, full of love, for all earth's shipwrecked wait?
Was that instruction lost on him, when at his mother's knee,
He learned to lisp his infant prayer: "Father! take me to Thee!"

All through his life, a brooding love could ne'er forgotten be;
That love was his bright, polar star, on land or on the sea.
The memory of that little prayer, in childhood he did say,
Kept bright, within his heart, a spark of love's eternal ray.

The mother and the child he saved, can ne'er forget to pray
For him, their rescuer from death; they cry to God each day,
For him who saved them from the storm. They do not know he stands
In spirit, close beside them both, with outstretched, loving hands.

No prayer is lost! The way to God is open unto all;
No soul can cry in its distress, and vainly voice its call;
God's angels are around, and they His messengers are made;
They come as they in ancient time came, where the patriarch laid.

Prayer is the ladder Jacob saw: your prayers are angels mounting up,
Answers are angels coming down, to place life's waters in your cup.
Be brave! the way to God is wide, and all may pass that way;
Desire to bless your brethren, then through pure desire you truly pray!

BENEDICTION.

May the prayer of your every heart, be an aspiration of perpetual work for man; and, striving to bless your brethren, may you realize the fulness of God's Benediction, and possess His Peace within your hearts for ever!

X.

THE TRUE GIFT OF HEALING, AND THE TRUE SPIRITUAL PHYSICIAN.

(Delivered on Hospital Sunday.)

ACCORDING to long-established custom in the Metropolis, one Sunday in every year is set apart for special consideration of the claims of certain very deserving charitable institutions, Hospitals, Dispensaries, and Convalescent Homes in particular, when collections are made at almost all the churches and synagogues in the city and suburbs, in aid of these philanthropic institutions, and philanthropic they truly are.

From this remark, you will see at once that our Discourse on this occasion will be in no sense condemnatory or oppositional. We have no fault whatever to find with the machinery already in motion for relieving pain and healing sickness, but the cry on every hand is, that the provision made is lamentably insufficient. Though the population of London, including all the adjacent towns included in the Postal District, is probably at the present moment nearer five millions than four, the number of beds, in all the hospitals put together, is very considerably under 10,000, and when we take into consideration the fact that at least half of this immense population is made up of persons whose circumstances will not permit of their having the best medical assistance the country affords, comfortable accommodation, and good, nourishing diet, anywhere out of a public institution, in case of accident or illness depriving them of their ordinary means of earning a livelihood; when we also remember the further fact that these institutions are frequently most painfully crippled in their means of usefulness by the inadequacy of the pecuniary support they receive, and when we remember also, that a very large number of persons dread going to a hospital more than words can express, it is surely high time that public attention was called to other methods of healing than those adopted by regular medical practitioners. especially to those methods which are so simple and yet so wonderfully efficacious that they can be employed in every home without danger or risk of failure.

The present medical knowledge of the world is a boon for which all should be thankful, and never against knowledge, but always against monopoly solely, should the voice of the reformer be raised. Undoubtedly there are cases at the present day which require the surgeon's knife and the learned physician's skill; at the same time we have no hesitation in declaring that the time is fast approaching when mineral medicines, at least, will be employed no more, while surgery will die a natural death as accidents become scarcer, and the Gift of Healing is so far developed and employed as to do away with amputations and excisions almost entirely.

As many of you are, no doubt, Bible students, and as some of you have only very recently severed your connection with orthodox Christian churches, while others again may still be members of one or other of the orthodox bodies, it will, no doubt, be interesting to most of you, at least, if we endeavour to explain the miracles of healing recorded in the New Testament, by the aid of such light as we can bring to bear upon them. through our experiences with healing by spirit-power and magnetic influence in the present day; while Jews and Christians, alike giving credence to the Old Testament, may be ready to hear what may be said from a spiritual point of view concerning those wonderful phenomena which are said to have transpired through the agency of the divine, working through the earthly organisms of specially inspired prophets among the Hebrews.

Perhaps the most marvellous of all the stories in the Law with reference to this subject, is that of Elijah healing the widow's son at Zarephath. The account of this stupendous miracle will be found in the first book of Kings, chapter xvii., truly a chapter of miracles from beginning to end, and one which we do not wonder has puzzled many commentators and drawn out many diverse opinions, as its interpretation has been diversely attempted. The story at its commencement, of Elijah and the ravens, is now largely discredited, but among scholars its meaning has been rendered clearer by the change recently made in the reading. Instead of "ravens" we are now told by scholars to read "Arabs," or the wandering, almost savages tribes, who infested the desert, and were far more notorious for their depradations than their acts of hospitality and kindness. No doubt they were originally rendered savage by the attacks made upon them by their neighbours, and other more powerful and better armed peoples, and like all animals and men when subject to attack from others, they had become warlike and deceitful. (It is absurd to blame the dweller in tents in the desert for his ferocity or his treachery, and then applaud the manœuvres of disciplined armies, and justify a man for springing upon a burglar in the dark and shooting him, while the death penalty is not yet repealed either in England or America.)

It is fear and constant exposure to hostile influences that make men and animals dangerous and savage. Even a domestic cat or dog will become very dangerous if it has been perpetually teazed and irritated from kittenhood or puppyhood while children who are unnecessarily thwarted by their parents or guardians, and who have to fight for everything they obtain, are not very likely to grow up docile men and women.

The story of Elijah and these wild Arabs is intensely instructive and suggestive, and while Dr. Talmage and other sensationalists and mountebanks in the pulpit, endeavour to persuade their unthinking followers that modern revisions of ancient texts do away with the spirituality and beauty of them altogether, these poor literalists have no eyes for the larger, while they gullibly endorse the lesser, miracle. Elijah was safe among the Arab hordes or Bedouins of the desert; not only was he safe among them, but he, a true servant and prophet of the Most High, was kindly, generously, and hospitably treated by them. They brought him bread and meat both morning and evening.

Our opinion is that this charming story forms part of the instructive history considered sacred by the wise old Hebrew fathers, because they saw in it a standing reproach to aggression and cruelty as means of subduing the hearts and wills of savages, and incorporated with the sacred canon many beautiful and thrilling tales, of how good and noble men found themselves safe everywhere, always conscious of God's protection, ever secure from danger, because they aroused not the hostility, but the love and respect for virtue, which ever lies latent in the breast of every savage, and even of every animal.

How much more helpful and inspiring is the new progressive view of miracles than that old literalism it is fast displacing; and may we not venture to predict, that, when the present wave of reactionary iconoclasm has spent itself in demolishing the rapidly decaying superstructure of superstition, which ignorance and priestcraft have built upon the rock of truth, the grand old Hebrew prophets will be revealed to the world, not as special favourites of Jehovah —in the old sense, for the new religion will despise favouritism and acknowledge one universal Spirit of impartial Love and Wisdom, as the Sovereign Ruler and Sustainer of all— but as men who were able to conquer difficulties others found insurmountable, by reason of the power within them, which gave them an authority and dignity none could withstand.

When we are told, farther on in the same chapter, that a hospitable widow at Zarephath entertained Elijah, and as a reward for so doing, found her barrel of meal and cruse of oil did not waste, we need not see in this anything more miraculous than the fact of kindness never going unrewarded; and if our eyes are not limited by purely earthly horizons, though we find sometimes that virtue goes in rags and wickedness in purple on the earth, and therefore cannot apply the story of that particular widow's immunity from loss in a literal sense to all outward benefactions, we may surely in the light of immortality take comfort with the blest assurance, that no one who ever takes compassion upon the sorrows and sufferings of a fellow child of God (and all are God's children), shall ever fail to be richly compensated in one way or another. either materially or spiritually on earth or in the hereafter: though it must never be forgotten that benevolence must be distinct from selfishness, or it is not, to use theological language, of the nature of grace. Should you give a large contribution to-day to some charitable institution, with a view to improving your worldly circumstances—remembering that the Bible says somewhere. that those who give to the poor and needy lend to God, and that whatever they lend to the Almighty will be paid back to them with liberal interest, good measure pressed down and running over—your actions are not benevolent except in seeming. Those who make merely a business transaction of giving, are like those in the 16th century all over Europe, who were accustomed to buy indulgences, and expected by sacrificing a little money, which the priests were always glad to receive, to be absolved from the consequences of sin in this world and the next. It was against this perfidious practice and atrociously immoral idea that Luther so vigorously protested, and though he was by no means a model man with a perfect theology, he was needed just when he lived, to bring into prominence the doctrine of justification by faith and not by works, which properly interpreted means neither more nor less than this, (that it is the spirit within, the motive which prompts to action, and not the act itself, which is precious in the sight of heaven, and entitles the doer of the deed to a place among the angels.)

But we must not linger upon this special topic to-day, except in connection with the work of HEALING, with which we have more directly to deal, and Faith as a necessary requisite in the *modus operandi* of Healing, has always excited considerable comment and controversy.

Throughout the New Testament we are told how inseparable are faith and the power to heal, or the ability to be healed.. In some instances the Evangelists tell us that Jesus said to those whom he had cured of painful maladies and long-standing infirmities: "Thy sins are forgiven thee," and at other times his words were: "Thy faith hath made thee whole." Then we are informed that under somewhat different circumstances, Jesus could do no mighty works because of the unbelief of the people among whom he went. Again it is recorded that he marvelled, or was filled with astonishment, at their incredulity, and in those places he could work no miracle; and then at times his disciples came to him complaining that *they* could not heal, and he attributed their want of success to their own lack of *faith*, saying unto them: "O faithless and perverse generation! If ye have faith as a grain of mustard seed, ye shall say unto this mountain, Remove hence to yonder place, and it shall remove: and nothing shall be impossible to you." All things are possible with God, and all things are possible to him that believeth unwaveringly in God, because the power of God through him can be perfectly expressed. In this hurried mention of many texts and circumstances scattered throughout the gospel narratives, we have given you a brief epitome of the general teaching of Jesus concerning healing, and that peculiar phase of it, the casting out of devils (unclean demons), allusions to which occupy a large part of the canonical New Testament.

We do not, of course, expect to be able to do anything more than give you the vaguest outline of the philosophy of this teaching in a single lecture, however, we shall not be so far discouraged by the shortness of our time and the magnitude of our subject, as to refrain from attempting to send you away from here with a few thoughts to turn over in your mind at your leisure, coupled with a few suggestions for the relief of suffering and cure of disease, which, we hope, you may all find of some use to you whenever called upon to minister to those whose minds or bodies are impaired.

We never read that Jesus, or his immediate followers or successors, carried cases of surgical instruments about with them, or that they prescribed or dispensed medicines of any kind. They relied entirely upon the word of power, faith, prayer, and similar spiritual and mental agencies. It is stated in one place, that Jesus told his disciples when they had not succeeded in performing cures and casting out impure spirits, that they must pray and fast, as the power to perform such wonders came forth only by prayer and fasting, and there is no reason why we should throw the slightest discredit upon this passage, though many advanced critics cast it out as an interpolation, for it agrees perfectly with the general tenour of the life and teaching of the great Galilean seer, as the Evangelists unitedly represent him.

He was a man of abstinence and prayer. He fasted forty days and nights prior to entering upon his public ministry, and constantly during his three years' active work he was accustomed to spend whole nights in prayer, and to withdraw himself to solitary places, feeding upon bread which fed the soul more than it affected the body. But whatever affects the mind reacts upon the body, while all physical ailments and conditions have a reactionary effect upon the spirit, so long as it remains embodied; therefore, food reform is not morally unimportant, while improved methods of sanitation are as effectual in helping to reform the morals, as they are in aiding the physical improvement of mankind.

It is fashionable to-day to ignore miracles, to laugh at the supra-material, to sneer at all the marvellous records of the past, classing them together as old wives' fables and nonsensical traditions, which the sooner we discard the better it will be for us. This is the Agnostic or purely negative and materialistic view of the subject, but among advanced thinkers of a higher and more intuitive type, the miracles afford a most fascinating basis for study and experiment. and while many eminently spiritually-minded persons discard the purely marvellous or magical, and lay no stress upon anything except what is purely moral, miracles lose nothing but gain a great deal by being lifted out of the letter into the spirit, for when spiritualized they are setters-forth of many of the sublimest truths the world has ever dreamed of, or longed to see made manifest on earth.

Theodore Parker was called an infidel by many, because he took an entirely spiritual view of the wonders said to have been performed by Jesus during his sojourn on earth. Had any one asked Mr. Parker during his ministry in Boston, thirty years ago, whether he believed in the literal raising of Lazarus, the literal opening of the eyes of men born blind, he would probably have answered No! but he would never have left the one, who addressed him seeking light, in the arid wilderness of blank denial; he would have at once begun to give you his views of how Jesus, as a great moral healer and emancipator, opened the mental eyes of those who were mentally and morally blind, and would have told you, in his gentle, persuasive, yet powerful and most emphatic manner, how much more important it was to improve morals and unfold mental capacity, to heal spiritual wounds and bind up broken hearts, than cure any number of purely physical ailments.

William Ellery Channing, another noted Unitarian, though of another school of thought, would, no doubt, have said he believed in the letter as well as the spirit; but Parker was so deeply imbued with a conviction of the eternal superiority of moral over physical changes, that he was, perhaps, too little accustomed to pay attention to the outward workings of the great spiritual law he so truly recognised, and fervently believed in, which renders possible, yea, probable, and, we may say, *certain*, those outward results, which though less valuable, perhaps, than the invisible and interior, are nevertheless the outward results and natural expressions in material life of the carrying out of those supernal principles of spiritual being, which have ever a material effect to produce in the upraising of man's material nature, when they are called into exercise in the mundane sphere.

It has often been appositely remarked, that extremes meet, and it is indeed strange to find that Roman Catholics have many ideas in common with the heresiarch Parker: though when he was in Rome, shortly before his passage to spiritual life, he so shocked some of the priests with whom he argued, that they pronounced his views favourable to idolatry. Only a short time ago we heard a Catholic priest declare, that the seven devils cast out of Mary Magdalene were the seven deadly sins, and this view is by no means uncommon among educated Catholics. Such interpretations as these go to the very root of the matter, and explain many very difficult and problematic questions which are constantly cropping up concerning sin and its connection with disease and suffering.

We are told in Genesis, that suffering entered the world by sin, that if man had never sinned, never rebelled against his Maker, never broken God's commands, that he would never have forfeited Paradise, but have enjoyed during his entire sojourn on earth, perfect immunity from distress of every kind; and this doctrine, usually considered the very quintessence of orthodoxy, is in perfect keeping with the views entertained by many Secularists, who declare that if the laws of nature are perfectly known and obeyed, that no one needs to suffer, and that when they are fully understood and implicitly followed, a Secular golden age will dawn upon the earth. On the other hand, Geology and all the natural sciences lead us inevitably to conclude, that animals died before man could appear on earth, while the New Testament rebukes the prevailing idea that all sufferers are sinners, and attributes to Jesus the following words concerning a man who was born blind, whom he afterwards healed: "Neither hath this man sinned, nor his parents, but that the works of God should be made manifest in him."

(No delusion is more painful, no doctrine more reprehensible, than that which teaches you to regard all sufferers as culprits undergoing chastisement for sins committed, while you, who are enjoying good health, pride yourselves upon your goodness. Such views are calculated to develop anything but charitable dispositions. The very best view we can take of suffering is, that it is an educator; it is a sign of imperfection surely, as we cannot expect suffering to be eternal, to have any part in the nature of God. No one wishes to suffer, and suffering is by no means capable of relieving monotony, and forming a pleasing change in the ordinary routine of life. Sin is the transgression of the law, says an Epistle, and if sin be merely a breach of law, either ignorantly or wilfully, then suffering, disconnected from pangs of conscience and remorse, may be due entirely to ignorance, while that suffering which is accompanied by the stings of an upbraiding conscience, can only proceed from wilful transgression of the moral law.

But it is no one's business to wait to know what has been the cause of suffering, before he sets to work to relieve it. Persons may have been ever so wilful, ever so profligate, their own evil acts may have brought upon them their present pitiable condition, but who shall dare to say that the present imperfect state of society is not largely responsible for the crimes and misdemeanours of the bulk of the people? Are we not all, in a sense, our brother's keepers, are any of us quite free from the imputation of having set temptations in the way of others, or failed to remove stumbling-blocks we might have taken out of our brother's way? It should ever be ours to treat the sinner, as well as the sufferer, as one wrestling with a painful and dangerous malady, and as you erect hospitals, not dungeons, for the physically sick and those afflicted with mental aberration, so you should abolish all loathsome prison-houses throughout the land, and see what constructive and reformatory measures will do towards ridding the world of the incubus of pauperism and crime which now oppresses it.)

The True Healer must be something more than a skilful medical practitioner, and he need not always be that. Healers must be born, not made. It is professionalism which produces bad doctors, bad clergymen, bad lawyers, and bad representatives of all trades and callings. Until very recently, only five occupations were considered fit for the sons of the gentry. A young gentleman, unless he could afford to live in idleness, which is often considered most genteel in the "upper circles" of society, must either enter the Church, or the legal or medical professions, unless he joined the Army or the Navy. Quite recently commercial life has been tolerated for the younger sons of the upper ten thousand, but even twenty years ago *business* in all its forms, as distinct from *profession*, was looked down upon with contempt. And with what result? The greatest injury to Church and State alike.

Many and many a young man has managed to take a degree at Oxford or Cambridge, and has entered the Church professionally. To him, conducting the public worship of God and exhorting the congregation was simply a means of obtaining a livelihood. Prayers were gabbled through as though ministers were parrots, sacraments were administered in so slovenly a manner that persons began to look upon all church ordinances as empty forms, meaningless ceremonies, while sermons, purchased wholesale for a few shillings the barrel, were read in so unedifying a manner in many churches, that it became customary in many places to sleep through them. Ministers of religion have been guilty of causing more than half the prevalent indifference to religion, and we can attribute the low ebb at which the life of the Church of England was found by the Tractarians at Oxford, when Dr. Pusey first became notorious, to nothing other than the making of the performance of what were called religious duties, a merely business act. The Dissenting Bodies in England have never become quite so formal as the Established Church, because it always needed some backbone, some pluck, some courage to be a Dissenter till very lately. In America, orthodoxy originally took the Congregational instead of the Episcopalian form of church government, therefore, across the Atlantic the Episcopal Church has rarely degenerated as much as in England, while all over the continent of Europe the Established Church has been the Roman, and there that church is losing, as rapidly as it is gaining in countries where it looks to the future to make progress, instead of to the past, as the time of its greatest triumphs.

(Professionalism is always dangerous when it creeps into Religion, Science, or Art, though it is only just and right that workers should receive a proper remuneration for the time and energy they expend in any pursuit, but something more than professional activity is needed in the Church and out of it, if this country is to experience a genuine *renaissance* of religion or art. Does not the genuine Artist love his art, and does not the lover of art love it for its own sweet sake alone, or for the good he sees he can do through its agency? Ministers of religion, Physicians, Lawyers, Singers, Teachers, Painters, must all be voluntary and enthusiastic workers in their special fields of industry, or they are not really in their right places. A person who loves public life only because of the èclat, excitement, and emolument connected with it, may be a brilliant professionalist, but can never interpret truly the beauties and the mysteries of his art.

Do you think Milton composed verse only for fame and money? Do you think Beethoven wrote music without feeling it in the very depths of his own soul? Could Angelo or Raphael have painted as they did, unless their souls were in their work? Did Massillon or Fenelon preach as hirelings, and have your truest physicians ever gone about among the poor and suffering, thinking only of their fees? Do not imagine we are denying the oft-quoted truism: "The labourer is worthy of his hire." If you reap spiritual advantages sown for you by others, as the apostle says, it is a small matter if the spiritual workers come in for a share, even a large share of your temporal wealth. But should any feel that were they wealthy they would work no longer, they have experienced within them their own unfitness for the work in which they are now engaged. We wish to especially emphasize this thought to-day, as it bears directly upon what we have to say of true Spiritual Healers.

We hear a great deal of Magnetic Healers and Healing Mediums, but do we sufficiently take into consideration the importance of those purely spiritual qualifications which, in their vast importance, far outweigh all the minor considerations of temperament and physique, which weigh so much with many. The true Healer is a sympathizer. No truly sympathetic person is destitute of healing power, or fails to exercise it, though often he employs it unconsciously to himself. The very food you prepare becomes charged with your life-emanations, and persons should beware of a discontented or ill-natured cook, for many are the evils consequent upon eating food prepared for you by persons who are not kindly disposed to you. Have you not often remarked that the very simplest food tastes better at home than most expensive fare in large and fashionable restaurants? There is an indescribable something about home cooking which renders all food pleasant and nutritious; if your home be a true one, and links of affection bind its inmates together.

Some persons laugh at the idea of personal magnetism being conveyed from one article to another, or from human bodies to whatsoever comes in contact with them, while they are quite ready to believe in infectious disorders, contagious diseases, &c., &c. In a word, they believe in the power of disease over health, but not in the power of health over disease. Such theories form part of devil-worship. They are a practical avowal of belief in the devil and disbelief in God, and it should be the special endeavour of every Theist to combat them as resolutely as he combats their counterparts in the realm of morals. "Evil communications corrupt good manners." "One black sheep makes many." These, and similar proverbs, are only half truths. Is not the other side of the question true also? Why not have a proverb: One white sheep makes many; good communications are antidotes to evil manners. These and similar aphorisms becoming common sayings, would do an immense deal to leaven the thought of the age with a purer philosophy than that which takes its rise in the odious and blasphemous doctrine of the total depravity of human nature.

How any one can deny total depravity, see its fallacy and not fight down the prevalent fallacy of the infectious character of disease, while good health is said not to be communicable, would be a paradox unless we knew how very slowly reforms make their way, and how relentless is medical bigotry, and how unwilling people are to think for themselves on questions of health, instead of employing doctors to think for them. A gentleman said to us one day, speaking of auricular confession, bringing forward an argument in its favour: "Do you not think it a good thing, perhaps, to entrust your soul to the keeping of a priest, as you would entrust your body to a physician?" Our reply evidently startled him. It was substantially as follows: "We think it so bad a thing to entrust your body to the keeping of a physician, that we scarcely think your illustration does anything more than afford another argument against the practice you are inclined to uphold." The gentleman said further: "But have not doctors special training, and are they not specially qualified for the work they take in hand?" We merely replied: "We hope so, and we hope the same of ministers of religion, but no more fatal error can be fallen into than resigning yourselves unthinkingly into the hands of anybody. You have reason and conscience of your own, and while you may profit by advice, you must ever turn for highest counsel and guidance to those inner voices, which have been in every age the special directors of man, from the times of the earliest history to the present moment."

God has specially revealed himself to his children, through the inner voice of the Spirit, and this inner voice, as we said in our lecture on "REASON AND INTUITION," is the final and authoritative court of appeal, to which each human being can turn in his extremity.

We hear so much to-day about animal magnetism, galvanism, and electricity as healing forces, that one is often apt to imagine that, as the terms magnetism and electricity are often employed by spirits as well as by Spiritualists when they speak of the means whereby cures have been affected, these purely physical agents constitute the total resources of the spirit-world and its instruments, and constitute together a universal nostrum efficacious at all times, under all circumstances. We certainly do not and cannot deny that great good has often been accomplished by material agents, when under spirit direction, but these material agents have no power to heal you unless intelligently directed. Now, it very often happens, that persons who have no idea that they possess any healing power, are the greatest healers, but these are usually persons of kind and sympathetic nature. They wish to relieve pain, and would gladly do so voluntarily if they only knew how, and it is a source of unceasing regret to many such, that they can do so little to relieve those around them. Belonging to this class are many true physicians, some are indeed in the medical profession, and these are the kind, good doctors you are always so glad to see. You never start nor shrink away when one of these approaches. No matter how ill or nervous you may be, the physician is your friend, your confidant. The very sight of his kindly face does you good, and you send for him whenever anything ails you, not so much because you have faith in the power of medicine to heal you, as that you instinctively feel you will get good if he only comes near you.

Men and women, who possess naturally this healing power, are the only ones who have really a right to offer themselves to the public, either as doctors or nurses; and as many of these sympathetic souls know nothing of *materia medica*, have had no hospital experience and no special training of any kind qualifying them for attendance in the sick chamber, it frequently happens that those from whom sufferers derive the most good, are persons who have no diplomas and no certificates. The world may call them "quacks," but they are invariably appealed to when ordinary methods have been relinquished as unavailing, and often by their means persons are raised to health and strength, even from the very jaws of death.

Of course, if accidents are simply local and physical, and persons are in no mental trouble and simply require the surgeon's assistance or the services of the herbalist, ordinary surgical and medical treatment does well enough, except in cases where physicians persist in employing mineral remedies, and these for the most part instead of being remedies are destructive to the constitution which they seem temporarily to purge, and to the use of such poisonous substances a large per-centage of unnecessary ailments, brought on no one knows how, may be traced.

Mineral electricity is now extensively employed as a therapeutic agent by many illustrious members of the medical profession, and when skilfully handled and judiciously administered it is a valuable acquisition, but in numberless instances, electricity pulls down but cannot build up. For dissipated and overfed persons, for all who are bloated, whose blood is impure and whose circulation is impeded by the presence of foreign matter in the blood and general sluggishness of the system, mineral electricity may be of service, but for sensitive, debilitated, nervous, overworked persons, of naturally delicate frames, with no great stock of vitality to draw upon at the best of times, electrical apparatus is often dangerous and destructive. Animal magnetism is far safer and far surer in its effects, as animal magnetism is in reality the concentrated essence of human life, vapourized and transmitted in the form of an invisible fluid from one organism to another.

Foods and medicines need to be digested and assimilated. Many systems are too weak to be able to do either. They cannot swallow food, they cannot digest or assimilate it, even if they succeed in forcing it down. In cases of utter exhaustion, and even seeming death, the body may be revivified by the infusion of magnetic life through the pores.) And to return to the story of Elijah—Has it never struck you forcibly, how thoroughly the prophet magnetized the apparently dead child, while he called upon God to return the soul to the body it had just vacated, or about which it was hovering ere it took its final departure? Here we find prayer, earnest aspiration, intensely strong desire, fervent calling upon God, accompanied by earnest endeavour to restore life by physical manipulation. Elijah combined the use of animal magnetism, will-power, and spiritual fervour, and thus became a conduit or channel through which healing power from the spirit-world and the surrounding atmosphere could flow into the inanimate form, upon which he stretched himself three times, respiring heavily, by that means breathing out his bodily vigour into the boy's physical frame. The warmth and vitality penetrating every pore, mingling with the departing life force within, and enabling the returning spirit, assisted by Elijah's fervent will and prayer, to upbuild the earthly tenement, and restore her son whole to his mother's loving arms.

(When Jesus healed a woman who had suffered twelve years from a painful malady, while she only touched the hem of his garment, it is said that as soon as she had touched him, he perceived that virtue had gone out of him. This virtue is the elixir of life, without which the body could not be sustained a single moment, and which, in forms invisible to ordinary sight, passes through the pores of the healer, saturating his dress, impregnating the air about him, and then reaching the negative, susceptible frame of the patient, finds an inlet and effects a cure. Health and disease are communicated in precisely similar ways. You know how timid people are about sending their clothes to a laundry, if they have the faintest suspicion of clothes being sent there which have been worn or used by persons suffering from certain diseases generally considered infectious. You know how alarmed some people are lest they should take the breath of a sick person, fearing it should contaminate them. All we ask you to accept is the demonstrable fact, that God was neither cruel nor insane when he ordained the laws of nature, and therefore in his universe it is not possible that while disease can be caught good health cannot be communicated from one to another. In the Acts of the Apostles, we are told that handkerchiefs and aprons were laid upon the apostles, and then transferred to the sick, and that these magnetized articles healed them, while so great was the faith of some in the power of one apostle, that they were satisfied if but the shadow of Peter passing by might overshadow them. The only physical means of cure of the ordinary kind mentioned in the New Testament, are clay and oil. The oil is recommended by James, and it must be applied accompanied by fervent prayer; while the clay, which Jesus used to anoint the eyes of a blind man, was made from his own spittle; and those who have studied the matter know that the saliva of a healthy person, or even animal, is extremely efficacious as a healing agent, as even the tongue of a dog has been known to heal wounds which resisted all other modes of treatment.

You will, however, be careful to observe, that purely physical remedies can only be adequate to effect a cure when the injury sustained is of the body only. But how many of the poor invalids you meet in your daily walks are suffering from bodily ailments only? If the distress is mental, then the angel of healing in the person of some ready sympathizer and tender friend, is alone able to do the needed work. If illness proceed from financial embarrassment, or the lack of sufficient food or raiment, then, of course, it is useless to say, Be ye clothed and warmed and fed! unless you provide things necessary for the body. But how many are there who are suffering from ailments, brought on almost entirely by unhappiness and discontent! How many homes are wretched, how many have skeletons in their cupboards, who strive to appear gay! How many have secret griefs preying upon their mind, robbing them of rest and taking from them all appetite, utterly deranging all the functions of the body! Such cases as these baffle the physician's skill at every turn. They are ordered to Brighton or to Hastings, to Scarborough, to Wales, to Devonshire, to the Isle of Wight. A sea voyage is prescribed, but they may go to the antipodes, and return no better. Neither the sea air, nor the mineral springs, nor the fairest country scenes, nor the gayest Continental life, has cheered them.

They are unhappy, and it is to these the Spiritual Healer can turn and say, "Come unto me, ye that are weary and heavy laden, and I will give you rest." Only sympathy, aided by direct spiritual ministration, can afford aid in such instances as these; and these are the most painful, chronic and important cases of all. To help these you need no great educational advantages or personal attractions. You need no copious supply of animal magnetic force, but you must have love for your neighbour; you must, at any rate, be willing to be an instrument under heaven for blessing and relieving your less fortunate and happy brethren; and if your soul goes out to others, and it is your prayer to help and heal them, you will inspire them with new faith, new courage, and the faith you have inspired will make them whole.)

Time forbids us to enter more deeply into this engrossing theme to-day. The little we have said will, we hope, induce you to inquire further into this beautiful truth.

IMPROMPTU POEM.

THE POWER OF SYMPATHY.

THERE is a charmed, potent spell, which bindeth souls in love's embrace:
No mortal tongues the bliss can tell, which to this sacred fount we trace.
It is a balm for every wound, for every sorrow, every grief,
And none can fly to it in vain, for speedy succour and relief.

This grace divine is known on earth but feebly, for the chains of clay,
Imprisoning your spirits here, full oft shut out its healing ray;
The laws and customs man has made, the barriers of land and sea,
Shut you away full oft from those, who are your own through sympathy.

But, wheresoe'er a kindred soul meets yours, in ways unknown to sense,
Striking a sweet, responsive chord within your breast, you go not thence
Without a rapture more divine than any earthly joy can bring;
It is as though an angel's voice did in your inmost being sing.

Throughout the realms of earth and mind, this subtle principle is traced,
Affinity together binds the atoms, so that they are placed
Nearest to those with whom they dwell in peace, attracted by some power,
Which, hidden deep in Nature's heart, compels them all to yield their dower.

As Goethe beautifully taught, there are affinitizing souls,
And heaven would scarcely heaven be unless this law of love controls.
Though, in a wide and boundless sense, angelic love flows free to all,
Still, e'en in heaven, there are some souls, whom yours, in special sense, you call.

Not through the ties of flesh and blood, are spirits bound through endless day;
Not by an earth-relationship, tread they the same celestial way;
But by a deeper bond than this, are they united on that shore,
Where only pure affection lives, when all the dreams of earth are o'er.

Sometimes a stranger crosses o'er your threshold, and you know him not
By any earthly bond, and still your spirit says, you've ne'er forgot
How, in some lifetime long ago, perhaps not on this earthly plane,
You've met and parted; now you meet again, and trace your kinship plain.

Sometimes when reading stories—old Iliads, and tales of long ago—
The author of some wond'rous prose or poetry awakes a glow,
Responsive to his thought, within the inmost circle of your mind,
In spirit, you for him enquire, and you will him hereafter find.

No link of love can severed be, which bindeth souls in love's great chain,
No tender throb of sympathy can fail some day response to gain;
And if not here at all on earth, assuredly, for aye in heaven,
Will sympathy make known to you her perfect power, when earth is riven.

Is there a heart within this room—is there a soul in any place—
Who strives some other life to bless, and knows not by what means of grace
The heart forlorn may reached be? Then, seeing not an open door,
You need not sigh, in vain lament, for him ye think so lone and poor!

Your sympathy can traverse seas! No continents can bar its course;
It flies as on the wings of light, impelled by love's resistless force.
And oftentimes, when ye have felt a thrill of gladness through your pain,
It has but been a loving heart returning to your side again,
In sleep, or reverie, or trance, or some bright angel from above,
One who has loved you many an age, consoling you with heavenly love!

BENEDICTION.

May Love's celestial power,
And Sympathy's sweet might,
Protect your every Life
From Sorrow's chilling blight;
And may ye Angels be,
To ease the world's dull pain,
And, through a Life of gentle Love,
Heaven's highest Homes attain!

AMEN.

XI.

THE SPIRITUAL SIGNIFICANCE AND USE OF FIRE.

OUR subject to-day is one of extreme interest and great importance from a spiritual point of view, and even from a material standpoint it is not an unprofitable or unattractive theme for consideration.

Fire was accounted one of the "four elements" by the Ancients, and was said to be inhabited by a class of beings called salamanders, the highest and purest of elementary spirits, whose work in connection with the earth was to purify and redeem it.

Many modern theorists, speaking of the past of this planet, state that once the earth was enveloped in a fire-mist, and that as this gradually cleared away the atmosphere was rendered pure and wholesome, and the earth slowly became fit for human habitation.

In the Kabala Fire always means the purifying or redeeming element.

Among the Rosicrucians Fire was considered necessary to accomplish the marvellous feat of transmutation, by means of which all metals were said to be at length convertible into gold.

Fire, in the Old Testament, is always introduced as a test of divine power, as in the story of Elijah and the prophets of Baal. We are told that Elijah and Baal's worshippers agreed, that the true God was the one who should make known his presence by fire. Shadrach, Meshach and Abed-nego were thrust into Nebuchadnezzar's burning fiery furnace, heated seven times beyond its usual heat, and because the fire consumed neither them nor their apparel, they were known to have been on the side of right, and genuine servants of the Most High.

In the New Testament, Jesus takes up the symbol, and employs Fire to signify corrective chastisment, and all processes of purification, both in this and other realms of being; while Paul, following in this respect closely in the footsteps of his master, says, the fire shall try every man and the work of every man, and those who can abide the test by fire, without suffering the loss of their possessions or the destruction of their work, shall receive a reward, but those whose work is burned shall themselves be saved, yet so as by fire.

The Roman Church, the Greek Church, and the high Anglican Church all endorse certain views of purgation after death, and admit the existence of the fires of purgatory for those whose sins are only venial. But unhappily for the interests of true religion, all these churches couple the infamous doctrine of everlasting torment for those who die in mortal sin, with the reasonable and scriptural fact of purification through suffering of those whose crimes are of a milder hue.

At the time of the Protestant Reformation, Luther and others found the doctrine of purgatory overlain with rubbish and overgrown with weeds. The reformers of the 16th century, like Cromwell and his followers in the 17th, honestly endeavoured to put an end to abuses, to root up tares, and save the precious wheat in all instances from destruction. But, unfortunately, in the one case nearly all the poetry of religion and much that contained spiritual truth was removed, while in the other and later development of Protestantism, everything beautiful in art was assailed, and sweet sounds were considered a profanation of the temples if they were supplied by instruments assisting the human voice.

In periods of reformation the sword always goes before the Prince of Peace, and has a part to play in making the way ready for those who are to sow germs full of spiritual vitality, in gardens long occupied by noxious weeds, which it seems in many instances impossible to uproot without plucking up some of the flowers of religion also. The task of an iconoclast is an extremely hard and unpoetical one, and in order to be an iconoclast or idol-breaker, one must have a stern, rugged disposition, a great deal of self-assurance, and very little respect for antiquities; yet the iconoclast need not be, and often is not, an unkind or heartless man.

Ingersoll, in America, who is one of the most determined opponents of the prevailing creeds, and whose lectures are often extremely denunciatory, bears a charming reputation among those who know him, as an excellent husband, father, neighbour and citizen. People say he is extremely kind-hearted, and we can quite understand how a very humane and tender-hearted man or even woman, can take just Ingersoll's position, without intentionally causing any real pain to any who seek to derive genuine consolation from what is beautiful in religious conceptions.

Surely annihilation would be a milder doom than everlasting torment; surely a universe that governs itself would be a better universe to contemplate than one governed by such a God as the one depicted by Calvin. All protest against what we feel to be religious truths, has been merely an inundation caused by a vigorous downpour of honest and needful assault upon doctrines so atrocious and so conspicuous, that to get rid of them, even at the expense of some poetry and even truth, was a desideratum, and when we feel certain, as we must if we have any confidence in the immortality of truth itself, that no truth *can* be destroyed, that though apparently dead it rises into new and more glorious life, seeming the stronger and lovelier for its every apparent defeat, we can but welcome the storm and tempest which lay it low, knowing that when seemingly crushed, it is only gathering strength for fresh encounters with error, and that its own intrinsic utility and self-evident rectitude, if nothing else, will render it at length acceptable to progressed and enlightened man.)

Let us, for an instant, look at the effect produced by literal fire in the material world. There is nothing nervous people dread so much as being burnt. Drowning is said to be comparatively an easy death. It is not the sinking of a ship but the burning of a ship at sea, with water all around it, that seems so terrible. You can scarcely bear to hear the description of a burning wreck, on which are human beings or even animals. It is the sound of the fire-engine which alarms you more than any other sound, until you get thoroughly accustomed to it, by hearing it so often and learning to place deserved confidence in the noble army of firemen, whose bravery and efficiency can scarcely be over-appreciated. But still the dread of fire in all large cities, and in large hotels especially, makes the lives of many people a burden to them, while the electric flash inspires terror in the breast of millions.

It is certainly true, that fire is in a physical sense a very dreadful and a very deadly thing. No one can witness a volcano in eruption, without being pretty thoroughly convinced of the real existence of the old traditional lake of fire in the bowels of the earth. No one can be out in a raging storm, without feeling deeply awed by the tremendous power of the lightning, which with its livid flame can in an instant fell the stoutest forest tree, and lay low a building whose foundations are in the granite rocks, and which has successfully withstood the action of all other elements. It is not hard to account for that old-world dread of evil deities, and of the anger of the Supreme, which was and is so fearfully manifest to superstitious minds in the action of the raging element.

But is not Fire the saviour as well as the consumer of the earth? Is it not through fire that earth and air are purified, being rid by the activity of this fell destroyer of what would inevitably produce its ruin, were it not for the interposition of this awful deliverer? It is the lightning which destroys blight. After a thunderstorm the air is purer, the earth fresher, and all conditions of life healthier. The maximum result of the work of lightning is good, only the minimum is evil; and is it not so with those fearful city fires, which have brought desolation in their train to thousands? If thousands have been made to suffer, millions have been made to rejoice, and if either the many or the few *must* suffer, then humanity and wisdom alike dictate that it is better to sacrifice the few and save the many, than to save the few and let the many perish. If fires are evils, then they are among lesser evils, not among the greater ones. They are impossible in a perfect state of civilization, and only occur where dirt, danger, and instability *must* sooner or later be removed, to make way for cleanliness, safety, permanence, and all the other necessary appurtenances and results of a perfect state of society.

Historically speaking, the praise of Fire is written in undying letters of flame, in the records of all great peoples. The fire of London in 1666 burned a great deal of property, very valuable to the holders of it, and caused much distress all over the city; but the fire burnt the plague also. Fire is in a certain good sense very often a most intelligent and discriminating respecter of persons and property. Electricity, its wild state in the atmosphere, seems to strike haphazard, but fires which break out in cities almost invariably burn down narrow streets of ill-built tenement houses. Wherever filth and disease are most represented, there the fire does its destructive work most quickly; wherever miserable shanties abound, and streets are so narrow that persons can almost shake hands with their opposite neighbours from the upper story windows, fires destroy most rapidly and effectually.

In America, the fires of Boston and Chicago have made both those cities much healthier, safer and more beautiful. The distress the fires occasioned awoke great sympathy with the sufferers, and did positive good, in awakening feelings of compassion for others in the breasts of those who were not grievous sufferers themselves; while, had those fires not broken out when they did, it is difficult to decide as to how far inferior in all respects those two great cities would have been to what they now are. Modern buildings, models of comfort, elegance and safety, almost perfect in their sanitary arrangements, now occupy sites formerly disfigured by wooden structures, which, had they lasted much longer, would have occasioned much disease and distress, and been great hindrances to the increase of commerce, unless they had been pulled down.

Some people will think, very naturally, that it would have been much better to have pulled them down, and built others before the fire broke out. Perhaps it would, but the fire had other work than merely to remove impediments to business, by destroying rickety buildings. Fire is a great purifier and transmuter, and has manifold uses to serve in the chemical changes produced in the vicinity of its activity. It is a well-attested fact among agriculturists, that fire so far changes the condition of soil, that plants and vegetables will grow on land where the soil has been burnt, which never could be made to grow there till after the fire had changed the soil, while other kinds of vegetation died out and could not be reproduced after the outbreak. (Fire destroys many kinds of animalculæ, which are the floating germs of disease in the air, and which would attack many hundreds of persons, causing a fearful increase in the rate of mortality, did not fire consume them; while in addition to these purely sanitary facts, we must not overlook some curious instances, which have come under our notice, of the effects of fire upon disembodied spirits, who are yet dwellers upon the earth or in its atmosphere, owing to the materiality of their states of mind, and the earth-bound character of their affections.

Of course, purely physical fire cannot affect disembodied spirits, therefore, one of the arguments against a literal hell has been, that it would destroy a physical structure almost instantly, and then the spirit would no longer feel pain. But there are fire-resisting substances, and chemical substances may be applied to the human body, causing it to resist fire, but with these we have not now immediately to do, and it surely cannot be supposed that God has ordained the resurrection of all who die in sin, in fire-proof bodies at the last great day, for the express purpose of securing to them an eternity of torment. Such an act can hardly be considered possible, if God be an infinite tyrant. If he be a God of Love, Wisdom, Justice, or anything men unitedly pronounce divine, such an action must be impossible to him.

There is a most remarkable passage in the New Testament which logically teaches that there are, and in the very nature of things there must be, limits to Deity, and limits so arbitrary that they are eternal fixities involved in the very nature of the Divine Being. The Infinite is necessarily limited by its own infinitude. The passage to which we refer is to be found in the account given by Paul of his view of the immutability of God's covenant, and the fixity of the divine decrees (see Heb., vi., 18). After enumerating many of the consolations naturally springing from a participation in the covenanted blessings, which are secured to all who obey the prescribed conditions for obtaining them, he speaks of immutable things in which it was impossible for God to lie. Can a God of Infinite Truth ever tell a falsehood? Can he ever wish to tell one? Can a God of Infinite Wisdom ever be guilty of folly or know a foolish wish? Can a God of Infinite Love ever think an unkind thought, or a God of Justice ever will to do other than justly to the meanest as well as to the greatest and noblest of his creatures?

It is impossible for God to be unkind, unjust, foolish or untruthful. He who is essential rectitude must do right. His Will is infinite in power, but that will can never be other than wise and clement, and it is just here that Theists throw overboard the infamous doctrine of everlasting torment, without even thinking it necessary to consider any fancied claims its apologists may think it has on the thought of the religious world. Orthodox Christians beg us to remember that Jesus advocated it, and therefore it must be true. To this plea, in its defence, we give the following shockingly heterodox answer: Even if Jesus *did* teach it, we still refuse to admit its claims, as there is that in the nature of the doctrine itself, which awakens a thrill of hatred and disgust for it in the hearts of all really humane people, who think about it, even while they are themselves assured that they will never suffer its agonies. But Jesus did not teach it! At all events, the Gospels do not say he did, though we admit there are passages in the New Testament which appear to favour it, and it is our province in this Discourse to consider the most notable of them, as they bear directly upon our present topic: the Value and Use of Fire considered Spiritually.

Only a few days ago, we heard a lecturer say Jesus invented the frightful dogma of everlasting torments. He did not. He preached against it, if the Evangelists speak truly, and it would be far too great a concession to the prevailing idolatry to allow that such a hideous dogma was ever conceived in the brain of any good and pure-minded man. It sprang from human barbarity and terror, in a savage age, and wherever it has prevailed it has been a destructive parasite, blasting religions and civilizations alike, justifying the sword of Mohammed and the horrors of the Inquisition equally. It is at the root of the upholding of unnecessary wars, and the death penalty in so-called Christian lands. Eliminate it utterly from the creeds of Christendom, and you have slain a viper which Christianity has nurtured for centuries in its bosom to its own undoing, so that the very term "Christian" is to-day held in contempt by many devout Theists, who have a strong admiration for the character of its alleged founder, as represented by the Evangelists.

Any student of Jewish history will see, in the reference made by Jesus to fire and worms as constituting elements of future punishment, direct references to the pit of Gehenna, a pit in which the fires were never allowed to go out. To a Jew, living in or near Jerusalem, the metaphor was singularly apposite as an illustration of the nature of future punishment. Gehenna was just outside Jerusalem, a pit where refuse of every kind was deposited. The fires, of course, were always kept burning as a sanitary precaution; they were everlasting fires, while the image of worms was drawn from the fact that worms were constantly found feeding on the rubbish which accumulated at the mouth of the pit. If the expression "everlasting fire" is used with reference to Gehenna, the allusion is very plain, the significance very clear. The fires are ever kept burning, not as a means of punishing the guilty with unending torment, but exclusively as means of consuming filth and keeping the city wholesome.

Crematories have been established just outside the gates of ancient cities, as cremation was practised by many nations of antiquity, and in hot countries especially cremation is very far preferable to burial, and with an ever-increasing population, will soon be found necessary in England and the United States, as well as all over Europe, and in the thickly populated districts of the Orient, where cremation is a sanitary necessity. Cremation was practised by many of the most illustrious Orientals, and Lord Lytton in his descriptions of the "Coming Race," declares that they join in a very beautiful and impressive, but by no means melancholy, burial service during which the body is almost instantly destroyed by means of "vril," and that the ashes of the departed are preserved by the family. This is a distinct allusion to very ancient customs, and to the best of these the world is now turning in its almost frantic endeavours to improve upon existing imperfect modes of burial.

In all allusions to cremation we find everything suggestive of purification, but nothing whatever of fire as a means of inflicting unending suffering. In the book of Psalms, you read the following words: "Thou hast tried us, O God, even as silver is tried; thou madest us to pass through the fire." Evidently the allusions are intended exclusively to refer to such corrective chastisement as purified the mind, and made the spirit of the warrior strong to encounter the difficulties and dangers of life, to which he would otherwise weakly succumb.

The Trial by Fire was one of the greatest tests ever applied to the initiate into the Ancient Mysteries. If the candidate for honours could successfully pass the trial by fire, he was considered worthy of the highest office, and was revered as one under the special protection of the gods; while many legends, traditions and superstitions are rife in many countries, not excepting England, testifying to a feeling or belief, prevalent in greater or less degree in all countries, that the specially inspired are impervious to the effects of fire. Thus fire-eating and fire-resisting are among the tricks of modern conjurors, intended to simulate the wonderful performances of the magicians of the East.

Since the advent of Modern Spiritualism, the fire test has been applied to several mediums, and well-authenticated cases, in which mediums have resisted this element, are now published, and are accessible to all who wish to read the record of such truly marvellous phenomena. A lady in Chicago, some years ago, had her hands washed and closely examined by eminent chemists, to make sure that no fire-proof chemicals were upon them, before she submitted to the fire test. Then in the presence of many competent witnesses, who bear willing testimony to the genuiness of the occurrence, she bared the flesh of her arm, thrust it into a mass of live coal, and her arm was not even singed or seared, ever so slightly. Her invisible protectors, being questioned through her entranced lips concerning the *modus operandi* of this startling miracle, declared that powerful spirits, acquainted with many facts in occult chemistry, unknown to the world at large, collected from the atmosphere and from the bodies of the medium and sitters, such material as when prepared by the spirits, in the form of an invisible preparation which they applied to the flesh of the lady, rendered her arm impervious to the flame. Spirits have declared on several occasions and through various mediums, whenever fabric has been protected against fire, that a similar process has been devised; and while the world is not expected to believe anything extraordinary without sufficient proof of its reality, it is surely unscientific, unphilosophic and, indeed, irrational to deny the possibility of that to which others bear testimony, merely because you yourselves have not personally witnessed the phenomena.

Fire-worship played an important part in the beliefs and ceremonies of the Ancients, and indeed the religion of the Parsees was so largely made up of the adoration of Fire, that they have quite commonly borne the name of Fire-worshippers. As it is now the custom to study rather than deride the worship of the Ancients, doubtless many of you are to some extent familiar with the peculiar tenets of the Parsees and others, who believed implicitly in Light as the expression of Deity, in the Sun as the home of the god of the solar system, and in Fire as the vivifying and purifying flame, without which nothing could exist, be born or renewed. Doubtless among some nations fire, heat or warmth was regarded as the manifestation of the divine emanation, or the Holy Spirit, and it is a noteworthy fact that fire and flame are the chosen emblems of the Holy Ghost in Christian records. The baptism of the Spirit is called the baptism of fire. John predicted that Jesus would baptize with the Holy Spirit and with fire, signifying both inward illumination and the purification of the affections from all dross. Fire is the regenerator and renewer as well as the destroyer, and we venture to say there was never a more sublime conception of the work of preservation and destruction, proceeding from one and the same spirit, than that grand old Brahmanical idea of Siva, the third person of the Brahmanical trinity, who is called both Destroyer and Reproducer.

To apply these ancient beliefs to the doctrine of purgation after death, as taught in the New Testament, is not difficult, and when we remember that Jesus was speaking to Orientals, and that Paul preached and wrote to Orientals also, it is by no means unlikely that all the incomprehensible and seemingly far-fetched allusions in the Gospels and Epistles, really referred, at the time the words were originally spoken or written, to beliefs and practices so common and universally known, as to render the peculiar form of illustration adopted, that most eminently calculated to impress the minds of those for whose immediate benefit the teaching was given under that guise.

(If, instead of denouncing, modern teachers would explain the dark sayings of old, the cause of spiritual liberation and true religious progress would make twenty times the headway it now does against blind and slavish idolatry of the letter on the one hand, and equally blind forgetfulness of all things spiritual on the other.)

The simple explanation now given by almost all intelligent exponents of the Gospel, of the illustration of a camel going through the eye of a needle, is a sample of how very easily most absurd and misleading dogmas have been built upon a misunderstanding of some local reference. One requires to know something of the city of Jerusalem and its precincts, to understand how the eye of a camel can have anything to do, even figuratively, with a rich man entering the kingdom of heaven, but when the camel's eye is explained, as a little gate leading into the city, through which belated travellers entered after the larger gates were closed, and when it is further stated that a laden camel had to be unladen ere he could enter through that narrow aperture, the illustration is peculiarly significant and apt. (Riches cannot be carried into the heavenly state. The ideal state of human society is communistic. Jesus taught equal rights and united interests. His early followers were practical communists: they did not allow ancestral privileges. They taught as did Paul: If a man will not work neither let him eat. They regarded it as a crying shame that some should possess vast acres of the country which they had not cultivated, and therefore not lawfully obtained except through the sanction of a partial, unjust and tyrannous law, favouring monopoly and crushing down the common people under the iron heel of the tyrannical aggressor. Jesus said these artificial distinctions must be dispensed with. Men must all be brothers, and so it is said, that when an early Christian church was formed, almost immediately after pentecost, the disciples had all things in common, and gave to every man as he had need. Henry George to-day might be a lineal descendant of the apostle Paul, and indeed of most of the early Christians, so closely do his views on "Progress and Poverty" agree with those of the great Apostle to the Gentiles, and the primitive Christians generally.)

There is perhaps no one passage of Scripture, certainly no parable, which has afforded a text for more frightful sermons than the story of the rich man and Lazarus, and yet no parable can possibly set forth the doctrine of future punishment, as a means of purification, more clearly than does that much misinterpreted and belied narrative of the only way by which an obdurate spirit can be brought to repentance in the life beyond. The Church of Rome has never endeavoured to teach the dogma of everlasting torment from this parable, but has always used it to justify the doctrine of purgatory. In the same way, the celebrated passages concerning fire, in Paul's epistle to the Corinthians, have been, and still are, brought forward by the Roman Church, to support the doctrine of purgatorial cleansing for all who do not die in mortal sin. Unfortunately, the Roman Church employs other texts of Scripture, as we think quite unwarrantably, to support the heinous dogma of unending torment for all who die in what the Church calls mortal sin; and as it is a mortal sin to neglect mass on a Sunday, or holiday of obligation, you may easily perceive on what a slender thread immortal life hangs, for those who accept all the dogmas of the Vatican.

The parable of the rich man and Lazarus, illustrates perfectly the lesson we intend to convey in our present Discourse upon Fire, *viz.*, that as material fire is a purifier in the material world, so spiritual fire is a redeemer in the world of spirits; and in enforcing this lesson we feel we are not taking up your time in empty quibbling or vain disputation. (We are setting forth a principle of nature, which it would be well for every legislator, employer, guardian and parent to remember, *viz.*, that punishment should never be other than corrective. Whenever vengeance or the retaliative spirit is made manifest, means of correction are forgotten, and methods of cruel and foolish torture usurp their place.)

We are told in the Gospel of a certain rich man (Dives), and of a certain beggar (Lazarus), who lay at his gate covered with sores, to whom the Eastern dogs, a very low branch of the canine family, were kinder than the opulent man, at whose gates the dying beggar lay. It will well repay us to prolong our meditation a few minutes, by endeavouring to fully take in the situation depicted, and analyze the characters presented to our notice.

Some interpreters have understood the rich man to represent the wealthy Jews, who in the time of Jesus neglected the poor; Lazarus, their poorer brethren; and the dogs, the Gentiles, who were called dogs by the arrogant Hebrews, just as Christians are still called dogs by Mohammedans, dog being an Oriental term of reproach, signifying an unworthy person, the dog in Asia and Southern Europe being a very different animal from the sleek, pampered and well-fed creature who feeds upon the best of the land in London or New York, and is his mistress's favourite companion in her carriage at the most fashionable squares, parks, boulevards or avenues. To live a dog's life in England to-day, or to be compared to a dog, would often mean that you were preferred before all others, and were entitled to a very great amount of consideration; but go to Constantinople or Damascus, for instance, and make the acquaintance of the dogs there, and they will fill you, for the most part, with mingled feelings of pity and disgust. They are mostly fierce, famishing, filthy creatures, almost utterly repulsive in their appearance and demeanour, but they are not destitute of fine feeling, however. Despite their degradation, they will be faithful to those who feed and succour them, and to the sick poor they are often extremely kind, and being possessed, as all dogs are in greater or lesser degree, of healing power in the tongue, they do to-day to the lazaroni of the South, what they did to the poor beggar, of whom Jesus spoke. (They give relief to the suffering by licking their wounds, and you will find in your own experience, that a dog's tongue will often heal a troublesome sore that no ointment will relieve.)

The dog of the East was a symbol of the poor, degraded and outcast, and also of the heathens, who were pariahs, or outcast from fellowship with the orthodox. Jesus took occasion to rebuke the pharisaism of the self-righteous Jews, and told them how their own poor were often ministered unto by the Gentiles, whom they called dogs or outcasts, while their own people neglected them. The consequences to the Hebrew race, of this inequality and injustice, he likened to the wealthy finding themselves in a lake of burning fire, tormented in a flame which nothing could put out. Not even a single drop of water could they get to cool their parched lips. They would, in the day of their dire humiliation, see Abraham, afar off, with the despised poor whom they had forsaken, in his bosom; Abraham's bosom being a Jewish figure of speech, a name for Paradise. To be with Abraham, the father of the faithful, was the goal of the Jew's most ardent expectations. The punishment of those who had had the wherewithal to relieve distress, and had not even relieved it among their own people, whom the law commanded them to treat as their own flesh, was that they should find the tables completely turned upon them in the future life. They would be filled with chagrin, remorse and anguish, realizing how utterly they were shut out from the covenanted blessings: not covenanted to the rebellious and the selfish, however, but to those who fulfilled the conditions of the covenant, *i.e.*, obeyed the spirit as well as the letter of the Law. (When the spirit is neglected, then even Sabbath observance and attendance at the Synagogue on solemn feast days become abominable in the sight of heaven, as it is a vain pretext and endeavour certainly to deceive men, and to deceive God also, if it were possible to conceal the heart from the All-seeing.)

The rich man, who is a representative of the opulent classes who shut up their bowels of compassion from their needy brethren, is at first only conscious of his own misery and loss. He cries out in his pain for water, and requests that Lazarus may bring it to him. He is told that is impossible, between them there is a great gulf fixed, and yet locally they are so near together they can see each other; at all events the denizen of hell can see the happy souls in paradise, and that sight adds to his misery, as it taunts him with what he might have become, and where he might then have been, if, with his many advantages, he had led as pure a life as that of the beggar he despised. He asks that court may be shown him still. Though he has fallen thus low, it seems to him but natural that Lazarus, on earth only a beggar, should be sent with water for his refreshment. (But he had to learn that there are no class distinctions in the Unseen World, that there promotion is only according to merit, and that one, who on earth was a lowly beggar, may be far too high to be commissioned even to take his station by the side of one of the greatest lords of the earth, who has feasted sumptuously and apparelled himself gorgeously every day, while he cared nothing, and perhaps knew nothing, except by hearsay, of the starving mendicant dying at his gate.) It is said that the beggar desired the crumbs from the rich man's table, but it is not said that he got them.

In London, and all large modern cities, Dives lives in a palace and Lazarus starves at his gate. Aristocratic Belgravia ignores the very existence of the slums at the East end of the city. Harrowing accounts appear in the papers daily, of deaths through starvation, in the cold winter months, of poor seamstresses who make the shirts which many of the fashionable gentlemen wear, and never pay for, at their elegant fêtes and parties. Many and many a tradesman is ruined, compelled to go into bankruptcy, because of the unwillingness or inability of the rich, or seemingly rich, to settle their accounts, and many are the poor laundresses and seamstresses, who are sent away day after day without their hard-earned pittance, because the opulent, or at the least, the make-believe wealthy consider them miserable inferiors, who should esteem it an honour to be allowed to work for the gentry and nobility, whether they get paid for their toil or not.

There are indeed many honourable exceptions: lords and ladies, earls and marquises, duchesses and counts, who not only pay all their just debts, but are positively benevolent, sympathetic and helpful to the poor, to the very farthest limit of their power. (And these, who are born to the purple, need not cast it off but wear it honourably; they do their duty in the exalted station to which they have been called, usually by circumstances beyond their own control. Were they to step off their pedestals, they might do less good than they are now accomplishing, and even Buddha, who left his father's house at midnight, and threw in his lot with the mendicant friars of India, might possibly have chosen the yet better way, and attained Nirvana earlier had he remained at home, faithful to his home, and fulfilled honourably and justly all the duties of exalted station.

There is an old parable in the Old Testament, about the trees choosing a bramble for their king, but they did not elect him to office until they offered the highest station to the olive and the cedar, and other beautiful and stately trees, more fit to represent them. The stately trees declined to serve, and therefore the bramble got in. There is a lesson for election times, and all whom the people want to serve as candidates for office. Somebody must serve; if a suitable person is not chosen an unsuitable one will be, so it is really hazardous and wrong for persons to cloak themselves with false humility, and refuse honours pressed upon them, by accident of birth, passing away of relations, or other similar causes.

They who trust in riches, and love them inordinately, are the only ones necessarily outside the Kingdom of Heaven. Not the possession of money, but the miser's love of it, is the root of evil, and only the miser or the egotist, who cares not who starves as long as he has his turtle soup and the best of wines, who cares not who goes naked so long as he is dressed in the latest style, in garments of the costliest material: only he who sneeringly asks the question of Cain, "Am I my brother's keeper?" refusing to take any interest in the welfare of others, ignoring the poor and the unfortunate completely; only he and such as he have a hell awaiting them in spirit-life. When death shall close their eyes upon all earthly scenes, death will be to them the thief, that steals from them all upon which they have placed their love, the moth which corrodes, the rust which eats away their fairest treasures. Then despoiled of all their boasted rank and powers, their spiritual eyes sealed against the light of heaven, their ears deaf to all celestial melodies, a burning fire of fury, remorse and impotent despair consuming their very vitals, will lead them in their pain to cry out for one whom they despised on earth, to be sent unto them to relieve their pain.

Had the rich man asked to see Lazarus face to face, that he might crave his pardon for the wrong he had done him on earth, perhaps he would have been sent to him, with water in his hand to cool the rich man's tongue. But the rich man still thought only of himself; the love of self was still supreme within him, dominating the love of neighbour and the love of God, and no reformation would have been worked within him if the torment he was enduring had been lessened, before the cleansing fires had burned away the dross of selfishness, which was his deadly sin, and the occasion of his doom. The fires must longer burn, his request must be denied, simple though it be, in seeming cruelty, though really in love.

God works in all the hells; the flames are lighted by his love, and they at length remove the rust of that most crying sin of all, the sin of selfishness; so when the rich man had endured his pain a little longer, he begins to think of his brethren and forgets himself. He had never troubled to set them a good example when he was with them on earth, and now it must add fuel to the flame that torments him, to remember that had he acted differently toward them, they would not be in the danger they are now in, of sharing this place of torment when they leave the earth. Though the parable closes indefinitely as regards the future of the rich man, it leaves him on the upward track, for surely no theologian or religionist of any school, can possibly deny that when, through bitter suffering, a nature is aroused from the sinful slumber of consummate selfishness, to express a concern for others' welfare, indeed for their eternal salvation, that that soul *can* be beyond the pale of redemption, hopelessly lost to goodness and to God.

If there were no such a thing as hell fire, it would be indeed a sorry look out for those who die in their sins. If people could be eternally satisfied with evil, or if God could be eternally satisfied with it, then all our confidence in the absolute nature and eternity of goodness would be destroyed, and not even God could be pronounced perfect. But all the traditions of the world point to one, and but to one, and that an inevitable conclusion, *viz.*, that all souls have deep within them something purer and better than the paltry self-love, which is often all that a spirit manifests during an earthly lifetime, and during a period of abasement in spirit-life, consequent upon misdoing.

Thank God for the fires of hell! Let us hope they are everlasting, if races of men are to be constantly born like unto ourselves upon this planet or any other. If there be an eternal succession of worlds, then everlasting fires are needed, not to make the everlasting punishment of any spirit in the universe a fact, but to render the everlasting evil, with which orthodoxy threatens the universe, an impossibility.

It is wisely said, that angels who kept not their first estate are the only devils there are. Innocence is forfeited during the battle of life, ignorance and wilfulness make unhappy combinations of things all good in themselves. Fire, the destroyer, reduces the state of evil to a pile of ashes, liberates materials from disorderly connections, breaks up the hells of strife and discord, fashioned by ignorance, and causes the Phœnix ever to arise from the pile of ashes, symbol of the Soul's perfect conquest over all that enshrouds and enslaves it.

Do not try to explain away the Eternal Fire which purifies the universe, for in doing so you may be trying to get rid of man's best friend and benefactor, the searching flame of Divine Love, which will utterly consume the tares of ignorance and vice, which grow now in the gardens of many lives, until at length, every spirit now in suffering will be able to say to the Eternal: Thank God for the discipline of pain! "Before I was afflicted I went astray, but now do I keep Thy Word."

IMPROMPTU POEM.

CLEANSING FIRES.

LET thy gold be tried in the furnace; let thy silver and gems be tried;
Let thy heart and thy mind be afflicted, that they may be purified.
If the stains of sin and error are all around them now,
Let the fire of correction cleanse them, and they shall be white as snow.

In the crucible of sorrow, God places many a heart
To cleanse it, and to purify, by the fire that makes it smart;
But men have vainly fancied, God places it in ire,
In an endless hell of torment, where his wrath lights the fire.

But 'tis not so, my brethren; ye who are suffering now,
'Tis not in anger that God sets His seal upon your brow;
But as on Cain, in old time, the brand was in mercy set,
So the brand of God's indignation, we pray you, ne'er forget,
Is a brand of loving-kindness, when seen in the spheres beyond,
A mark of God's pure endeavour to save you, a sacred bond
Which will draw your spirits unto him, however widely they strayed,
The cord, or the chain of sorrow, on your hearts in love is laid.

Sometimes on the one foundation, silver and gold ye lay,
Then, in the day of judgment, God recompense will pay
For the silver and gold ye have given, to ease another's smart,
Will bring you sweet consolation, and satisfy your heart.

The silver and gold, ye'll remember, are not from an earthly mine;
They are thoughts of pure loving-kindness, which clearer than diamonds shine
The gems, which shall sparkle brightly in heaven's illustrious crown,
Are born of your efforts for others, when ye've laid all selfishness down.

Sometimes, but hay and stubble ye place in God's temple seat,
Ye bring to him naught but rubbish—chaff for the burning meet;
Ye bring cowardice, hypocrisy, self-seeking, thirst for gain,
Falsehood, and many an error that cannot in heaven obtain.

Sometimes on the earth ye suffer the loss of all you love,
Sometimes in the fire of sorrow, which descendeth from above,
You lose, in an earthly trial, your love of the base and vile,
And then, ere ye leave the mortal, heaven's sunshine once more doth smile.

But many there be, who go outward to the Land of Souls, unblest
With any desire for heaven, without the sweet secret of rest;
Without love of God in their bosoms, without any care for his poor;
For these, when this earth-life is over, there remaineth God's threshing-floor.
He will purge his floor most thoroughly, will gather his wheat into barns,
Will burn up the chaff, as the fuel which keeps that Gehenna alive,
Which, ever outside of earth's cities, is burning, for spirits who need
To be cleansed, ere they enter those portals, which nothing but pleasure can breed.

Not in anger doth God send affliction, but Dives, in anguish most dire,
Is suffering only by reason of God's love, which lighteth the fire
Which parches his throat, and consumes him with sorrow and grief for his sin;
His selfishness dies in the bright flame, he cries: "Let my brethren begin
To lead a new life, lest they, also, to this place of torment are brought;
Send an angel, or send me, I pray you, that these sinners in time may be sought!"

"They will hear not the law nor the prophets," said Abraham unto him then:
"If one rose from the dead, they'd believe not," heaven's doctrines are far 'bove their ken;
But their brother himself, he must seek them, undoing the wrong he has done,
Must return to the earth as a preacher, and preach till they've new life begun.

Are any of you clothed in purple? Do you sumptuously fare every day?
Do ye think naught of brethren in danger? Do ye drive the poor beggar away?
Then, surely, when earth-life is over, the fire in your bosom will burn,
And ye'll ask, when too late, how to succour the homeless, the sad, the forlorn.

Too late! yes, to you it will seem so, until all your selfishness dies.
And, then, when pure love of your neighbour lights up with sweet mercy your eyes,
A way will be opened, your spirits will see how to rescue the sad,
And, employed by some glorious immortals, through your work will others grow glad.

The fire must burn on till all error is expunged from your inmost desire;
Bless God for the hottest furnace, for the fiercest, torturing fire,
For surely hell fires are reserved for all, who impenitent die,
But in mercy, not anger, they're lighted: not to doom, but to raise you on high!

BENEDICTION.

May the Light of God's Love burn brightly,
And enter your spirits below,
While yet upon earth you must labour,
Then, whenever from earth you go,
Your transit may be to regions
Where you need not the cleansing flame,
But where, numbered among the angels,
Heaven's radiance your souls may claim.

AMEN.

XII.

THE ASCENSION OF JESUS INTO HEAVEN, AND THE DESCENT OF THE HOLY SPIRIT.

IN our Lecture upon "THE RESURRECTION," you will remember, we started a train of thought which we were not able to elaborate to any great extent on Easter Sunday. Now that we have been requested to give our views upon the ASCENSION, and also upon the Descent of the HOLY SPIRIT upon the disciples after the ascension of Jesus into heaven, we shall endeavour to be yet more explicit in the expression of our opinions concerning the method of the Resurrection; as we believe the appearances of Jesus to his disciples after his physical death, to have been nothing other than ancient spiritual manifestations, recorded for the benefit of mankind by those chosen disciples and holy brethren, who were specially privileged to hold communion with the triumphant spirit of the great teacher and loving friend, from whose material form they had so recently been called to part.

There is a growing tendency among all really advanced thinkers, to spiritualize rather than to explain away Scripture narratives; and while recent Oriental discoveries have led many to abandon the name of Christian, and withhold their allegiance from a restrictive Christianity, which exalts one teacher at the expense of all others; while some have gone so far as to deny the personality of Jesus altogether, no one who is really a student of Oriental and classic history, can fail to be struck with the surprising fact that all the religious systems and sacred books of the world extant, have similar traditions and similar accounts of ancient spiritual marvels. The astronomical theory, and many other modern theories account for some things, but they do not cover the entire ground which must be covered before we can offer to the world anything like an adequate solution of the difficulties presented to students, and indeed to almost everybody, who reads anything now-a-days concerning the mysteries of past ages.

Spiritualism can and does offer the only really intelligible and satisfactory explanation of the spiritual phenomena of past times, and it is a great pity when professing Spiritualists, instead of calling public attention to spiritual truths, imitate materialists who have no knowledge of spiritual things, according to their own declaration, and therefore cannot be expected to give it forth to the world—as to give what one does not possess is an impossibility—and indulge in scoffing assertions with regard to ancient marvels, which by reason of their purely negative character, add nothing whatever to a controversy, except fresh fuel for the inflammation of party feeling and sectarian strife.

We have no blind or superstitious veneration for the Bible, as you very well know, neither have we any foolish and unreasoning dislike to it. We wish to treat it fairly, but then we endeavour to treat every book fairly. Thus, the Bible, in our hands, receives no better and no worse treatment than any other literary compilation, and we shall rejoice to see the day when sacred anthologies are so common, that go where you will, you will have placed in your hands compendiums of the choicest literary and moral extracts, which wise and far-reaching minds shall have gathered from all available sources, ancient and modern. Moncure D. Conway in England, and Giles Stebbins in America, have done something in this direction, in the publication of two very valuable works adapted especially for reading in schools, and at public religious meetings, but much more remains to be done in this direction, and we only hope lovers of truly great sayings of truly great men, will ere long make some decided effort to place such works as those to which we have alluded, in the hands of all readers, and not at a prohibitory price, as expensive works of that character are scarcely needed, as only the rich can purchase them, and the wealthy owners of good libraries would find little or nothing unfamiliar to them in such a treatise. Still a portable volume of moderate size, filled with choice selections from the best ancient and modern authors, is always valuable, as large, cumbersome works can with difficulty be carried from place to place, and are often practically useless, except to the very few, on account of their bulk and costliness.

We are often asked why we so constantly allude to the Bible narratives, rather than to others, in our Discourses, and also, why we usually preach from a Scripture text? Our answer is: It is the province, both of the pulpit and the platform, to teach morality and to unfold spiritual truths, and as we can just as well do this work as we are able. by taking up narratives with which the public are familiar, and expounding them in the light of universal laws and principles, as by alluding to incidents unknown to the greater portion of our audiences, we take the popular Bible, and preach from it, not to the exclusion of other works, but merely because by so doing we the sooner gain the public ear and arrive at desired results, *viz.*, the unfoldment of those spiritual truths which the Bible narratives certainly do set forth as well as any others. and better than many; while we add to this reason another, and that is this: the Bible is used as a weapon for the advocacy of the most pernicious doctrines. Once convince the public that the Bible itself does not teach what orthodox people say it teaches, and you have broken asunder the last link which binds many sincere though timid and rather superstitious people, to the now rapidly dying errors of the past.

Oh, but the Bible says so! is a phrase often used to silence any one and every one who dares to put forward an unorthodox doctrine. The user of the phrase means, of course, that the Bible says exactly what he says, and, therefore, the setter-forth of the strange doctrine is deluded, or an emissary of Satan. This foolish habit of endeavouring to silence every objector to one's own ideas of what the Bible enforces or substantiates, will be dismissed when the prevalent superstitions concerning the Bible are at an end; but they never will be vanquished until some one enlightens the public mind on the subject of inspiration and spiritual matters generally, to put to flight the old infallibility dogma, and all notions of plenary inspiration, in the old orthodox meaning of that term.

That the Bible is a record of the spiritual experiences of an important section of mankind, is indisputable. The Bible, indeed, is not the record of the spiritual experiences of the whole human race, but it does embody the most startling revelations made to Jews and the Gentile peoples also, from whom the Anglo-Saxon race has gradually developed. Orientals have their own records, somewhat similar and somewhat different, but these records are not, as some suppose, superior to the Bible; they are, if anything, inferior to it, probably because they are older, for one thing, and during the past several thousands of years the Eastern and Western parts of the world, north of the equator, have been slowly but surely advancing, every new race attaining to a higher stage of civilization than its predecessor.

Ancestral influences are acknowledged by all students of heredity, as playing a very important part in the development of races and individuals. Truly the modern student is very apt to ignore spiritual communion with ancestors altogether, but the very doctrine of ancestral influences, as taught by externalists who believe in heredity, is the outside shell of a great spiritual truth; yea, their conclusions are quite correct, only they go no further than effects and secondary causes. The first cause, in such instances, is always spirit influence, and when this is clearly demonstrated to all people, no scientific facts will be set aside, but the theorizings of scientists will be vastly improved and grandly supplemented.

The story of the Resurrection of Jesus is incomplete without the Ascension, and the Ascension is again incomplete without the Descent of the Holy Spirit, and it will be well for us to spend a short time this morning, in endeavouring to account for the marvellous events recorded by the Evangelist, on the basis of such spiritual laws as render them explicable, without the setting aside of any known law of nature. A law may be overpowered by a mightier law, as a strong man may be overcome by a stronger, but then it is the *law* that this should be so, and whatever takes place under the operation of law, must be, correctly speaking, a legal or natural event, though it be a supermaterial occurrence.

Supermaterial, superhuman, and superterrestrial are words that still convey some meaning to our minds. Supernatural we have outgrown, not because our views of spiritual action over matter have become narrowed, but because our conceptions of nature have so far enlarged, that we confess our inability to see beyond it.

Every miracle ever recorded may have taken place in obedience to some immutable law of nature, which rendered possible that which to most minds was strictly impossible. The mere plea that something is incomprehensible, is no argument against its reality, and they are poor philosophers who cannot make room in their system for accepting the genuineness of many things, which to them are truly miraculous. (Marvellous, inexplicable, even though perfectly natural.)

The disintegration of the body of Jesus seems to us the only rational interpretation of the story of the Resurrection, when we consider it literally. If the record of his life be true, then for three years, at least, and for how much longer the New Testament does not tell us, he had been practising the most rigid self-denial, and had acquired the power of stilling tempests, multiplying loaves and fishes, healing all manner of diseases, delivering those suffering from demoniacal possession, and what seems even more startling still to some readers, there were times when he transported himself to a distant place, or changed his appearance, so that his enemies were powerless to lay hands upon him.

On one occasion it is said that because he offended the rulers by the plainness of his speech, they took up stones to hurl at him, and would have thrust him over the brow of the hill, but he eluded them and thus saved himself from his persecutors. It must be remembered, however, that this story, or a similar one, is not told of Jesus only, and therefore the application becomes more powerful and universal, as it cannot be said that only one man, and he the special son of God, was endowed with this extraordinary ability, or was subject to so signal an instance of spiritual power exerted over him on his behalf.

We are told that after Elijah was taken from Elisha, the spirit carried Elisha to a place far distant, and there was enacted the scene with the bears, which has excited such heated controversy in many quarters. The Acts of the Apostles informs us that Philip was carried a long distance by invisible agency, so without calling to our aid any of the records of the Orient and tales of the magicians, which would probably be regarded as spurious by a majority of professing Christians, we find in the Bible itself many accounts of such phenomena as are in rare instances duplicated at the present time, and which in connection with Modern Spiritualism have been vouched for by Lord Lindsay, and other notable persons, whose witness on any other subject would be accepted anywhere, and that without cavil.

That is a natural and very reasonable disposition of the human mind, which refuses to accept as true anything peculiarly uncommon, until the unusual phenomenon has been observed so often and under such circumstances as to render delusion and imposition alike impossible; but when the testimony of the ages and the records of all peoples agree, surely such testimony as this is worthy of the profoundest consideration of all thoughtful people. But had we no lessons to teach, no moral truths to gather and illustrate by a recital of the marvels, either of the past or present, we would let magic, mystery and miracle rest for ever; but as the supreme triumph of the Spirit over Matter is the object of material embodiment, and all initiatory discipline on earth and in probationary realms of spiritual being, we feel our subjects to-day are neither fanciful nor unimportant. They are of vital interest to all seekers after truth, and can be made the means of setting forth the object and results of many of those toilsome earth experiences, which many persons are inclined to think are as objectless as they are hard to bear.

It has been suggested by some that Jesus never died and came to life again, and indeed that no one ever rose from the dead. This doctrine has found favour with Essenes or Essenians, both ancient and modern, who account for the seeming resurrection in this wise: Jesus, say they, was an adept, a member of a mystic fraternity, the members of which had power to apparently lay down their lives and take them up again. Many of these brothers are said to have been buried in swoons and trances from which they afterwards revived. The Essenians would account for the resurrection of Lazarus, the widow's son at Nain, the daughter of Jairus, and others, all by reference to the powers of this mystic fraternity over seeming death; and so far as the explanation goes, it is adequate in some cases (though not in all), as it illustrates the powers of human will or psychological influence, and opens a very broad field of investigation into the mysterious power which highly developed and mediumistic people can exert, or be compelled or enabled by spirit power to exert over the minds and bodies of the afflicted and the dying.

Perhaps it has struck some of you that the early Christians built upon a false foundation, when they made all their system to hang upon the resurrection of the man Jesus. Suppose he never did rise in any literal sense, are all hopes of immortality delusive, and is all preaching and prophesying on the subject of immortality vain? These are very great and awful questions for the orthodox, who repose their every hope of life immortal, on the testimony of those who declare Jesus had risen from the dead and reappeared to them, conversing and eating with them. The resurrection of a physical body, however, would be no proof of immortality, unless the immortalization of the body were a demonstrated fact. and when we read the account given in the first chapter of Acts, of the ascension of the body of Jesus, we are struck with the awful incompleteness of the testimony to the ascension there furnished; for we are only told that, as the disciples were gazing steadfastly up into heaven, Jesus vanished: "A cloud received him out of their sight, are the exact words used in the authorized version.

True, it is stated that angels said unto them, that Jesus had gone to heaven, and would come to earth again, but they (the disciples) did not witness the entrance of Jesus in a physical body into the spiritual world. The material body vanished; it became invisible, it was disintegrated, in our opinion, as physical bodies according to universal testimony do not enter the spirit world, and could not exist there, certain physical conditions being required for the sustentation of a human body, composed of matter, which are not present except within the atmosphere of the earth.

Jesus may have had the power to take up his body and lay it down at will, without having carried a single physical atom into the spiritual universe, and that he had this power is abundantly proved, if the records of his *post mortem* appearances are to be relied upon. It is not to the physical body and its immortalization, that the world looks for consolation in the hour of bereavement and the loss of all earthly things, and it was not to this the disciples were taught to look by Christ. The appearance of Jesus to Saul of Tarsus, as he journeyed between Jerusalem and Damascus, is one of the proofs of immortality which seems to have the greatest weight with that celebrated teacher and controversialist, who from a persecutor of the Christians became their warmest friend and foremost advocate, through the conviction brought to his mind by that singular apparition.

Renan, in his life of St. Paul, suggests that Saul was attacked with ophthalmia, a disease of the eyes common in

Asia, and frequently occasioned by exposure to a severe storm in districts where storms are both frequent and terrible, and that when struck by lightning he saw his past life pass before him, much as drowning people often are enabled to review their past. In that condition of helplessness, he no doubt experienced a change of heart and mind, and as suffering and fright often produce reflection, and bring one into a state of spiritual receptivity, this explanation is extremely feasible; while Paul's thorn in the flesh has been considered by many commentators to have meant his weak eyes and very defective sight, which made it necessary for him to employ amanuenses to write epistles at his dictation, as, when he writes a short epistle with his own hand, he calls it a long letter under the circumstances, suggesting the idea that it was written with great difficulty, and probably much pain to the writer.

Stephen, we are told, saw heaven opened, and beheld Jesus, but there is not a shred of evidence that in the cases cited either Saul or Stephen saw Jesus physically or objectively, for no one else is said to have seen anything except the changes produced by the visions upon the countenances of the seers. If you have had any experience, no matter how limited, with clairvoyants and clairaudients, you must have observed the peculiarly beautiful expression which the face of the somnambule wears when in the condition of trance, rapture, or ecstacy. For this reason it has been the custom for celebrated painters to study the psychologic art, and entrance their "models" in order that an expression of almost superhuman loveliness might be transferred to the canvas. But when faces are all aglow with heavenly rapture, and you know the expression of ecstacy cannot be feigned, you see and hear nothing which causes you to understand why the sensitive or medium should appear so wonderfully happy, while if visions of a distressing character are presented to the seer, you see nothing which enables you to account for the horror and fright, which will sometimes render the features of a medium positively livid. There are so many avenues of perception open to exceptionally-endowed persons, that are not open to the majority, that it is the height of folly for any one, no matter how gifted or widely experienced, to taboo as spurious or even unlikely, that which has formed no part of his individual experience. The world progresses through the accumulation of facts and their application to religion, art and industry, and it is a safe position for everybody to hold to, that he will deny nothing but what is in direct opposition to some demonstrable reality.

We are often told that it is the part of every one, who makes an affirmation, to prove it, and that no one is logically called upon to prove a negative. Reasoning from such a premise, it has often been remarked that neither Materialists nor Christadelphians are under any necessity of proving that man is not immortal. That is a very one-sided way of looking at the matter. Such people do not satisfy themselves with anything short of dogmatic assertion, that man is mortal only; now in the face of almost universal testimony to the fact of human immortality, it is quite as reasonable to demand proof of man's mortality as of his immortality; and it is just here where all materialistic evidence breaks down. No one has ever been able to prove that the real essential life of man has ever become extinct. Bodies of flesh and blood we know have dissolved and corrupted, but it is impossible to deny the great probability of an ethereal and invisible condition of human embodiment, over which death has no power. If material substances can become invisible, and if the atoms of life are all invisible, then the statement that the essential body of man is invisible, does not appear fallacious to any true scientist.

The testimony of the New Testament is not really, as many have supposed, to the material resurrection and ascension of Jesus, but to the fact of many persons having been quite satisfied that they had communion with him after his material death. The concurrent testimony of many clairvoyants constitutes the bulk of evidence furnished by the New Testament, while a spiritual certainty possessed the minds of many, who do not claim to have had any such such vision of Jesus, that he was really alive and present with them; this spiritual certainty being so powerful a conviction of their minds, that they were ready to suffer martyrdom in support of their faith in the true resurrection.

Paul was far too great a scholar, had a far too philosophic mind, and was far too mediumistic a man to have hinged all his preaching upon the reanimation of an earthly body, which had once become a corpse. It is he who speaks of the witness of the spirit, of knowing Christ after the spirit and not after the flesh, of a spiritual body as totally distinct from the material form, and of the impossibility of flesh and blood inheriting the Kingdom of Heaven. Doubtless Jesus did materialize for the satisfaction of honest doubters, as many spirits are materializing to-day as an accommodation to the gross materialism and arrant scepticism of the present time, but no matter how valuable and even necessary physical manifestations may be for the enlightenment of sceptics, there will surely come a time when they will no more be needed: they will have done their work, and will cease when the spiritualization of humanity renders them superfluous, as staircases and ladders may be dispensed with when people can fly or transport themselves through the air.

We have constantly observed that those Spiritualists who attach most importance to physical manifestations, with which they are never satisfied unless they can observe them under "crucial test conditions," are always seeking to impose new and yet more crucial tests, often cruelly afflicting and disgracefully villifying and insulting the sensitives with whom they experiment; and still they appear to derive less and less satisfaction from their experiments, the longer they continue them. Why is this, but because many of these medium testers are persons almost wholly destitute of spiritual perception. Phrenologically they are Materialists: they must handle the spirits as they would handle material merchandise. They would make mediumship a mere matter of buying and selling; they would look to nothing higher than the accumulation of worldly wealth; they would want the spirits to tell them who would be the winner of the Derby, how they could amass a fortune by gambling in stocks, and as for the mediums who are brought under such accursed influences, they soon become so morally corrupted that they do not care whether manifestations are genuine or otherwise, so long as they receive a handsome remuneration for legal or illicit transactions, as the case may be.

Now, were the disciples of Jesus and the early Christians a set of impecunious showmen, who went from place to place vending their wares,—was it their object to make money by exhibiting marvels before an open-mouthed public, ready to swallow the latest fiction got up for their pastime? The temptation to make merchandise of spiritual gifts may have constituted the third and last temptation the devil offered to

Jesus, called the temptation to worship the devil in order to acquire material wealth and power; but it was ever held in execration by the primitive Christians, who were an honest, self-denying company of spiritualized men and women, who communed with each other and with the spirit-world for the purpose of enlightening humanity on matters of the utmost importance to one and all of the human race. Therefore. Simon Magus, and the man who employed a damsel as a soothsayer to bring him wealth, were severely denounced by the apostles, for the strife was then as now between the conscientious and the avaricious workers in the Spiritual Movement.

We are told that Jesus promised his friends, that wheresoever two or three were gathered together in his name, there he would be in the midst of them, but only when they were assembled in his name did he promise to bestow his presence. Ere he took his departure from the sight of men, he promised a Comforter, even the Spirit of Truth, which the world of orthodoxy and self-seeking would not receive. It could not embrace the Spirit of Truth, because that spirit would not sanction its intrigues or gloss over its hypocrisies, which are made to do duty for virtue. When he promises this spirit, he does not only say he will send a Comforter. he says he will come himself, and be their teacher and consoler, declaring it is expedient for his disciples that he should depart. because if he remain in material form among them, they will not be called upon to exert their spiritual faculties in clasping hands with a soul in immortality, across the borders of material life.

Truly the spirit-world stoops to earth: it stoops to conquer pride and prejudice, and man's benighted state of spiritual darkness; but the highest attitude of the receptive mind is that of desire to rise to a spiritual level over material doubt and strife, rather than to drag the spirit down to the plane of material things once more. Spiritual revelation is truly a Jacob's ladder, but the descending angels only stoop to earth that they may lift earth's children into communion with them on their high rounds nearer the summit. All communications alleged to be spiritual may be so, but if they are, then those which come in response to man's greed or lust, are only revelations from those hells and purgatories within the atmosphere of earth, where spirits, destitute as yet of spiritual perception, are dwelling amid the murky shadows of the outer earth. The Hindoos were not wrong when they declared that one of the spiritual spheres was upon or within the earth itself, for peopling the earth's atmosphere are countless millions of disembodied men and women, who are ever ready to enter into converse with those upon earth, who seek communion with them.

The great question at allseances is: In what name are you assembled, or in other words, what motives and desires have brought you together? Are you, or are you not, with one accord in one place, as you are told those were who received the Holy Spirit on the day of Pentecost? If evil thoughts and vain desires possess your minds, if uncharitableness or selfishness are dominant within your breasts, then it is in vain that you sing sweet hymns and utter wordy prayers. Spiritual beings are attracted or repelled by your thoughts, and neither hymn nor prayer can be of any use in invoking the Spirit of Truth, unless such effusions are the honest expression of your inmost desires, or unless they promote charitable and loyal dispositions in the hearts of others.

When the Spirit of Truth came, how did it manifest itself? According to the second chapter of Acts, almost every conceivable type of manifestation was produced. The physical came first, to arrest attention and prepare the minds of those assembled for what was to follow. The rushing mighty wind, which shook the house where they assembled, the visible cloven tongues of flame, came before the speaking with many tongues; and when those many tongues were employed, they were not brought into play to merely startle or astonish the multitude, but because all could not understand one language, and the message of truth would be no message at all to the people to whom it was addressed, unless it were delivered to them in a language they could understand. A jargon of unknown tongues in an English-speaking audience, would be no evidence of the coming of the Holy Spirit; but if different minds must be approached in different ways, and different understandings require different versions of the one Gospel of Immortality, then the self same spirit, even the Spirit of Truth, makes use of divers instrumentalities, and as Paul says, in 1 Cor., xii.: "There are diversities of administrations, but one Lord."

The Spirit of God is ever present when divine results are

accomplished, and there is no other way of testing spirits or teachings, but by watching the effect produced upon those who embrace or give heed to them. In coveting earnestly the best gifts, one only needs to have pure motives, and be wishful to be made use of by the higher powers, for the benefit of the race; and then whether his gift be healing, prophesying, or any other gift, the Spirit of Truth will be his guide, his comfort, and his reward, in this and in every stage of existence.

IMPROMPTU POEM.

ASCENSION THROUGH SORROW.

CAN earth confine the Spirit, throughout eternal day?
Say, are we doomed for ever to tread earth's toilsome way?
Shall bodies resurrected imprison still the soul,
Even when it has conquered, and reached the wished-for goal?

Earth-bodies are to spirits, what earth is to the seeds
Of flowers and of grasses,—each one on matter feeds;
And in the dim, strange darkness, buried beneath the sod,
Each germ of life unfoldeth, and seeks the light of God.

How wondrous is the pathway! through which all spirits move;
How mystic are the lessons! which every heart must prove:
Ofttimes the anguished spirit cries out in grief and pain—
What is the use of sorrow? Oh! need I grieve again?

The lesson of life's turmoil—of all its pain and strife—
Is never fully learned, till on the sacred height
Of perfected self-conquest, your souls enchanted stand,
Viewing celestial mountains, from some fair Beulah land.

Along the toilsome pathway, the pilgrim-soul must speed,
Sometimes on fruits and nectar, again on griefs to feed;
Sometimes by flowing waters, where flowers brightly bloom,
Sometimes through arid deserts, as lonely as the tomb.

God leads his children onward, through sunshine and through storm,
Their brows oft kissed with radiance from Heaven's bright centres, warm;
But oftentimes the desert develops most that power,
Which sends a Christ to battle, to win the victor's dower.

Temptation by the devil, ye every one must know:
Tempted by avarice and pride, by passions, by each low
And selfish earthly motive, ye must to Satan say:
Get thou behind me, Tempter! and triumph in life's fray.

Oh! were it not for Olivet, for Calvary's sad cross;
Oh! were it not for earthly death, crowning all mortal loss;
The resurrection angels for you would never sing—
Another soul has conquered, and death has lost its sting!

Ascending 'mong the angels, behold the Soul arise,
The conqueror in triumph, through highest paradise,
Mounts on and up still higher, till realms celestial see,
Are opening to receive him, while angels chant with glee:

Welcome! oh, conquering Spirit; welcome! oh, Soul divine:
Welcome! to this your birthplace, the Kingdom that's now thine
Is empire o'er all matter, death's icy hand to thee
Henceforth will be a symbol of perfect victory!

BENEDICTION.

(May the Ascension of the Spirit over all material strife, be yours in blest experience now, and in fulness of glory hereafter. May Heaven's best blessings rest on you all, and may you become one with all true conquerors for ever!)

XIII.

A SPIRITUAL VIEW OF THE TRINITY.

IN our last Discourse, we led you up in some measure to where you were prepared to see (if you followed the drift of our argument) how without one making three or three making one, in any nonsensical manner suggested by way of ridicule by opposers of the doctrine of a Trinity in Nature and a Trinity in God, the idea of the three-fold expressions of the Divine Mind, prevalent all over the earth from immemorial ages, may not after all be inconsistent with Monotheism, or the most uncompromising declaration of the Israelites: The Lord is One.

Upon the question of the unity of the Godhead, Unitarians and Trinitarians are professedly agreed: they only differ as to what is meant by absolutely unity, and so mystifying have been the definitions of the Trinity put forward under the name of Athanasius especially, that it is scarcely possible for any person of ordinary mental calibre, to gather anything like a definite idea of what the Fathers of the Church really thought of the nature of God, judging by such a compilation as that called the Creed of S. Athanasius, yet that creed was laboriously compiled by many of the most learned doctors of the fourth century, gathered in solemn council to obtain from the Holy Ghost a clear and definite refutation of the heresies of Arius and his followers. So say all orthodox Church historians, while even the candid Unitarian feels compelled to credit some, though not by any means all, of those engaged in the Arian and Athanasian controversies, with at least a sincere desire to arrive at truth, and defend the true faith from all successful attacks in future.

The doctrine of the Trinity is certainly not one of those doctrines which are "plainly revealed in Holy Scripture," so that no one carefully reading the Bible can fail to come to the conclusion that God has revealed Himself in that Book as three in one or one in three. The three persons and one

God, of the Church of England litany, are certainly not plainly revealed as constituting the true Godhead, but quite the contrary is the case, for the word trinity does not occur even once in the whole Bible, and Jesus taught his disciples to pray to one only God, the Father, who is in heaven, whose personality must certainly be one, if the term Father conveys any idea to the human mind.

The most that can be proved from the New Testament is, what the Arians endeavoured to prove, that there is but one God, the Father, and one Lord or Master, Jesus Christ, and a Spirit of Truth, whom Jesus said the Father would send in his name. You may possibly make your case good by reference to Scripture texts, if you are Arians and believe in the superiority of Jesus Christ to all other created beings; but you must in that case regard him but as a creature of God, though the first and highest of all creatures. Arianism deduces, from the plain language of the New Testament, that we are commanded to worship God the Father, that our prayers should be addressed to God through Christ, for the Holy Spirit; therefore, Arianism, though distinct from Modern Unitarianism, is a purely monotheistic system, as it regards Jesus as only a finite being, even though a super-angelic personage; but the difference between God and any creature, no matter how exalted, must ever be the difference between the finite and the infinite, which is an infinite difference.

Arianism permits of a secondary worship being offered to Christ, much as the Roman Church allows of a secondary worship being paid to Mary, the mother of Jesus, and numerous saints and angels; but though their prayers and intercessions are asked for by devout Catholics, they are never adored in the Catholic Church as parts of Deity.

The creed of Athanasius is not only utterly unintelligible, but with its damnatory clauses it is one of the most objectionable and preposterous compositions ever palmed upon the world, as an embodiment of truth, while the damnatory clauses are strong presumptive evidence of its internal weakness, for whenever a position is insecure, it is necessary to fortify it by threats, so as to suppress inquiry. To the timid and superstitious, what can be more awful than questioning the veracity of a creed, which tells you if you do not believe it in its entirety, you will perish everlastingly? No doubt multitudes have suppressed their honest convictions, from sheer dread that, perhaps if it were true, and though they thought it was false they were not absolutely certain of its falsity, they might be bringing upon themselves and others the terrible penalty of everlasting torment. Believe or be damned, is a very convenient motto for those, who having usurped power on false premises, desire to maintain their hold upon the people through fear; and as certain passages of Scripture appear to favour this dogma, it has been peculiarly easy for interested parties to twist texts to suit their own arrogant assumptions.

The New Testament is not a book which can be taken literally, from end to end, as a divine compilation, neither is it so plainly written that every one can understand exactly what it means. Again, no original MS. has yet been discovered, dating further back than the fourth century, the three oldest MSS. being the Vatican and Sinaitic MSS., traceable to the fourth, and the Alexandrian MS., only traceable to the fifth century. These three MSS. are not literal transcripts of each other, thus it is evident to any scholar, even of the humblest pretensions and narrowest opportunities, that it is absurd as well as cruel and unjust, to endeavour to decide any point of doctrine by reference simply to a few ambiguous statements in the Gospels or Epistles.

The declaration in the Epistle of John, that there are three who bear record in heaven, the Father, the Word and the Holy Ghost, and these three are one, is considered an interpolation by students almost universally, while the damnatory clauses, apparently justified by the reputed saying of Jesus: "He that believeth and is baptized shall be saved, but he that believeth not shall be damned," is open to quite another interpretation than that usually put upon it. All such passages are true in a prophetic sense, especially when "condemned" is substituted for "damned," as it is in the Revised Version. In the old law, "Whosoever sheddeth man's blood by man shall his blood be shed," does not necessarily prescribe capital punishment as the doom of murderers; it makes a prophetic statement, signifying that those who wrong their brethren shall eventually suffer as they have made others to suffer; while David's prophesying against wicked men, declaring that their wives shall be widows and their children fatherless, when understood in the letter only, becomes offensive as a prayer.

We have no time to enter upon these topics now, as our subject is the Trinity, but as we have touched upon the law of compensation, or just retribution, we promise at no distant date to speak more fully upon methods of compensation in spirit life; showing, as far as we are able, how (every act of life brings with it its own punishment or reward, not as an arbitrary act of divine sovereignty, but as a result of infinite wisdom, displayed in the natural law of cause and effect, which governs the spiritual as well as the material world.)

The greatest objection which can ever be brought against the popular Christian view of the Trinity, is that it makes evil everlasting, and declares an opposition between different attributes of the Divine Nature. Take the attributes of Justice and Mercy, for example, as they have ever been the principal subjects of contention in the Church. Justice is always regarded as the especial attribute of God the Father, Mercy, of God the Son. Now, it is invariably stated by the orthodox, that the Son came into the world to appease the Father's wrath, but if Father, Son and Holy Ghost are all one, as the creeds of Christendom declare, then the wrath of God must be the wrath of the Son as much as of the Father.

Old pictures of the Trinity represent the Father as a stern-visaged, elderly man, the Son as a younger man, and the Holy Ghost as a dove: that is the popular picture of God, put into the hands of children by Roman Catholics and Ritualists, while Gustave Doré, the celebrated French artist, in his celebrated Illustrated Bible, has intruded this distressing caricature of the world's belief in a Deity. (Doré's picture, as a work of art, is exquisite, and perhaps when spiritualized by the imagination of him who gazes upon it, it may illustrate some occult truth concerning the operations of the Divine Mind, but Madame Blavatsky, in her "Isis Unveiled," commenting on this picture, has to our mind given utterance to a far deeper meaning, doubtless in the artist's own mind, when she says, that to her and to all true mystics and deep students of divine things, the chaos in the background, dim, vague, awful though it be, is far more suggestive of the Eternal, whom no man has seen with fleshly eyes at any time, than the two men of different ages and the bird, in the engraving.)

The very fact of the Son being represented as younger

than the Father, in the picture, shows that nothing can have been originally intended, than the Law as given to Moses, and the Gospel as revealed by Christ. Age may apply to divine revelations to man; one dispensation of truth on earth may antedate another, but one person of the Godhead cannot be of unequal age with another, if all three are alike eternal. Thus the Catholic doctrine of the Trinity, that the three persons are co-equal and co-eternal, is defied rather than expressed in many phases of Catholic art.

How extremely significant appear the grand old words of the second commandment of the Decalogue, as they recur to one's mind when gazing upon Christian pictures: "Thou shalt not make unto thee any likeness of anything that is in heaven above, or that is in the earth beneath, or that is in the water under the earth." Knowing how prone to idolatry the people were, knowing how readily the Israelites would lapse into the idolatries of the neighbouring peoples, if they were allowed to have images and pictures in their synagogues, Moses sternly forbade them to cultivate what is ordinarily termed religious art. Col. Ingersoll and others have made much capital out of this prohibition, and have endeavoured to show how obedience to such a command robbed the Hebrew people of all the inspiration they might have derived from a pure and ennobling art; but the dangers are so great, of bowing down to the creature and worshipping it as the Creator, limiting Deity within the narrow groove of man's conception of some finite object, that after all it may be well to exert a wise, restraining power, and prevent as far as possible the introduction of objects, calculated to lead the mind astray, into places of public worship.

This is an age of *renaissance*, however. Puritan supremacy has despoiled cathedrals of much of their ancient beauty, and a work of restoration is now going on, by means of which painting and sculpture are being brought back into something like their old prominence, in places of religious assembly. We are not sorry that the tendency of the age is to artistic revival, but we do regret the craze which possesses the minds of those who desire to have everything mediæval. As in mediæval times art was crippled and dwarfed by corrupting and corrupt theological phantasies, the great masters were like chained eagles: they longed to soar, and the

Church doomed them to paint and sculp as it directed. The working of theological bigotry is discoverable in the subjects chosen and the manner in which they are treated, even when the workmanship is so perfect that no artist of to-day can rival, much less excel, it.

But what is a perfect skull or dragon compared to something intrinsically beautiful, outwrought with equal accuracy, care and skill? What is the perfect delineation of an emaciated misanthrope, compared with an equally perfect portrayal of some form radiant with beauty? In a brighter and freer age, Art will be again the handmaid of Religion, but even if the execution be not so grand in a hurrying age, as in one of loneliness and contemplation when years passed as months in the completion of some exquisite work of art. Art is destined not to live as a memory of the dead past simply, but, resurrected in more glorious apparel than any in which it has yet arrayed itself upon earth, it will take humanity captive, in a period of true *renaissance*, when it stands as the embodiment of the loftiest conceptions of Deity, the human mind can possibly attain unto.

In the art of the future, Christs, Madonnas, angels will multiply, but finite forms will never be expressive, to the true reader of the language of art, of the Eternal Infinite, but only of those real and ideal forms in nature, which express godlike powers, and enable man to see through the windows of the eyes of those, whose souls have most expanded the life of God within, which is the perennial spring of happiness, the fount of true greatness, and essential life for ever. Take the Christian's picture of Father, Son and Holy Ghost, along with Madame Blavatsky's suggestion as to the chaos illustrating, as far as can be illustrated, the unfathomable nature of the absolute Godhead, who is beyond all lords, angels, and messengers who have appeared to man.

In ancient Egypt, as we have previously reminded you from this platform, the ideas of Deity were three-fold as well as unitary, as among Christians, and indeed almost all ancient peoples have introduced triangles and triadations, to set forth their ideas of Eternal Mind; even the original Monotheism of Israel has not excluded the number three from the name given to Deity, as there are three consonants in the name Jehovah, J H V H, vowels not occurring in Hebrew writing, and the H being repeated, there are but three letters in the name Jahveh or Jehovah. By many scholars these three letters or three syllables have been regarded as expressive of the past, present, and future of the Eternal.

Of course this Israelitish name for deity, gives no clue as to how the tri-personality of deity crept into the beliefs of the world, disfiguring all of them except the Jewish; for the Jews, in spite of their innumerable persecutions at the hands of Christians, wandering through all the Christian countries, have never renounced their unswerving fealty to the religion of their fathers, touching the unity of God. Here and there a Jew becomes a convert to Christianity, not generally with very beneficial results either to himself or others, and usually not until almost a fortune, collected from the credulous contributors to missionary societies, has been spent on his "conversion." Though the Jews never preached the doctrine of the tri-personality of the Deity, almost all the ancients were deeply imbued with it, but the original conceptions were nothing like the disfigured and distorted versions of the Trinity, which have made the Athanasian Creed possible.

In Egypt the Trinitarian idea was beautiful, poetic, and natural: God the Father, God the Mother, and God the Child. Osiris, the Father, was worshipped under the similitude of the sun; Isis, the Mother, under that of the earth; and Horus, the Child, under that of the atmosphere; but beyond Osiris, Isis and Horus was the Grand Central Sun, the centre of the Universe, around which all worlds revolve. To this supreme central orb, ineffable and eternal, all loftiest thought was directed, and if any outward form was ever introduced to symbolize the absolute centre, it was that of Alcyone, the centre of the Pleiades, and of the "sidereal heavens," because the most distant orb known to the ancient world.

(In India, Brahma, Creator; Vishnu, Preserver; and Siva, Destroyer and Reproducer, expressed the three-fold powers of Deity to the Hindoo mind; but beyond the three was the one Brahm, the Divine Essence, the Unchanging Being, who had no visible forms, and was beyond all outward adoration. Nirvana is said to signify the perfect absorption of the mind of man in a contemplation of the Infinite, till the finite becomes lost in the infinite. To Brahm no altars or temples were erected: he was worshipped only in the heart of man, and was truly the spiritual Deity of the Ancients. Is it not singular that the Church of England litany addresses three persons *and* one God, following, even if accidentally, directly in the track of those very Brahmans it sends missionaries to convert to Christianity? The enlightened Brahman cannot comprehend the mission of the Christian missionary, because, reading the religious text books of England in the light of his esoteric knowledge of the inner meaning of terms and symbols, he finds Christian conceptions completely analogous with those of the wisest and purest of the ancient Brahmans. But both Brahmanism and Christianity have become corrupt, so missionaries are needed both in England and India; but for the Brahman of to-day and the Christian of to-day, to try and convert each other, is truly a blind man leading another, and both falling into a ditch.)

The idea of divine incarnations, in the persons of Avatars or Messiahs, is extremely natural, because no one can fully realize or sincerely love the abstract. Abstract goodness to us is unintelligible. Impersonal being we can scarcely conceive of. The incarnation idea is an attempt of the human mind to introduce reality into the thought of God. Three persons are two too many, as they produce a confusion in the mind, and belief in them leads naturally to tritheism or polytheism, which certainly prevails to a large extent in Christendom, though all Christians most positively declare that they cannot endure the idea of more Gods than one. But who has ever joined in Trinitarian worship, without feeling the strange incongruity of addressing three separate persons, and yet maintaining that these three are but one.

The mischief which Trinitarianism always accomplishes, is the division of the thought of God into, at least, two irreconcilable parts. The Holy Ghost and Jesus agree very well together in the mind, as the fourteenth chapter of the fourth Gospel, which mentions the Holy Spirit particularly, so closely identifies the Spirit with Jesus, that the coming of the Comforter always seems to mean the coming of Christ in spirit, though his physical form is not present. The attributes of the Son and Holy Ghost are also in accordance. Both reveal truth, both breathe forth loving-kindness, and the mind very naturally associates the idea of Christ with the appearance of Jesus upon earth, and that of his holy spirit as the manifestation of Jesus to his disciples after his removal from the external world. "Wheresoever two or three are gathered together in my name, there am I in the midst of them"; "I will not leave you comfortless, I will come to you"; "The Lord is that Spirit," and several similar passages in the Gospels and Epistles, favour the idea of the Holy Spirit being really a spiritual manifestation of the ascended Jesus; but between the idea of Father and Son there is no such agreement, unless we get rid entirely of every cardinal assumption of orthodox Trinitarians, with reference to the mission of Jesus and the attributes of God the Father.

The New Testament certainly does not teach orthodox dogmas. If we carefully note such passages as "God so loved the world, that he gave his only begotten Son"; "His name shall be called Jesus, for he shall save his people from their sins," we can trace a perfect unity of feeling between God the Father, and that Great and Holy Teacher, who said, "I and my Father are one"; but if God so loved the world that he gave his Son, then surely God was never so angry with the world that his Son was compelled to assume human nature to assuage his wrath, in order to deliver mankind from everlasting torment. If the mission of Jesus was to deliver his people from their sins, then it was not to save them from the penalty due to transgression, but from sin itself.

All orthodox views of the Trinity are built upon erroneous ideas of justice, sin and the consequences of sin. It is mere absurdity, insult to common sense, to indulge in fiery but meaningless rhetoric concerning the sin of a finite creature, committed in time, being an infinite transgression, meriting an eternal punishment. No human act can possibly be infinite; no human act can possibly merit eternal doom; neither can any act of man possibly merit everlasting happiness or glory.

Now we come to a point of issue, not only with the orthodox believers in everlasting torment, but almost equally with those kind-hearted Universalists, who have represented the God of Calvin without the devil of Calvin; for Calvin, like Mohammed, was really a reviver of the Persian duality, Ormuzd and Ahriman, the power of Light and the power of Darkness, though conjoined in one person. These Universalists, who have taken away the fear of hell and the wrath of God from their theology, have left us with a good-natured, easy-going Deity, who is too kind to damn any of his creatures.

and who takes them all immediately to a heaven of happiness when their earthly life, however short and unsatisfactory it may have been, is ended.

Universalism, as taught in America a century ago as a protest against Calvinism, was an excellent and necessary antidote to the harsh and bitter theology which it supplanted, but to the logical mind, thinking deeply upon the nature of justice, Universalism was a beautiful but unsatisfactory poem; and though the truths it realized have permeated all other denominations to a greater or lesser degree, Universalism itself, even in its sectarian form, has considerably advanced during the past half-century, till Universalism and Unitarianism are now almost identical in America.

Unitarianism is the stronger and healthier system of the two, though it often lacks the intuition, discernment and keen spiritual perception of immortal verities, necessary to make Unitarianism the prevailing religion which speaks to the heart as much as to the intellect. We have known many warm-hearted and deeply spiritual Unitarians, but we have known many extremely agnostic and sceptical. Their religion has seemed of the head rather than of the heart. Their discourses have been learned and extremely intellectual, but they have lacked spiritual power, and have failed to include a strong grasp of immortal life. It is on this account that Unitarianism does not keep and hold many of the greatest thinkers of the age, who are strictly Unitarian in their thought of God. No religious system is complete unless it has the clearest and fullest grasp of Divine Justice, and of the law of Divine Retribution, hereafter as well as here. Some Unitarians, indeed many, have this. Many of their sermons are full of living appreciation of the very highest truths which Spiritualism can possibly teach, and these men require no phenomenal evidences to convince them of the immortality of the human soul, and of progression after death.

The only satisfactory doctrine of the immortal world, which commends itself to reason and intuition alike, is that God is one, and his law is one. As the results of yesterday's activities appear in your condition to-day, as you are to-day preparing yourself to be to-morrow what you could not be, were it not for your having been exactly what you now are, so in the future state, every day prepares you for its successor. When your body dies, and your spirit is emancipated, it does not find itself at the end of a journey, but only at one halting place along the road. Death only introduces you to another state of being, where you can gain fresh experiences, but in the spiritual world you must go on earning whatever you obtain, meriting whatever you enjoy, and thus perpetual misery could only be possible if a spirit were to go on incessantly committing sin, and thus bringing upon him constant punishment for constant sins committed. Immortal happiness is only possible to those who are everlastingly living in accordance with the divine laws of being, which ordain that true felicity must ever follow upon the performance of deeds of genuine benevolence; and it was this gospel Jesus taught, when his mission was to save mankind from the misery consequent upon wrong-doing, by leading persons out of evil and the love of it, into the green pastures of philanthropy, and beside the still waters of integrity.

Justice is to us the one complete and all-expressive word, which pronounces the sum of Divine perfections. Justice we regard as the perfect sphere, the absolute whole. Some people seem to think by employing the phrase—God is Justice, we take away all the softness and beauty of John's delightful declaration—God is Love; but when the poet Bowring wrote that hymn, which has found an honoured place in almost every hymn book, every verse ending with "God is wisdom, God is love," did he take anything away from the beauty and the poetry of the statement—God is Love, by prefacing it with—God is Wisdom? Do we desire to be governed by a being who is unwise, indiscreet, foolishly fond? A merely sweet-tempered ruler, who lacks force of character and true wisdom, may be amiable, but he will certainly be weak, and often make mistakes which will work disastrously to the governed. Perfect wisdom blended with perfect love—these are the elements which go to make up a perfect character, and to us the word Justice, properly interpreted, means love and wisdom in equal proportions. Love is one hemisphere, Wisdom is the other, Justice is the sphere, therefore, when we gain a true idea of justice, we do not mean anything distinct from love and wisdom: we mean love and wisdom both.

Thus the unity and the duality of the Divine Nature are not irreconcilable but perfectly in accord. Our Father and our Mother! should be the cry of every true aspirant to the

Divine. We need a *Mater noster* as well as a *Pater noster*, in our theology. We need new pronouns to express the thought of God. He and she, not he only, should be used when the Deity is mentioned. Let us make man in our image, after our likeness, said God to himself, or rather said the divine Fatherhood to the divine Motherhood, and man appeared, rational and emotional, spiritual and intellectual, male and female.

As we watch the organisms of the lowest types of animate life, we find they possess the organs of both sexes. Life starts with masculinity and femininity conjoined, and only as the progress of life is upward and onward through material forms, do the sexes appear in separate organisms. The grand old philosophers of ancient days followed nature's suggestions perfectly, when they taught the duality of the human soul: and told how the soul in its paradisiacal home, ere it came in contact with material substance, was male and female; and how, again, when earthly pilgrimages are over, it will be reunited, and form a perfect sphere.

The very highest spiritual truths are in such perfect accord with nature's material revealments, that we are convinced that in the New Dispensation, when knowledge shall be disseminated among the multitude, instead of being confined as of yore to a privileged minority, the deepest mysteries of spiritual being will be deduced from a study of external life; as nature's outward form is but the vesture of the Spirit.

Now, if we have a perfect Sphere as our symbol of Deity, if our conception of the Eternal Mind, be of a Being of infinite and perfect Justice, a Father and a Mother in whom Love and Wisdom are blended in eternal union; if we go one step further and regard all life, all creative and sustaining power throughout the universe, as an emanation from the Divine Centre, as the proceeding influence of God, then we have accounted, we think, satisfactorily for the world-wide belief in a Trinity as expressive and interpretative of Unity.

The Circle is the whole, the Triangle the expression of the Circle. God is Love; God is Wisdom; God is Power: three manifestations of Deific Life. God is Justice, one perfect unity of nature, one divine sum of attributes. Justice is comparable to the perfect ray of white light; Love, Wisdom, and Power are as the three primary colours. Say white, and you mean the whole; say red, or blue, or yellow, and you mean one of the three primary constitutive parts of white.

Such a view of Deity, while it utterly destroys the caricature of the natural and spiritual Trinity prevalent in Christendom, nevertheless explains the origin of the idea of three persons (properly manifestations) but of one God. In the future, as in the olden Trinity, it will be God the Father, God the Mother, and God the Child; and the Child (Son and Daughter), in essence like the Father and Mother, who gave it birth, is none other than the *Logos* or Word, the Divine Light, which is the life of man; the Divine Energy by which all things are formed and are sustained; the Divine Soul of the laws of Being, who is within you all; the Wellspring of your Immortality; the Divine Nature, deathless as the Eternal, which, having had no beginning, shall also know no end!

IMPROMPTU POEM.

OUR MOTHER WHO ART IN HEAVEN.

A LITTLE boy knelt at his father's side,
When fell the shades of even,
Repeating the old familiar prayer—
"Our Father who art in heaven."
And when he had ended his evening prayer,
And had chanted his little hymn,
Ere he kissed his father and bade him good-night,
He looked up with his eyes all dim
With unshed tears, and with quivering lip
Said: "Father, why may not I say—
Our Mother in heaven, whene'er I kneel down,
At morning and night to pray?

"Is God only Father? In his mighty heart
Is there throbbing no *Mother* love?
And if I shall see him in heaven so fair,
If I reach to the realms above,
Will God but appear as a strong mighty man?
Oh, tell me, dear father, I pray,
Why manhood is only expressed in our God,
While woman is purest, men say?

"I love you, dear father, you've always been kind,
And dear mother loved you when here,

But mother and father together are best,
  Two parents I want to have here,
And you were so happy when mother was well,
  It seems to me God cannot be
Quite happy in heaven, if he's all alone,
  Ruling worlds by his sovereignty."

The father made answer: "God's word has declared,
  That Jehovah, the God over all,
Is far beyond mortal conception and thought,
  His glory must mortals appal,
Unless they behold him in Jesus, his Son,
  And through him alone can ye trace
The tenderness greater than dear mother's love;
  Some day you will look on his face,
And when you are cleansed from every stain,
  From all earthly foibles set free,
The dear loving Jesus will be to you more
  Than the tenderest mother can be."

"But why," said the child, but half-satisfied yet;
  "Why is Jesus a man, why is he
To be ever expressive of God's inmost heart?
  Why may not my mother, to me—
The one whom I've loved, who has tended me here
  With all love's devotions so free,
Oh, when I'm in heaven, say, shall I not find
  My own mother nearest to me?

"You say that good Jesus atoned for my sin,
  Bore the pain which he bore on the cross,
To redeem me from sorrow and save me from hell,
  But still I remain at a loss
To know, why the Father of Jesus should send
  His Son to this dark world of pain,
That those who had wronged him might, freed from all sin,
  To the heights of his glory attain."

"Oh, child! 'tis a mystery, you must accept
  All that God in the Bible declares,
Or never in heaven, my child, will you sing
  God's praises; for he who dares
To question His Word, or to doubt that the Lord
  Is our Saviour from sin's endless night,
Shall never be found in the Lamb's book of life,
  Or be clothed in garments of white."

The child said no more but betook him to rest,
  He was tired with the heat of the day,
And his poor little brain had been heavily tasked,
  To try to find out God's true way;
His father had baffled him, caused him to doubt,
  When fain he would make him believe,
But the germs of inquiry were rife in his mind,
  And new truth he was nigh to receive.

As he knelt by his bedside alone in the dark,
He prayed that God's Spirit might come,
And reveal to his spirit the truth of the world,
Which his Mother oft told him was home.
He prayed that God's angels, who came in old time
To Joseph, in dead of the night,
Might come also to him, and reveal God's great law,
And into his spirit shed light.

Was he sleeping or dreaming? He never could tell,
Throughout all life's after years;
He only remembers a beautiful form,
Which still often in vision appears.
He thought he was standing on high table land,
Where the spice islands dot all tne seas,
Where bright birds, with gay plumage, incessantly sing,
And melody make with the breeze.
There were hill-tops and valleys, and beautiful lakes,
The sky was than sapphires more blue,
The waters were emerald, sunbeams did shine,
Golden with radiant hue,
Beaming forth on the waters in colours unknown,
Unperceived by the flesh eye of man,
Till the landscape was covered with flowers which spoke,
As a friend speaks to his fellow man.

In the midst of that beauty an angel appeared,
But no wings on her shoulders saw he,
She was guiding a vessel, and onward she steered,
While the children on deck sang with glee;
Till at length, close beside him the ship sank to rest,
And the face of the angel beamed bright,
And when she came closer, and touched his dim eyes,
He beheld her, with spiritual sight,
As his Mother, transfigured, grown young, and grown free
From the wrinkles care traced on her brow,
And she whispered: "My darling, I answer your quest,
Come up into heaven, come now!"

She touched him with pressure more tender and mild,
Than mother on earth ever knew,
She took him on board, and presented him there,
As her son, to her beautiful crew,
Saying, "These are my children, who gathered from earth,
In infancy's earliest bloom,
Need guidance and training in spiritual life;
Look there at those flowers, whose perfume
Makes grateful the atmosphere, they whose bright forms
Are so matchless, so choice and so rare:
These are words, these are letters, in language of heaven,
Their voices sound forth in prayer,
In praise, and in answer; wherever we go
The flowers instruct us in love,
They are all living creatures, have voice of their own,
And their songs make sweet music above."

He saw one bright blossom, more fair than the rest,
Far fairer than flowers of earth,
'Twas a typical flower, which bloometh in heaven,
From breath of the angels its birth
Is perfected through stages of growth, which express
The efflux of heavenly truth.
And that flower is immortal, it sees no decay,
It lives in perpetual youth!

That flower ope'd its petals, disclosing its heart,
And that heart was as white as the snow,
As the white beams of pure light, in perfected ray,
Shines forth from the heavens, aglow
With the light of God's presence, this beautiful flower
Disclosed two hearts blent in one,
Two lives which were blended in perfect accord,
And together they shone as the sun.

The flower said: "You ask me of God and the Soul;
You say: Have I mother in heaven?
God 's father and mother to every child,
To whom his love life has given;
The angels are dual, and God is the same,
For celestial life doth display
The life of God's image, which feebly on earth
Is enshrined in your bodies of clay."

The flower ceased speaking, the boat glided on,
The Mother just kissed her child:
He felt the warm imprint upon his red lips,
He awoke from his dream, and smiled,
And knew that the vision had answered his prayer,
And, henceforth, he knew not doubt's carking care.

BENEDICTION.

May the light of God's perfect Love,
And His Wisdom, eternally kind,
Lead you all to discover His Justice divine,
And to the Eternal Mind.
May your praises for ever and ever flow,
In deeds, thoughts, and words of peace,
Till you reach those fair regions where griefs enter not,
And doubtings forever cease!

AMEN.

XIV.

WHAT IS PROPERTY?

THE subject with which we have to deal this evening, is one of paramount importance to the whole human family. Its importance, indeed, cannot possibly be over-estimated, as the proper distribution of Land lies at the very root of the question,—How can the ever-increasing population of the globe be adequately sustained, or if the increase continues to be as great during the next century as it has been during the past, how can man manage to exist at all?

There are some who think it safe and wise to leave everything blindly in the hands of fate, but these are not the reformers of the world, neither are they the men and women by whose activities the world makes progress. The true reformer is ever a genuine philanthropist; a whole-souled worker for the mass of mankind, caring for the race rather than for a few privileged members of it; therefore, the reformer is ever opposed by those who have vested interests in monopoly, and there are always to be found in abundance those who think their own personal welfare, and that of their offspring, is of so much more importance than that of mankind universally, that they most vigorously oppose every movement which is set on foot for the abolition of partisanship, clannishness, and all other narrow and exclusive frames of mind, which deny the right of all God's creatures to enjoy an equal share in the good gifts provided by the Eternal for all His children.

Of course there are those who believe in the divine right of kings, in the justice of the laws of entail and primogeniture, which yet hold sway in England, and some even go so far as to say that God has ordained some to positions of honour, and others to positions of dishonour in this world, and that it is sacrilegious to try to alter the divine decrees. But in precisely similar ways has slavery been justified, while polygamy has also been upheld as both sanctioned and commanded by the authority of Holy Writ. But advanced thinkers of all schools, in the churches and out of them, are now beginning to regard nothing as sacred or divine which contravenes justice or interferes with the equal rights and liberties of all sections of mankind, and so desperate are the people at large now becoming, that unless rights and liberties be allowed to the multitude, through the adoption of pacific measures, the passing and enforcement of wise, humane, and equitable laws, England will soon be convulsed with as fierce insurrections as have ever desolated any country of Europe.

The entire question of human emancipation from practical slavery—and the slavery of many nominally free-born children in England is worse than the negro slavery of the past—hinges upon a correct and decisive answer being given to the all-important enquiry: What is Property? If Land be Property, if private property in land be permissible and even just, then in course of a very short time, comparatively speaking, very few people will be anything but abject slaves utterly in the power of absolute and tyrannical masters. If land positively belongs to a few wealthy landowners, and these owners of the soil choose to deny all except their own particular favourites to tread upon their ground, then the bulk of mankind will be forced into the air or the water, in neither of which elements they can live, or even should they be allowed to walk the earth on sufferance, by what possible manner of means could they make provision for their simplest and most pressing wants, if they are denied the right to cultivate the land or build upon it?

The present terrible depression in trade all over England is consequent upon land usurpation. The monopoly of thousands of acres of valuable territory by persons who not only do nothing themselves to increase the value of the land to which they lay claim, but who veto the industries of all who improve it, by taxing the working people of the country so heavily for all improvements made, that it is in many instances impossible for persons to continue to live and pay the ever-increasing rates and rents, which go up as fast as the slightest addition is made to the value of the land claimed by nobles and millionaires who have perhaps lived out of England, or, if at home, far away from the scene of those industries which are daily increasing their revenues, though they have done nothing whatever to deserve the addition of a single farthing to their incomes. There is surely something radically wrong in a system which allows property to increase to an unlimited extent for the personal aggrandisement of a few privileged persons, who are the drones, not the workers, in the great hives of human industry; and it is to the finding of a remedy for this disgraceful and dangerous crime, that the Land Nationalization Society has been established in all parts of England.

You have doubtless all read, or at least heard of "Progress and Poverty," and "Social Problems," two very valuable and instructive works from the pen of that earnest American champion of right and liberty, Mr. Henry George. Those works have been, as all such works are sure to be, most severely criticized, and perhaps they are open to criticism in many particulars, and we must, always remembering that no author is final or infallible, regard criticism as a compliment rather than an insult to an honest agitator, for it is the work of every reformer to set people to thinking for themselves, and we are convinced that whatever makes people discuss these great problems, these burning questions of the day, fearlessly and candidly, must lead, and that very soon, to so complete a revolution in popular sentiment with reference to these matters, that if the theme be only kept prominently before the public, the word Property in the next generation will have an entirely different signification to that commonly accepted at the present moment.

Property is necessarily subject to increase, and can increase without loss or injury, and even with constant gain, to those who assist its increase, as well as to the individuals who are said to hold, own, or possess it. Land cannot be property in the same sense in which the results of labour constitute property, because no one by his own exertions can add to land, except to a very small extent. Certainly there is such a thing as "made land" here and there, as may be instanced in the filling in of the Back Bay, in Boston, U.S.A., and the building of palatial residences, gorgeous churches, and imposing public buildings, where a few years ago it was all water. But the immense bulk of land upon the earth was simply found by man, and could in no possible sense be the property of the finder, as nothing can be rightfully any one's property unless it represent the result of his own personal industry. Still, it is quite just and reasonable to admit that all who discover unoccupied or uncultivated land, have a right to take possession of it for building purposes, and have a right to cultivate it for the supply of their necessities. Therefore, property may consist in what is built upon land, and in what is produced by the cultivation of the soil, as every one has a right to the fruit of his own toil, to the reward of his own labour. But the assumption we entirely repudiate is that made by those who claim that land itself belongs to certain individuals, and that these persons have a right to hold it in perfect idleness, that they may practise cruel sport upon it, or simply retain it for their own amusement.

In many instances the land thus claimed has been actually stolen from its original inhabitants, and has been stolen in the most merciless manner, by usurping tyrants who turned it into a hunting ground, after they had pillaged it and driven the dispossessed inhabitants to starvation, or slain them at the point of the sword. The story of the Black Forest, in every child's History of England, tells the story most truly and graphically, of how the land was cruelly wrested from the people, and profligately spoiled by a company of heartless nobles. From some of these dishonest men, people of great gentility and family antiquity boast descent, and when we hear of people's ancestors having "come over with the Conqueror," and how they are numbered among the upper ten thousand, because their ancestors were ruffians who despoiled countries and put whole populations to death, we cannot but mourn for the false heredity and senseless vanity which allows people of any degree of common sense to glory in tracing their descent from men whose boast it was that by the triumph of might over right, by simple brute force and the use of barbarous and bloody weapons, they gained a foothold for themselves and their descendants on land which only became theirs through grossest acts of heartless tyranny and dastardly destruction of the means of others' subsistence.

This, we are told on every hand, is an age of progress, and so it is in mechanical invention and labour-saving appliances; but is not labour often so saved that the saving of labour in many instances means starvation to those who are dependent upon labour for the means of life? Formerly women could earn good wages as seamstresses, and there were many trades and industries at which they could earn a comfortable living, at which they can now scarcely earn a penny. Everything is being done by machinery, and the machine has brought in its trail many a thousand evils, unfelt by your hard-worked though healthy, happy, and sufficiently-fed ancestors.

This is an age of luxury, and the wants of the people seem to be ever on the increase; but does human happiness or the prosperity of the multitude keep pace with this constant increase in visible signs of wealth? Ostentation and display are rife on every hand, but do we not come face to face every day with poverty, the most abject, crime, the most infamous, and misery, the most hopeless? Are not the streets of every town and city throughout the civilized world. pictures of the most frightful contrasts? On the one hand churches, public buildings, mansions vie with each other in magnificence and costliness. Splendidly-appointed carriages roll by filled with the devotees of rank and fashion, while across the way, the beggar covered with rags is as desolate in modern London as was he who lay covered with sores, with no friends but dogs, at the gate of Dives, in an old Oriental centre of mingled luxury and misery.

The great problem of the age is what to do with the ever-increasing number of those who are born, and who continue to exist unclothed, unwashed, unfed, unsheltered. Gospel Temperance Societies, Total Abstinence Leagues, and many other worthy organizations are formed to counteract vice and misery and put down the sin of intemperance, the prolific source of so much misery and so many abominations; but, was Mr. George, when he replied to a question in Leeds, not so very long ago, very wide of the mark when he declared that drunkenness was occasioned by misery and squalor fully as much as misery and squalor were brought on by drunkenness? The root of the matter lies far deeper down than the excrescences upon the surface of society, and while they do well who strive to banish intemperance, they do still better whose views and measures are yet more radical, and who, seeing a deep-seated cause for the manifold evils all reformers unite in bemoaning, and are endeavouring to suppress, are not content with paliative measures, but going to the very root of the matter, find in the Land Question the only real basis for practical, solid and effectual reform.

Dr. Watts was a sound philosopher, when he taught children to sing, that Satan always finds mischief for idle hands to do. He needs to preach to the sentimental advocates of indiscriminate almsgiving to-day, who, while supporting the lazaroni, who make begging a profession, are also supporting the public houses far more than they support the poor. We do not wish to suppress any natural and spontaneous outburst of charity which any kind-hearted person, touched with sympathy at the sight of human woes, may feel. We do not say, never throw a penny to a beggar in the street, or give a gratuity to an itinerant musician; very often the poor are forced into the streets to beg and sing, because they can get no work to do, while they are both able and willing to work; but work is scarce, wages are low, and labourers are plentiful. Thus, many who would fain work, must either beg or starve; but as discretion is the better part of valour, and we all admire bravery and account it a virtue, though in these days it is not the only or even the highest virtue, as it was among the ancient Romans and the old Latin races, who had only one word for virtue and bravery, as there were not two ideas but only one to express, even charity may not be the less beautiful or sincere, because it is discriminating and has a brain as well as a heart. The goddess Love need not be blind or thoughtless, in order to retain her sweetness, her gentleness, and her poetry. She may well lose the mawkish sentimentality in which she often disguises and disfigures herself, but when people, who are really kind-hearted, add to their sympathy common sense, sound judgment, and real work for the poor, charity will not be the enervated, crippled goddess she often appears to-day, provoking a sneer rather than applause from many, who though they do not wear their hearts upon their sleeves for every daw to peck at, are nevertheless sound, practical, political economists, who though not characterized by sentimentality, are keenly alive to the sorrows of the world, and do all in their power to remove them.

We can never confine ourselves to the advocacy of any one system of reform, when we see so many springing up around us, all proceeding from sincere good will to mankind and earnest effort for the improvement of the race; but if there is one scheme more important than all the rest, it is the Nationalization of the Land, as this scheme enters into the cause of direct suffering, and while aiming at the immediate relief of present distress, as do all other and less radical measures, it aims also at preventing a recurrence of these disasters in the next generation.

Work is the sovereign remedy for every ill. Labour, which occasions suffering and painful exhaustion, may be traceable to the transgression of a divine law, or to human imperfection; but work itself is divine. All religions picture an active God, and all who tell of angels speak of them as busy as well as happy beings. Every child is born with a love of occupation, and no system of school education or home training is anything like complete, or even praiseworthy or worthy of recommendation, unless it makes provision for the employment of every faculty of mind and body. Mischief is the misdirection of energy. Never aim at the annihilation or suppression of a faculty, taste, appetite, or talent, but aim at harmony in the use of all. Aim at symmetrical unfoldment, aim at roundness of character, and remember that everybody is good for something, and, given a fair chance, every one may become useful if not great.)

Mrs. Weldon, whose name is now a household work to all readers of the daily newspapers, when conducting an orphanage, entirely her own enterprise, some years ago in London, says she found every child who could be picked up in the gutter good for something; and that brave, philanthropic and cultured lady, who loves children and makes them love her, has discovered means for calling forth their latent powers, so that every one may be an ornament to society, if his or her education is only persevered with.

Some reformers are Malthusians, and see no other way of limiting distress than by limiting the population, and while we are quite ready to admit that in the present state of society many children are born only to grow up as criminals and sufferers, we do not anticipate any evil from the birth of any number of sound, healthy children who, coming from good parents, and being themselves well educated, shall be able to fill useful and honourable places in society. The population of Great Britain, without Ireland, at the present time is about thirty millions in round numbers, and it has been computed that were it ninety millions, the country would be quite large enough to sustain the people were the land properly distributed and cultivated, and were monopolies abolished and political rings broken up. In America the land can sustain twenty times its present population, and then not be at all overcrowded. Australia, amply large enough to sustain hundreds of millions, is now occupied by just a few millions of Anglo-Saxons and a handful of Aborigines. The land, not yet under cultivation in the British colonies and dependencies, can be made to sustain so great a number of persons in comfort and even affluence, that the overpopulation of the world is something so remote that it is quite useless even to discuss it. But unless the Land Question is decided, and that very swiftly, the world will be practically overpeopled with perhaps a twentieth part of the number which could be easily sustained, without any further improvements in agriculture or the practise of any superior economy than that which already prevails.

Turn where you will, and you are on somebody's land. Someone has set up a claim to private property in the very earth you tread, therefore, you are on that land by permission or on sufferance. It is not your own, and should you improve it entirely at your own expense, the bulk of remuneration would not go to you, who are the active, and, indeed, sole cause of the bettered condition of that spot of earth. The revenue derived from your labour increases the rent-roll of your landlord, who is very likely, at the present moment, on the Continent, spending his money abroad, and not adding even to the support of trade in his native country, or in any manner to the wealth and prosperity of the people whose earnings he is squandering on selfish luxury, at some fashionable haunt of dissipation abroad.

One of the greatest and loudest outcries against oppressive landlordism in Ireland, began with the protest against the Irish land-owner exacting higher and higher rents from Irish farmers, because they, his tenantry, improved the land, while he squandered their earnings abroad, and had a larger profit every year, if they were only industrious enough to keep on improving his property. Had they received the use of the land, with the understanding that improvements were to be accepted in lieu of rent, the scheme might have been fair enough, and have been an incentive to the tenants to work; but who cares to improve land to fill fuller still the already overfilled coffers of some peer or landlord, who cares nothing whatever for his tenantry, and appoints bailiffs and stewards to enforce extortionate rents, and evict all tenants who cannot meet his disgraceful demands? (Do you wonder at the present disorganized and dangerous condition of Ireland? Blame the Land League, and Mr. Parnell, if you will;

protest with all your might and main against the iniquitous outrages which the infuriated Celt has resorted to in his desperation, but be not hard on the sinner whom injustice has turned into a criminal, and then let the original offender receive your compassion and laudation, while you condemn to imprisonment, or even death, the lawless champion of freedom, who, though acting ever so rashly and unwisely, is still, in his rude way, uttering his protest against that tyranny and oppression, which you all, as Englishmen, affect to hate.

Home Rule may not be the means of saving Ireland, even if it is obtained. England has Home Rule, but here the condition of many of the working people, and of paupers generally, is little better than in Ireland. England has not been desolated by famine so much as Ireland. Englishmen are not quite so improvident and impetuous as Irishmen, but if things go on for another fifty years in England as they are going now, England will be the scene of as much fighting and desolation as Ireland is the scene of at the present moment.

America has Home Rule, and yet across the Atlantic the self same evils are threatening the nation of the United States, as are threatening England. There the Stewarts, the Vanderbilts and other monopolists and millionaires, are fast buying up all the available land, and if they are ever induced to sell, though they buy cheap, they are determined to sell dear, and, by controlling the stock markets, are the means of bringing frequent panics upon the country. These panics, of course, mean suffering to multitudes of innocent persons, and though these men are spoken of in many avowedly Christian circles as honourable and religious gentlemen, no thief or highway robber can really be more dishonest than he who, taking advantage of his neighbour's necessity, compels him to pay an extortionate duty upon the very necessaries of life, as is the case when railroads are under the control of individual monopolists. Rates of passenger travel and freight transportation are regulated by the arbitrary decree of the man or men to whom not only the railroad property, but the land through which the trains pass, belongs. By controlling railroads and steamships, freight can only be transported if the owner of the means of transportation gives leave, and his permission gained, he charges whatever he thinks fit. This makes the necessaries of life extremely dear.

Therefore, in the Eastern States, Western produce can only be obtained at fabulous prices, and though the States are nominally united, the monopolist does all he can to keep the union a fact in name only.

Co-operation has been suggested as the sovereign remedy for all these ills. Societary *versus* individual property has been advocated, as peasant proprietary in land has been suggested by many as the true solvent of the land difficulty. Now, as to co-operation, theoretically it is irreproachable. The ideal co-operative schemes, of which we hear so much, are well nigh perfect. So were the Owens' communistic plans, and the failure of either Co-operation or Communism, in an actualized state of society, is due, not to an error in the ideal system, but in the means of carrying it out. There is a danger everywhere from the tendency of large organizations soon coming under the dictation of a very few wealthy and influential men, and these are considered, by the country at large, extremely important because of their wealth. No matter how they got it, the vote of a man of immense capital is worth more, in the eyes of all aspirants to political power, than that of a labourer.

Make all votes of equal value, establish manhood, yea, and womanhood suffrage, too, and if there be evils accruing to the nation at first, from the adoption of so broad and liberal a policy, these evils will be but the excrescences by means of which the bad blood of the nation, the virus which innoculated its veins in the old feudal times, and has been lurking as a deadly poison within ever since, will be thrust forth; as the agitation, and even revolution, consequent upon the franchise, cannot be permanent, though for a while a sudden accession of liberty sweeps down like an avalanche upon the land, and the timid fear for the future, not knowing that the turmoil of the present is but the harbinger of happier and more peaceful days.

Co-operation, independent of officialism and party strife, will be a fact so soon as the great mass of men and women find it to their interest to club together, and stand shoulder to shoulder as one man, against a common foe. While individuals cannot easily become large capitalists, except in very rare instances, the accumulated and united capital of a multitude can be a power sufficient to offset that of any and every millionaire.

Now, should the great People arise in their might, and determine to counteract the existing evils, they must compete with the monopolies of the day, and can do so provided they can trust one another, and work together as partners in a common firm. A railroad built and managed as the property of a million, controlled by representatives chosen from the people, might leave undisturbed the manœuvres of monopolists, and yet at a cheap rate do all the business of the country, and leave the monopolists' enterprise to sink or swim as best it might. But the great question which arises is—How shall the people get possession of the land whereon to build and create wealth? For nothing can be done without land, and that is fast disappearing even from those who are ready to pay a fair price for it. It is in the hands of an ever-narrowing few, who hold it with a death grip, and who are starving the million to support the handful.

There is at present an old land tax of four shillings in the pound on all English land, a mere fraction of which is now paid. Enforce that tax as a step towards the absolute nationalization of the land, and the burden of taxation will fall, not upon those who make good, but bad, or no use of their property. If four shillings in the pound should be the tax levied upon the justly-estimated value of land all over the country, then those whose land was of little or no use to them need not pay the tax: they could at once allow it to become the property of the Government. Those who cultivated land, and built upon it, would be the means of employing many who are now idlers, able and willing to work, but without employment or the means of subsistence. Houses would become more plentiful, food would be cheaper, clothes would find purchasers, and by the proper employment of the unoccupied thousands, strikes and panics would be averted, and the country saved, and all through the settlement of the land difficulty. No one should be allowed to claim what he does not employ for the general good, and no one should be permitted to so underpay labourers as to allow the rich to be ever growing richer, while the poor are ever becoming poorer.

Peasant Proprietary has been suggested as a means of settling all the present embarrassing and pressing questions with reference to land, but while peasant proprietary may be an ameliorative or palliative measure, it does not partake of the nature of a radical reform. It would temporarily reduce the evil, it would allay some immediate distress, it would split up vast estates and farms into many small ones, but it does not propose a radical change in the present system of land proprietorship. Private property in land is admitted by the peasant proprietor as much as by the wealthiest earl or duke, while the advocates of peasant proprietary, of course, cannot object on principle to the ownership of land by individuals, and until we clearly understand the injustice of any claim to the ownership of land, we shall not have solved our problem or settled our dispute.

The Peasant Proprietor says he has laboured hard to possess himself of a small estate, which he shall be able to bequeath to his children after him, and he asks, very naturally—Have I not a right to do what I will with my own, and is not that my own for which I have industriously laboured, year after year? Is that which I have earned to be taken from me? Am I to forfeit everything, and see my property distributed among the multitude? Our answer is—You can never have worked for or earned land, though you may by your own industries have rendered land valuable which was comparatively worthless before you took it in hand. You may have procured the right to the fruitage of certain acres of ground and to the buildings upon it, but the land itself does not belong to you, merely because you have discovered it, or brought forth its latent powers, causing it to yield a luxuriant harvest. But if you, possessed of this land as you think justly, should be compelled to deliver it up to the Nation, you must of course claim and receive compensation for what is reasonably your own. The Nation, or the State, having the right to take the land, has not the right to grasp the fruit of your toil. Now, you did not make the land, therefore, it is not yours. The ground is the property of God, and you did not buy it of the Creator. It has been decreed to you by no special gift from Him. The land belongs to all men equally. The Creator has given it to the inhabitants of the earth, without favour or restriction, and no one person can possibly say he has a greater right to land than another has.

But how will you divide the land from the results of the labour which has made it fruitful? How will you separate between the property of the man from whom you take the land, and the land itself? The answer, to us, is very simple. If the State takes your land as it is, with all the improvements or buildings upon it, which are results of your industry, you must be compensated for all that is yours; as the State has no right with anything except the land itself. An offer may be made to you to retain possession of the land, by payment of ground rent to the State. You must pay your tax on the land instead of on the property, and we do not think if the taxation were shifted, if you were all obliged to pay for using land because the land is national not private property, and were then excused from all tax upon legitimate private property, that any one of you would be injured. A reasonable scheme of land nationalization merely forces all persons to pay the public for the use of land, which is public property, but does not extort money from any one because he improves the land, and thereby cheapens the commodities of life, and by increasing lawful competition benefits the entire community.

Now, the immediate advantages of land nationalization would surely be these. The nation claiming the land, but not its produce or the buildings erected upon it, would compel all who keep land idle, as pleasure or hunting ground, to pay dearly for the privilege of playing dog-in-the-manger, or devoting some of the best parts of the country to purposes of cruel sport. Fox-hunting, grouse and pigeon-shooting, and other sports indulged in by the nobility and landed gentry, are surely of no use to the country, and why should a privileged few be allowed to amuse themselves at the nation's expense, without paying, and that pretty dearly, for the privilege. Suppose the land tax of four shillings in the pound were rigorously enforced in every case, on the evenly estimated value of land, and the valuation were determined and fixed at a uniform rate by the chosen representatives of the people, assembled in convocation, then if any chose to pay this tax, they would be pouring into the nation's coffers an amount of wealth by no means inconsiderable, which could at once be utilized in many schemes of improvement. But those who make no use of land at all, and really receive no enjoyment from the nominal possession of it, would surely, in most instances, deliver it up to the nation, or else improve it or build upon it.

Now, if it were improved, cultivated, built upon, these

works could not be undertaken without the employment of a large number of men to do the necessary work. As the land became fruitful or covered with houses, which could be sold or rented, the wealth of the country would positively increase, as wealth is created by labour, and the enrichment of the masses does not necessarily mean the impoverishment of any body. If land cannot be added to at will, while capital can be increased by labour to a practically unlimited degree. as all property was originally the result of labour, we do not see that any one needs to suffer by the nation's claiming the land. If those who are now holding it unoccupied shall be obliged to pay the nation for their tenure of it, they will simply be forced to make it productive, or in some way remunerative, that they may still afford to hold it; and by making it fruitful, or building upon it, they enrich the nation, and have an opportunity of enriching themselves also, as labour creates capital, thereby adding to the wealth of all who work or furnish the means for the carrying on of any industry.

If this land tax were at once rigorously enforced in every instance, a very large amount of land would at once be given up, and that land could be utilized in providing bread for the starving millions, and clothing for the multitudes who now go naked in the streets. We want more houses, more clothing for the masses. Hundreds of miserable creatures are huddled together in foul, unhealthy tenements; thousands go supperless to bed, and starve in nakedness in the streets, while the cry is everywhere, that the warehouses are overstocked, that work can only be allowed half-time, that England is producing more than she can consume. Labourers and workmen of all trades are striking for higher wages. Many mills and factories are only working half-time, and others are closed altogether. A general panic seems imminent, unless some radical plan is at once devised and carried into execution for the remunerative employment of the masses.

England does not produce too much, she produces too little. Every unlet house is required as a home for many who are homeless, every unsold yard of cotton or linen stuff is needed absolutely, imperatively demanded, to cover the almost naked limbs of the many who wander from place to place without rags to cover their nakedness. The present condition of

England is as bad as that of old Rome ere she fell, and unless England be warned and repent in time, her place among the nations will know her no more. She will miserably perish, as did the great nations of the old world, who, when they were priding themselves upon their greatness, fell, not from the attacks of Goths and Vandals who swooped down upon them from the North like vultures eager for their prey, but because the plebians were many and the land was not theirs; they would not fight for the masters, who oppressed them in times of peace, and commanded them to take up arms against the invader in times of war. The patricians dug their graves with their own hands, they pulled down their houses about their own ears, and when they fell, the free world rejoiced as it ever must over the downfall of a tyrant.

If England were besieged to-day, how would she sustain herself, in the present disaffected condition of her children? Where would that union be found, which alone secures invincibility? England has so many vipers hugged close to her bosom, that she needs to set matters straight at home before she arouses the ire of all lovers of peace and justice, by seeking to add to her foreign dominion by aggression and bloodshed. The war with Egypt is a miserable fiasco, a wretched burlesque, calling forth the contempt and ridicule of all onlookers. England's present condition is not what it was in the eyes of other nations, and should the time arrive when England shall again become the scene of bloody conflict, how will she sustain herself, how breast the storm which even now seems gathering thick about her? There is but one means of prevention for coming disasters, but one means of securing to England a great and noble place and name in the annals of future history, that is—make Englishmen a unit, let the masses be so employed and remunerated that England becomes self-sustaining, not longer so miserably dependent as she now is on foreign countries; and this can be done in the course of a few short years, solely by employing her own subjects upon the land which now lies idle, and relieving the masses from the terrific burden of supporting a few land-owners in luxury, while the million starves as soon as it can no longer work, or starves, as is in many instances the case, while it is able and willing to work, but can get no work to do.

You will perceive that the scheme which we propose is

both an equitable and simple one; it is, moreover, a very practical and easy one. We do not wildly and quixotically propose to divide the land into as many pieces as there are inhabitants, and then give each individual a share. We propose to make the nation itself the steward of all the land, then if you wish to hire land the State is your landlord. You pay for the use of the land you occupy, not to a private individual, but to the nation, in the persons of its chosen representatives, who are bound to employ the national capital in national improvement. To-day the multitudes are working for tyrannical masters, many of whom hoard their wealth or squander it abroad. If you work for the State you work really for yourselves. The governors must be elected by you; they must represent you and use the money you contribute to the general fund for public improvement. Thus can the nation support itself, and you have no taxes to pay nor higher rents, because you are industrious and use the land. You pay for the use of land, if you claim it, whether you use it or not. If you cannot afford to hold it in idleness, you must employ it, and by employing it you benefit all who work for you, and increase your own revenue into the bargain.

Every one knows that if a thousand or a million able-bodied, skilful men should take possession of some unoccupied ground, and build upon it and make it fruitful, they would be adding to the wealth of mankind, without robbing anybody of a penny; and as this has been done abroad, and is still being done in the Colonies and Western States of America, why not turn the estates now lying idle into habitable and productive ground? By employing under Government a large number of workmen, who would work for the State instead of the individual employer, and be well paid for their labour, what results would accrue to the nation at large? Why, very shortly all the unbought goods in the warehouses would be upon the backs of those who at present are almost naked; work would become more plentiful and wages higher; the demand and supply would alike increase, and by this simple addition to the amount of work in demand, a panic would be averted, strikes would die out, and the working people would become self-supporting, and more, they would earn enough to live in comfort, and to make provision for a rainy day.

If parents can take care of their children and educate them, let them do so, but in cases where children are brought up to beg and steal, and have no proper homes, the State might well step in (or better, private parties), and see that no child is allowed to grow up without an education, enabling him or her to earn an honest living at some useful trade.

We believe in the sanctity of Home as much as any one; we advocate independence and self-ownership as much as any; we do not believe in an abstract State swallowing up all individual homes and property, though the time will come when communism will be rendered practicable, and be found the highest state of society;—all we ask for now is that the one who works may have the benefit of his labour; that no dogs-in-the-manger be caressed; that justice reign supreme; and no one be allowed an undue advantage over his neighbour.

In these few and imperfect suggestions for the nationalization of land, we know we have not gone sufficiently into detail to make our views clearly intelligible to all; but in a single lecture, that is, of course, impossible. What we have said has been said merely in the hope of inducing you all to consider this great question, and to place before you our honest conviction as to what may and should be done, and that without delay, to minimize distress, and at length remove it from the globe.

IMPROMPTU POEM.

THE CRY FOR BREAD.

WHY are the children hungry? They cry for bread in the street;
Surely the earth produces enough for them all to eat!
I have seen the loaded fruit-trees, in the orchards all so fair,
I have gazed on the golden corn-fields, and, on resounding air,
Have heard the song of feasters, and seen them cast away
The bread, for which men perish in many a street each day!

Why are the children naked, or covered but in rags?
Why do they wander sadly? While each one lamely drags
His tired form from door to door, and through the bustling streets,
Petitions, with heart-rending cry, of every one he meets,—

Oh! buy my pretty flowers, all withering in the sun;
But if he cannot sell them, then, when the day is done,
He sleeps within some shelter, so hard, and cold, and rude,
Or, left out in the dreary streets, he starves for lack of food.

Why are the people homeless? since there are mansions fair,
Unoccupied, yet beauteous, and gardens sweet and rare,
Where flowers bloom but none see them, for high walls built around,
Fence in these sacred precincts, where luxuries abound:
The children freeze and hunger, the women faint and die,
With weary babes pressed to their breasts, in want and misery!

Shall no one feed the children, take off the beggar's rags?
Is charity so tardy that every day she lags;
While death and sorrow increase, while land lies idle still,
That the noble may but own it, though it should the peasant kill?

Have ye no homes made ready, to invite the children in?
Have ye no schools to teach them to build, to knit, to spin?
Have ye no food to give them—those waifs along life's way—
Those foundlings, whom the city swallows like beasts of prey.

Are there no empty homesteads, where children could shed light?
Are there none, tender-hearted, who'd make their own lives bright,
If they would take the children and lead them in the way—
The path of honest labour—which brings the triumph day?

The cry for bread goes upward; the angels hear the cry;
And when the children perish in want and misery;
Their loving arms embrace them, their loving voices cheer,
And the angels draw to heaven those who on earth are drear.

Are there no angels dwelling upon the earth to-day,
Embodied here among you, to drive this curse away;
This dreadful curse of hunger, this poverty so dread:
Are there no means of succour; can the children ne'er be fed?
The Angel of the Earth declares, that it can render bread
For all the starving millions: then raise such food, we pray,
By dint of honest labour, that all have enough each day!

If mighty lords and ladies control the land of God,
If wealth stalks by in purple, while pressed against the sod,
Are the weary forms and faces of those who long to die,
Workless and wealthless, striving in ceaseless misery;
Then pass good laws, we pray you, that all may sow and reap,
That all, through honest labour, may smile where now they weep.

Let loving justice guide you, let love for all mankind
Direct your every measure, till laws become refined
From ancient, feudal cringing to nobles, but in name;
Take ye the rich, broad acres which now the proud lords claim,
Take them by legislation, by voice, which raised for right,
Clamours for Justice only, for Freedom's pure delight!

Take all that now lies idle: there build, there reap, there sow
For future generations plant good seed, that will grow,
And call that man the noblest, who truthfully can boast,
That his work is the bravest, and does of good the most.

The barren lands rejoicing, the wilderness will sing,
Where now the cooped-up children, in dens which miseries bring,
Playing in fields and meadows, breathing the country air,
Eating the bread of honest toil, these will full shortly share
The blessings God is ready to freely shower on all,
Delay not to obey it—the spirit's urgent call;
But go ye and deal justly, let loving justice guide,
And the laws that are most loving, most stable will abide.

BENEDICTION.

May the light of love, so brightly,
Shine on your every way,
That darkness, injustice, and wrong,
Like clouds shall pass away,
Before the rising brightness
Of the sun of the New Day,
Which rises (healing in its wings)
To drive all want away!

AMEN.

XV.

TRUE SPIRITUAL MARRIAGE.

THE question of Marriage, is one ever recurring, ever interesting, ever important, as marriage is essential to the constitution of home and the rearing of offspring; and as you all very well know, the sanctity of home invaded, children neglected, the true union of man and woman annulled, necessarily leads to the disintegration of society, the destruction and overthrow of all that is most worth preserving in the social order. But a question may well be asked, and that is—Whether the prevailing ideas of the marriage covenant are the highest conceivable, or whether, in a further advanced and more perfect state of human society, the marriage union may not be one of greater solidity and felicity than it ordinarily is at present?

(Unquestionably, Marriage is both a divine and natural institution. The union of one man with one woman is ever higher than polygamy, as it approaches nearer to the divine ideal of celestial union, which union is nothing less than the perfect blending of the two halves of one soul, in the perfect bliss of angelic association for eternity.

Swedenborg, when discoursing upon the loves of the angels and describing the married state in heaven, declares that angels are dual beings; that the highest degree of life attainable in this direction, is that marriage of the individual which makes two one. Within the human soul itself this union is consummated, and to this Jesus doubtless alluded when he said, that in the resurrection they would neither marry nor be given in marriage, but would be as the angels. This allusion to angelhood would be meaningless and vague, unless those addressed were familiar with the idea of angelhood, and knew what the teacher meant when he said, that all who participated in the blessedness of the resurrection would be as the angels.

The word angel, of course, literally and simply means a

minister or messenger, and it is said in the Psalms, that angels are spirits; in the Apocalypse angels are mentioned as having charge over the seven churches of Asia; and there are those who so interpret the angel in that connection, that they ordain ministers to take charge of congregations, and call them angels, as is the custom among the followers of Edward Irving, the highest minister in the "Catholic Apostolic Church" being designated an angel. This interpretation may be in no sense erroneous, as an angel certainly does mean an exalted minister and a divine messenger, and when in its highest sense it is used to designate those who in spirit-life have attained to the celestial degree, it signifies those who, having completely conquered every material temptation, and learned every lesson earthly experience can teach, no more require the discipline of earthly suffering and pain, neither the sorrows and separations, which may be encountered in spirit-life, until the spirit has become quite delivered from the bondage of all earthward desires and inclinations.

Plato, alluding to the inmost soul of man, declares that the soul itself is dual, and therefore no human life, as expressed on earth to-day, expresses more than half the primal life of spirit. Thus a soul is two spirits, as a globe is two hemispheres, and on account of this division of the soul on earth, it is not good for man to be alone. Every human life seeks companionship, all desire the complement to themselves, and this perpetual longing for companionship evidences the fact of the soul not being perfect upon the earth. Merely earthly unions are for time only, but that marriage which is the best you are capable of making at a given time, may serve a useful purpose in time, though no place can be given to it in eternity. Those companions, with whom you may have pleasantly and peacefully passed a portion of your earthly lifetime, may greet you as dear friends in spirit life, but the earthly partner there may not be the conjugal mate.

No earthly law can bind except for time, no ordinance or statute of the Church or State refers to the life beyond the grave. Thus the minister of religion or the civil magistrate, pronouncing the marriage blessing over the husband and wife at the altar, can declare no further than that the union, which is there and then consummated, may last until death parts. Even the Church of Rome, most inexorable in the tying of the marriage knot, not permitting of divorce, allows widows and widowers to marry again. If the Church sanctions second marriages, and yet believes in immortality, evidently the Pope himself admits that the marriage covenant on earth is a covenant for time only; and if any one reads the introduction to the marriage service in the Church of England Prayer-book, he will soon discover that that church has no idea whatever of the perpetuation of earthly union in the immortal world. Nevertheless, the Gospel says, that those whom God has joined together no man can put asunder. If the Church has joined you, the Church can divorce you, if the State has united you, the State can separate you. But if your union be a union made by the Eternal, then no earthly power, civil or ecclesiastical, has power to break the bond.

We have often alluded in your hearing, to the soul's priority to the material form, and have told you that the soul's consciousness, not ending with the animation of the body, has not begun with it, and is certainly not derived from it. The soul unembodied, in the paradise from which you came to earth, in that scarce-remembered home where you dwelt before matter attracted you to the earth, and caused you to take on a physical embodiment, was pure as the snow as yet unfallen, unsullied as the water from the clearest spring, ere yet it has encountered the dust of earth.

The old-time fable of primeval paradise, the Eden state of humanity unfallen, portrays in glowing Oriental allegory the purity and peace of the primal home of souls. The Soul itself, both primal and absolute, a unit of life, imperishable and uncreated, ancient as the Divine Mind, immortal as the Eternal Spirit, prior to assuming a material form dwelt as a perfect globe or ultimate atom of life, in that paradise of which the poets speak. When Schiller speaks of his spirit's reminiscences, when Shelley speaks of trailing clouds of glory accompanying the spirit earthward from its primal home,—these poets sing of that pure life of innocence and peace, which souls have left to tread the troubled round of earthly being.

Some ask—Why should the spirit fall? But then—Why should the seed be planted? Why should the infant lose the innocence of babyhood, and with maturity encounter the storms of earth, and buffet with the billows of a thousand ills and dangers? As every possibility of future glory is embedded in the tiny seed implanted in the ground, as only what is involved in the typal germ can be outwrought through evolution in the full-fledged blossom, as the acorn enshrines, though latently, every possibility of the oak's fruition, so every babe holds in his inmost life every promise of manhood, womanhood and angelhood, which shall ever burst forth from out the infant being, as it progresses towards the perfection of eternal life.

Darwin may boast of having found the law of evolution, Spencer may follow him along his labyrinthine path, and seek the soul imprisoned in the dust, as though the dust first gave it birth. All the scientists, which the earth has ever produced, may enquire of protoplasm, of animalcules, of the lowest signs of vitality on earth, but the dust will never unravel the mysteries of Spirit, no material combinations evolve intelligence, no "evoluted" outward forms can ever prove the origin of spirit, though each one may register some attainment of the soul, which on its outward journey has fashioned the monad ere it formed the duad, and the jelly-fish and monkey ere the earth was ripe for man. Then when human life appeared, one half the soul was embodied in the form of man, the other in the form of woman.

The Spirit of God, working through all the processes of nature, formed man (humanity) at first, both male and female. How many human beings were first formed, or where they first appeared, the records do not say, but Genesis declares, when God made human life in the image of the Deity, he made that life both male and female. When first the soul approaches earth, the soul divides, and the philosophy of counterparts is, that one spirit is but half the soul. The two halves seek each other through earthly life, and through the spheres, until at length the celestial union is attained. The two discover that they are but one, and in the bliss of life eternal there is neither male nor female, but the perfect life in which the two are one.

Paul, writing to the Galatians, says, "In Christ there is neither male nor female," meaning that the divine life, and that of humanity perfected, is not single but dual; and when in Genesis God speaks to God, or angel speak to angel, saying, Let us make the human race in our image and after our likeness,—the allusion is to the duality of life. The half of the soul addresses the other, and in that is expressed the true duality, which is the perfect unity of God. King David said, whenever he should wake up in God's likeness, he would be satisfied; and no soul is satisfied before the celestial marriage, for nothing short of it contents the spirit, and only to the extent that earthly unions resemble the divine, are they felicitous or spiritually lawful and enduring.

We do not deny that many unions upon earth are spiritually lawful and accomplish good, even though they may not be eternal. All human acts on earth can be but relatively right, as only a relative amount of light is given to earth's children, and if when at the marriage altar you can say to the man beside you—This man I love more than all others; I have singled him out from his fellows to be my spouse, not because of rank or wealth, but because of the love I bear him,—then your husband is such to you in more than name. But if for gold or lands you shall allow the form of marriage, submit to the outer rite, while the heart is a stranger to the ceremony, then though your bridal array be ever so pure, and you conform ever so perfectly to the laws of man, your marriage is but mockery in the sight of heaven. The earthly law is not clairvoyant, its representatives have not the power to read the heart, therefore earthly ordinances are often unavailing in the sight of heaven, because they are but cloaks, disguises, resorted to to cover shame and wrong.

No one can positively foretell the future, no one can know all that is in store for him. The best may be deceived, or may unconsciously, unwillingly deceive themselves: and if you find you have made a mistake, you are not a sinner; you are free from blame if the mistake be nothing more. Thus we do not say that all unhappy marriages began in sin or wilful deceit, but if they were free from this dishonour, they certainly took rise in ignorance, and can be nothing higher than painful and humiliating experiences, needed, to teach the spirit which passes through them, lessons which can be learned successfully in no other school than that of such experiences as these, painful though they be.

Those, who make such mistakes unconsciously, deserve pity, not censure. They suffer quite sufficiently in their own lives, without having to encounter the jibes and jeers and condemnations of their pharisaical accusers. Even if adultery be committed, the policy Jesus adopted was not to curse the sinner, but to seek her reformation. If those who follow

Jesus nominally would follow him in reality, instead of recrimination and abuse we should hear of sympathy and kindly exhortation, not condonence with iniquity, but the helping hand outstretched to enlighten the benighted and reform the evil doer.

Angels never indulge in harsh invective, they never censure those who are not as pure as they are themselves, for well they know that censure only drives the sinners deeper and deeper into the pit of degradation. Those who draw in their skirts and pass by on the other side, considering themselves too holy even to touch the garments of a fallen sister, may be the very first to fall when temptation is presented to them; while those who have risen superior to it, can afford to sympathize and uplift, not dreading the contagion of another's vice, then can safely seek the reformation of the offender.

The present deplorable condition of morals, both public and private, in all centres of modern culture, is due not only to the weakness of human nature, as is often said, but in very large degree to the extremely faulty and incomplete training of girls. This defect in their education, coupled with the false notions of woman's rightful sphere, instilled into the minds of girls almost from infancy, is one of the most fruitful causes of woman's degradation, where vice flaunts itself unblushingly in the streets of all your towns and cities.

Man is styled the lord of creation, woman is to be his vassal, the creature of his will, the child of his caprice. the toy that he may play with to-day and ruin to-morrow. The man who blasts a woman's name, deceives her when she has confided in his honour, is said to have been "indiscreet." He "sowed wild oats" in youth, but all men are alike. He is received with honour in society. He may pick his bride from among the fairest in the land. He may lead a spotless virgin in her teens to the hymenial altar, and is considered a suitable partner for the flower of some illustrious flock of pure and trusting maidens; while the woman whom he has deceived, whose life he has cruelly blasted, is no fit company for such honourable gentlemen as he.

Far be it from us to wish to degrade women to the level of fashionable society men; far be it from us to do other than seek to secure in its fullest beauty the purity of woman; but, in common justice, let there be but one law for man and woman, and let not that be accounted excusable in the stronger which is condemned as inexcusable in the weaker vessel.

According to the present law, woman is inferior to man, no matter what her mental power or moral excellence may be. Because she is a woman, she is therefore man's inferior. A drunken and illiterate man of brutal habits enjoys the franchise; he can go to the polls and assist in electing a member of Parliament, or a member of the Senate, but should a woman be ever so talented, ever so worthy, ever so qualified to vote intelligently, she must be denied a voice in the affairs of State, merely because she is a woman.

It is both nonsensical and unjust for the opponents of Woman Suffrage to say that woman's rightful place is home; it is equally unjust to deny the ballot to all women, because some say they do not want it. Some men do not vote, and no one can compel them, but suffrage rightfully considered is a duty as well as a privilege, and as right laws affect women as much as men, and women can earn property as well as men through their own industry, what can possibly be a grosser injustice than taxation without representation?

Of course, if women prove themselves incompetent for certain kinds of work, now undertaken by men only, those particular fields of labour must ever be the scene of man's undivided operations. Truly, woman does not go to battle, and is not often fitted for a soldier's life, still there have been women who, like Joan of Arc, have headed armies and displayed a bravery on the field of battle, which if man could imitate he has never been known to surpass. But we have had too much of warfare; we need not to deify those who can excel only in works of slaughter. It is not he who drives the knife into his brother or shoots him dead with a revolver or slays him on the battle field, who will be accounted worthy of renown in coming days.

It is Bright, the advocate of peace, who, even more than Gladstone, powerful and eloquent though he be, is looked up to as the greatest statesman of the times, by those whose spiritual vision is least beclouded. The altars of gods of war are fast falling into decay. It is not the god of battles who is adored by the most refined and spiritual of earth's inhabitants to-day. Thus woman's disinclination for cruel sports and cruel battle, will be her passport to honour in the coming days, for she who renders strife impossible, is surely greater than he who engenders it.

It is to woman that all the world looks, as the bringer-forth of the Redeemer. A virgin must conceive, and bear a son, and call his name Emmanuel, which means God with us. The virgin-mother of Christ, Mary immaculate, brought forth a sinless babe, according to the records, and because of the purity of her conception it was styled miraculous. A miracle, indeed, it must have been, if ever wife or maiden brought forth a child unpolluted with hereditary taint, in the days when Israel, sunk in degradation, was a vassal of the profligate and declining Roman Empire! Not to be wondered at, is it, that a legend passing strange was woven around the history of so remarkable a mother and her child.

But whenever an unusually-divine result has been obtained, the world has attributed it to a miracle, deeming it necessary that the laws of nature should be set aside, that a child should be born without the stain of sin. But it is not obedience to the law, but disobedience thereunto, which brings sin and sorrow to the world. God's laws, the laws of nature, are not themselves impure, and when the time shall have arrived that they are thoroughly obeyed, every birth will be a divine incarnation, every mother will be pure as unpolluted maid, and God's sons and daughters will people the earth, and life celestial shall at length be ultimated upon earth.

The dreams of sage, poet and prophet, concerning the Golden Age, are not too bright and hopeful to be real. No picture of the future of the world is any too highly coloured. Isaiah's prediction of the perfect people, whose swords are converted into plough-shares and into pruning hooks, will yet be perfectly fulfilled; and when that day shall dawn, the age of harmony shall be heralded by such divine messengers, as with the dual voice of man and woman, the blended powers of mind and soul, of intellect and of affection, shall demonstrate that perfect union of all faculties of mind and spirit, which are never truly understood or rightfully applied till every organ of the brain and conception of the spirit fills its own distinctive niche, and contributes its own peculiar part to universal harmony.

The highest life must be a symphony; the powers of human nature must play together like many instruments in an orchestra, or many voices in a choir: as in the Book of Revelation, the perfect life is symboled in the woman, whose diadem shines bright with the blended lustre of twelve stars. Twelve and its multiples ever signify completeness. The head adorned with diadem of twelve stars, is an allusion to the twelve-fold glories of the perfected reason, while the clothing of the body with the sun, means that the inner light of love, with all-encompassing sheen of golden glory, must robe, as in a vestment of perpetual and unsullied light, she who is to bring forth the Male Child, who is to rule the earth with Rod of Iron, signifying power and might invincible, strength adequate to accomplish the final overthrow of ignorance and wrong; while the moon beneath her feet, emblem of all material desires and all external wealth, signifies the ultimate conquest of the soul over matter, and the complete subjection of the material to the spiritual being.

Have you never pondered over the story of the Sphinx, grim and hoary with years, with woman's head and lion's body? This mystic figure stood in ancient Egypt, propounding her question to every passer-by. What was the riddle of the Sphinx, but the query of to-day: How shall power and gentleness, how shall love and law, how shall intellect and affection, how shall science and religion, how shall man and woman be so united, that there be no more conflict between the material and the spiritual realms? If any one can answer that interrogation, the veil is rent in the midst of the temple of human life, the glass, through which truth is but darkly seen, is broken, and, face to face, is the vision of truth discerned. The destruction of the Sphinx is but the end of mystery, of conflict, of all gloom and doubt, the unveiling of the secrets of eternity, the acceptance by man on earth of truth in the celestial degree. The letter killeth but the spirit giveth life.

How shall justice be merciful and mercy just? How shall infamy be slain, society protected, the criminal reformed, and yet the death-penalty be abolished, and dungeon cells give place to light and airy schools of industry, reformatories and hospitals for the morally sick and mentally deformed? How shall more than Plato's dream of an ideal republic be made practical, and a state of society be attained where the weak are made strong, the crooked straight, no one harshly dealt with, and no one slain?

The voices of the angels of the New Messiah are on the air: their songs upon the breeze proclaim deliverance to the captives, emancipation for all in bondage; and this New Dispensation of truth, even now dawning, is the age of man and woman, of reason and of love, the age of reconciliation and mutual understanding, when neither science nor religion, the brain nor the heart, man nor woman shall be unduly exalted, the one above the other.

True marriage means equality. Woman is to be man's helpmate, and a helpmate is not a servant or an inferior, but an equal. We often hear men speak of their wives as though they were less than themselves intellectually. If that be so, and sometimes it is, the woman is either superior in her intuitive perceptions, which removes the inequality and balances the temperaments, or the marriage is an unhappy one.

It is often said, that a couple cannot agree: they are too much alike. Though that expression sounds strange to unaccustomed ears, and the prevailing idea has usually been, that persons must be very nearly alike in order to blend well, there is great truth in the expression—they cannot agree because they are too much alike. No one is perfect, no one has all the elements of greatness within himself, and it stands to reason no one will be satisfied with a mere echo or repetition of himself, unless he be so insufferably conceited as to live in perpetual thirst for flattery, able to conceive of nothing more delightful than the heaven of the egotist, which would be a hell to all sensible or unselfish persons.

Good contrasts are always better than bad matches. Colours which are very dissimilar offset each other, showing each other up to the best possible advantage. But a very brilliant red or blue close beside the same colour, a shade paler, is not usually an artistic success. Either one colour must reign alone, or when there are but two, those two must be such contrasts that the one helps the other, so that a pleasing harmony of blended effect is produced.

Now, with regard to the blending of temperaments. A great deal has been said about positive and negative being brought together, and the prevailing idea has been that a strong, proud, masterful man should marry a gentle, docile, confiding, and simple-minded woman. Some such unions have been relatively good, and the outward results have been apparently satisfactory. There are some men, and women also, who are never happy unless they are playing the part of king or queen, master or mistress. They have a greater desire to be obeyed than to be loved; they want some one to control, some one to look up to them, and follow their lead unquestioningly. A man or woman of this type wants a servant rather than a companion, a pupil rather than a confidante. Then, on the other hand, there are those who are never happy except when they are ruled. They love to look up to someone else, and are seemingly unable to originate any ideas, or take the lead in any enterprise.

We know men who have absolutely ruled their wives, and wives who have absolutely ruled their husbands, and have yet been extremely happy and well-suited to each other. But these unions are not the highest; they are certainly not the closest earthly approximations to the blessedness of celestial oneness of life, for in the angelic state, one is as positive as the other, one as negative as the other, only where the one is positive the other is negative, and where the one is negative the other is positive. They both are equal in all the elements which go to make up character. They may be likened to a world in which land and water are equally divided. They are never wearisome to each other, can never exhaust each other, for the one has what the other lacks, and in such exact proportions, that the two really make one. That is the spiritual theory of counterparts; that is the prophecy of future marriage; and whensoever you have attained to so well-balanced a state of mind, that you are equally poised and have found your equilibrium, there will be no stronger and no weaker vessel, no masculine superiority, no feminine inferiority; for wheresoever one is superior to the other, one is a mystery to the other, and one is a disappointment to the other.

Similarity of tastes is necessary to a happy union, and yet similarity in occupation may often be a mistake on earth. Nevertheless, in the case of the poet and poetess, Mr. and Mrs. Browning; in the case of those eminent and noble Spiritualists, Mr. and Mrs. Howitt, or Mr. and Mrs. S. C. Hall, both have been literary, both have taken up the pen, both have worked in the same field, yet there has been no rivalry. They have always spoken affectionately and approvingly of each other's work, and, though engaged in similar pursuits, the one mind has suggested what the other could not have perceived, and so they have complemented each other's labours, and given the world a glimpse of what true marriage union may be, will be, and must be.

But when the outward work is not similar, the appreciations and sympathies of the pair may be united. The man, for instance, may be a great statesman, a man of letters, a politician, or he may be a physician, a surgeon, a lawyer, or a minister of religion. The woman, who is his wife, may be a poetess, an artist, a singer, one who spends her time entirely with the muses, yet she has a fine brain, quick intellectual perceptions, a keen, analytical mind. She is far more intuitive than her husband. She looks at matters from the other side, but she is no ignoramus; she is no soft, simpering woman, who writes silly sonnets, sings sentimental songs from morning till night, and goes into hysterics at the slightest disappointments. She is a brave, strong, sensible woman; musical, artistic, poetic, æsthetic; and yet her husband can discuss with her the merits of Gladstone's latest speech in Parliament. She can read his law books with him, and help him to solve a knotty problem in theology. Perhaps she could not take his place, and he certainly could not fill hers; but she is charmed with his discourse, her mind gladly drinks in the wisdom he imparts, while he, tired with unceasing mental strain, finds in her love of the beautiful and cultivation of the arts, the very balm he needs to soothe his weary brain, after the struggles and turmoils of his professional or business career.

Without extending our observations further along this line, we have said enough to illustrate a principle, and that is, that true equality does not mean that one shall be in all things exactly on a par with the other, but that one shall always be able to fill the void, or supply the defect in the life of his or her companion.

Women should be brought up to fill any place in society which man can fill, not that they may need to fill it, but they must be ready for it in case it is opened to them.

The duties of motherhood are often so pressing, that women who have families of young children cannot, in duty to their offspring, leave home to appear in public; and, indeed, their time may be so occupied with home duties, that to neglect them, even for important literary work, would be a sin. A woman who intends to entrust her children to the care of hirelings, should never become a mother. Her own child, not a dog, should be a mother's constant companion wherever she goes; as a child needs to imbibe a mother's life by constant contact with her, if the mother is to become really the parent and guardian of her offspring.

But if some of the very best years of a woman's life are spent in rearing children, is that any reason why she should not be a highly-cultured woman, capable of filling the highest place in Church or State, should occasion demand? No qualifications can possibly be too great, to render one a pattern mother, and if, when she has leisure from domestic duties, she devotes herself to the improvement of society, by efforts of tongue or pen, instead of spending her spare hours in foolish and unhealthy dissipation,—will not the world at large, and her own husband and children in particular, be immensely benefitted, if the wife and mother, instead of striving to be a fashionable belle, a queen of society, endeavours to work with heart and brain for the improvement of the race?

Alas! for those husbands, sons, and brothers, who feel that the women in their families are their inferiors. Alas! for those who cannot confide in the wife or mother, feeling that only a man can understand them, and have sufficient common sense to pass an opinion worthy of their consideration. Superior women make superior men, and that woman alone is fitted to be the wife or mother of a man of real power, who can be in all things his confidante and bosom friend.

The present system of training girls, leads to the desecration of home, the support of men's clubs, where husbands learn to forsake their wives, fathers to neglect their children. The education of girls, not simply in accomplishments, the training of daughters to be useful more than ornamental, and the throwing open of the doors of every hall and college in the civilized land to woman, is imperatively demanded, to open the way for the purification of society, and the breaking up of those infamous assemblies, where man rules alone to oppress woman, and where no other means are devised for the healing of the nations than that warfare, strife, and aggression, which sooner or later, unless it be abolished, must lead to the overthrow of any nation which allows it.

Not to render women unfeminine, not to disqualify them for the duties of wife and mother, but to render them the better able to perform these duties well, do we advocate the acknowledgment, before the law, of man and woman as the perfect equals of each other.

IMPROMPTU POEM.

TWO HEARTS THAT BEAT AS ONE.

BEFORE the World from Chaos was brought forth!
  Before the sea or air or sky were known!
Before yon glorious orb of light portrayed
  The glories of that light which suns have known!
Before God's Spirit breathed upon the slumbering clay,
  And woke man into being by His mighty word,—
In realms afar, beyond all mortal ken,
  Two human spirits tidings of God's plan had heard!

At that far-distant time they were as one,
  Had never known a separate life, for there,
In paradise, before material birth,—
  Knew not how souls must human bodies wear,
To unfold their powers, and bring into relief
  The native graces of that life within,
Which unto God for evermore must turn,
  As it in God for ever must begin!—

These spirits—cherub, seraph, two in one—
  Were like two children happy in their play,
Like two sweet infants who, in babyhood,
  Can know no shadow of life's dark dismay;
Obeying all God's will, they sweetly moved
  Like two Æolian harps, who aye respond
Unto each breath of air, which reaches them.
  In closest union were these spirits, fond,
United in such true, seraphic bliss,
  As in the paradise unforfeited, those beings know,
Who have not yet heard matter call to them,
  And earth appeal to draw them into clay.

But one day came an angel, radiant, bright,
  With golden crown upon a lofty brow,
Where wisdom sat, while from her eyes sweet love
  Shone forth, such as God's servants show,
Who, through life's pilgrimage of trial and pain,
  At length to homes of perfect bliss attain.
So, soon as she approached, these spirits said:
  "Oh! why are we not beautiful as thou?
We are content in our pure innocence,
  But then we have no crowns upon our brow,
No palm of conquest, and no victor's dowers:
  Oh! say, how can such bliss be ever ours?"

"My children," said the angel, bending down
  In tenderest fondness o'er that childlike pair;
"I am a guardian sent to you, that I
  The mystery of life's unfoldment may declare.
Ye have just felt the pain of strong desire,
  To be more beautiful, more fully blest:
The earth attracts you downward unto it,
  And ye must needs descend, then enter into rest.

"But if ye follow these impulsions, strange,
  Then through long ages ye must separate be,
Endure all earthly ills, and wear all earthly chains,
  And, for a while, of heaven forgetful be.
Ye needs must dwell apart, and union crave,
  But when ye meet in heaven for evermore,
Then, beautiful as I, will ye appear,
  And sing the angel's song, upon celestial shores."
"Oh! let us go," the spirits answered; "we
  Can bear a little parting, though 'twill be such pain,
If in the future ages we, like you,
  Can such transcendent height of glory gain."

"Then, be it so," the angel then replied;
"And, lest ye wander all too far, I'll be your guide;
Ye will not always know that I am near,
But, though unseen, your every cry I'll hear;
And when ye think you're all alone, I'll be
Beside you, ever watching faithfully."

* * * * * * *

Into a quiet garden came an angel form,
So beautiful and bright, it startled one who knelt
In lonely prayer and anguish inexpressible.
A yearning in her heart for love she felt.
She had known honour, wealth, and power and state;
Had been caressed and feted, made to taste
All that the world calls sweet and most desires:
But still her heart for something more aspires.
Suitors had she, and those who loved her well,
Yet in her heart a burning prayer did swell
For one, she felt most sure would some day bring
All she desired, upon life's rosy wing.
This was her guardian angel who drew near,
One whom she loved and trusted, and felt near;
E'en when her earthly eyes were holden most,
She felt the nearness of her brighter sphere,
And while thus weeping, musing upon love,
And what would fully satisfy her heart,
This angel said: "Go quickly to a scene
Of pain and woe, where, in death's sharpest smart,
One lies in suffering, calling on the name
Of some dear maiden, whom he seems to see
Before him always in his every dream:
She only soothes him in his misery!"

* * * * * * *

Beside a solitary couch a woman kneels:
  A man is dying, in his palid cheek
No hue of health is left, and in his eyes
  There is no lustre; but, with love so meek,
So saintly, so angelic, doth she look
  Into his fading eyes, while he in hers
Gazes, until his deepest soul, within,
  With tender memories of distant ages stirs.
His voice is faint, his eyes can scarcely see,
  But yet he murmurs in his broken tone:
"We were together once, in some sweet paradise,
  And when we both from this dark world have flown,
Then once again together shall we move,
The depths of wisdom and of love to prove!"

* * * * * * *

'Tis summer-time, and over hill and dale
  The sun shines brightly, and the flowers are gay:
But in one grave two hearts, that beat as one,
  In peaceful quiet, softly, calmly lay.
They passed together from these scenes of care;
  They both had suffered, both through pain grown strong;
They were prepared for the angel's crown,
  Ready to join in heaven's triumphant song.
And when their eyes were opened, in the life above,
They knew that theirs was an eternal love:
Its birth in paradise they then discerned,
And the two mortals to one angel turned!
One in so far, that every thought agreed, and yet
  Companions were they and for aye will be;
And when ye all have fully vanquished sense,
  And over earth gained final victory,
Then will some beauteous angel unto you
  Make known the dual mystery of the spirit birth,
And teach you how two hearts that beat as one,
  Though long times sundered while upon the earth,
At length *must* meet, and will for ever prove
The eternal sweetness of the soul's abiding love;

BENEDICTION.

May the light of the Spirit of Truth be your constant guide through earth, leading you day by day ever nearer and nearer to that Divine Estate, where no life shall be sad or lone or solitary; but where all bask in the fulness of joy immortal, and are satisfied for ever in the likeness of God! Amen.

XVI.

THE SPIRITUAL SIGNIFICANCE OF THE APOCALYPSE.

The Woman, the Male Child, and the Beast.

THE book of Revelation, though one of the books of the canonical Scriptures, is so mystical and abstruse to general readers, that it is anything but a revelation to the majority of Bible students. To Martin Luther this book (the Apocalypse) was so incomprehensible, that he rejected it, refusing to allow that it was a divinely-inspired document; but to Emmanuel Swedenborg it was, with the book of Daniel, the most fruitful source of spiritual instruction and delight.

In his "Apocalypse Unveiled," Swedenborg undertakes to unfold the esoteric or inner meaning of the book, in the light of a spiritual history and prophecy concerning the earth as well as the spiritual world; and while we do not intend to confine ourselves to any particular methods of interpretation, we certainly intend to treat the Apocalypse, not as a mythical history of a golden Rome, which is all it appears to be to many modern critics of the sceptical type, but as a figurative embodiment of those essential truths and principles of being, which the Ancients were ever wont to set forth in Kabalistic form, for the enlightenment of all who were sufficiently advanced spiritually to comprehend the metaphorical language which, while it hides from the uninstructed, reveals to the student of the figure-language of the ancient Orders of spiritual scientists and historians all over the world, not only the past but also the future history of the earth and its inhabitants.

Time was when but one language universally prevailed among the learned, and even now that language has not become obsolete, though it is understood only by the comparatively few, as masonic signs, emblems and pass-words have no meaning to those who are not Masons.

The confounding of tongues at the time of the building of the Tower of Babel, doubtless alludes historically to a period when diverse written languages were substituted for the simple, universal and expressive language of numerals, adopted by the Grecian sages in latter days, as well as by the Egyptians, Chaldeans, and others at much earlier periods of human progress.

You have doubtless most of you heard of the Pythagorean system of Numerals, and of how Pythagoras, the sage of Samos, was wont to convey spiritual ideas to his pupils by means of numbers. Almost the first thing which strikes the reader of the book of Revelation, is the constant reference to numbers in that book, and no one carefully perusing it can fail to see how persistently the same numbers are employed in similar connections. In order to make the way plain for what is to follow, it will be well for us to give you the generally-accepted significance of numbers, only reminding you at the same time that there is always room for some differences of interpretation, as it is not every Order that subscribes to the original formularies of the most ancient Spiritual Orders upon the earth. We would further remark, that these numbers have a definite place and value in nature, and that whether you turn your eyes to the starry heavens above your heads or to the flowery sward beneath your feet, you are constrained to allow that nature herself, or the power that maps her out, is versed in the kindred sciences of mathematics and geometry. Nature mathematizes and geometrizes at every step of her way. The number of stars in a system is fixed, the number of petals in a flower is fixed, and these perfect expressions of exact principles in geometry, go on from age to age, duplicating themselves, with no power to guide them other than that law, immutable and eternal, the law of nature which is the law of God.

Behind all phenomena, mind may be traced by those who have ability to discern it, but not by those who are so utterly engrossed in the senses that their spiritual perceptions are too dormant to be employed. The idea of a Divine Mind to-morrow will be far clearer than it is to-day, even as the doubt of to-day is healthier than the unreasoning credulity of yesterday. But doubt is only transitional: revolutions in popular sentiment are always accomplished by the demolition of much that is old and something that is beautiful; but revolutions and reactions are not permanent, uncertainty and doubt are not ultimate conditions of the human mind, and thus the progress of mankind has ever been through periods of sorrow, difficulty, doubt and strife, which have at length resulted in the establishment of kingdoms or republics, of greater harmony and justice than any which have been overthrown at the time of a political crisis or social inundation, which has dethroned despots but uplifted the mass of mankind.

You must have been forcibly struck, if you have ever attentively read the Apocalypse, with the remarkable recurrence of certain numbers always in similar connections. 7 is always applied to things divine; 12 and its multiples to a completed gathering, in which all states and conditions of life are represented; while 6 is the number of the Dragon, the Beast, False Prophet and Accuser, which from times immemorial has expressed its baneful power in all institutions founded upon selfishness and supported by oppression, injustice, tyranny and strife. The number 1, of course, signifies perfect and eternal unity; it may mean the essential primary or ultimate atom of life, whatever that may be, or it may mean the Eternal Spirit, or the perfect whole of God's Kingdom may be intended; but whenever and wherever introduced, it always signifies the sphere of life unbroken and undivided.

The Circle was the most ancient symbol of Deity and of the Soul itself, and must ever be the perfect symbol of unity, in heaven or on earth. All suns and worlds grow spherical as they advance towards perfection. The ultimate condition of the earth, will undoubtedly be perfect sphericity of form, and when it shall have attained to its ultimate estate of progress as a globe, then will it describe a perfect circle round the sun, and be itself perfect as a globe of equal land and water. All temperaments and temperatures will be blended into a harmonious whole; the race of man will be unitary, languages will have lost themselves in one perfect and expressive tongue, which all will speak and all will understand; while Science and Religion—the one employing the intellect chiefly, and the other making the more direct appeal to the emotions or affections—will traverse the beautified earth, hand in hand as a perfectly united pair, the one complementing the other, but with never a word or thought of discord or division between them.

The number 2 is, of course, expressive of duality. It divides the Circle into two equal halves, breaks the Sphere into two equal hemispheres, as justice, we told you in a previous lecture, was divisible into love and wisdom, and the Divine Spirit should be adored as our Father and our Mother, the infinite Two-in-one, even as the soul of man is also essentially dual; and yet duality and unity are in such perfect accord, that the one is dual and the two form a unit. The number 3 carries you just a step further outward from the Circle or centre, and as the Triangle perfectly breaks and interprets the Circle without detracting from its essential oneness, so the figure 3, in all masonic and ecclesiastical emblems, means not only fatherhood and motherhood, but offspring in addition. Thus Justice may be the one, sovereign, all-inclusive attribute of the Deity. Love may be the one hemisphere and Wisdom the other, so that love and wisdom form a compound when perfectly blended, and that compound is justice; love being one half of justice, while wisdom is the other half; and then when this perfect justice operates, it fills the universe with life and light and law, so that the Divine Word goes forth, the *Logos* is embodied, only you must ever bear in mind that prevailing notions of the Trinity are mistaken, because they separate the Child from the Holy Spirit, and call the Child the Son only. The Child and the Holy Spirit are one and the same, the offspring of Deity; and the offspring or proceeding influence of a unitary and yet dual parent, must necessarily be dual also. The Son and the Daughter must constitute the Child of God, while the sole-begotten of the Father and the Mother, must be the perfect number of all souls in the universe, who in their primal and ultimate estate must be all pure and immaculate as the soul of that great teacher, whom all Christendom adores as the brightness of God's glory and the express image of his person.

The personality of God can never be fully explained to human thought or understanding, by reason of man limiting the idea of personality to that which is circumscribed, and has definite size, form and strength. Perhaps *individuality* is a clearer and better word than *personality*, and conveys to the mind a clearer idea of persistent and unchanging unity and self-conscious identity. In man outward personality has no stability, only the soul which is the primal unit is immortal, and while no one has approached the soul through the avenues of any one of the five bodily senses, as the soul cannot be seen, heard, tasted, touched or smelt, and is therefore ignored by Materialism altogether, as it requires intuition or interior perception to ascertain that there is a soul, even as it requires an eye to discern colour, an ear to detect sound, nostrils to distinguish odours, a palate to appreciate flavour, and bodily sensation to know how objects feel, whether they be rough or smooth, hot or cold; and as it is easy to imagine the possession of four senses without the fifth, or even of only one without the other four, so it appears to us quite logical, in the absence of demonstrated proof of a spirit or a spiritual world, to accept it as not unlikely, that those who hold interior communion with the spirit world, are simply possessed of more than ordinary quickness of perception, in specified directions, or may have the use of some subtle, discriminating sense, called intuition, which transcends the bodily organs, but never denies what outward perception can positively reveal.

The mystery of God is no greater than that of man. To account for a universe without a Supreme Spirit, is far more difficult than to admit the existence from eternity of a self-conscious and all-controlling Will; and surely if atoms may be regarded as eternal, if motion may be thought to be eternal, you can logically proceed one step further and admit one more proposition, and that is, consciousness and will are eternal. If this admission be not made, than nature is all blank, chaotic, meaningless and void, and the order of the heavens and of the earth is the result of a blind force, to believe in which requires far more gullibility than to admit the existence of Deity.

But time warns us that, if we diverge in any measure from our subject, we shall have to finish our discourse without having explained, ever so slightly, those mysterious personages who figure so prominently in the book of Revelation, with which you will naturally expect us somewhat to deal. We must, therefore, hasten our explanations of numbers and their significance, and at once proceed to giving you, in the light of the values ascribed to numbers, the meanings we attach to the characters introduced upon the stage of this profound and glowing allegory.

We have finished our allusions to the Deity and to the Soul when we have passed beyond the number 3, for 1, signifying unity, 2, duality, and 3, trinity, exhaust the figures which are consecrated to the embodiment of the idea of God, and the first principle of nature. 4, which stands next in order, is, as you all know, indicative of the Square, and this is the basis of all equitable rule, of all true masonry, of all fellowship between men and nations, of all propagation of truth, or evangelization of the world. Upon the Square, the Great Egyptian Pyramid, and all minor pyramids, built later and after its pattern, repose. The Square is the base of the Triangle, and with its 4 corners, one directed to each separate point of the compass, eloquently describes the perfect thought of Universal Brotherhood. To act on the square is a common expression, signifying to deal fairly with each other. 5 signifies Government, or the hand of power, the active employment of that ability and intention which the square embodies. You have all heard of the five points of human fellowship in masonry, and to those who are Masons, it will be unnecessary, if they are at all indoctrinated into the mysteries of their craft, to do more than allude to this emblem, while to all who are not connected with any Secret Order, a further explanation of the symbol would be scarcely intelligible. 6 is the one number out of all, which distinctly indicates failure and incompleteness. It is the Number of the Beast, and of the Man of Sin. It is never mentioned in the Apocalypse, except in connection with the seeming triumph of ungodliness. Following next in order after the 5 of Government, it indicates government in which the spirit has no part, for 7 is the number of the Spirit, and of all spiritual things.

There are 7 golden candlesticks, 7 spirits of God, 7 lamps of fire burning before the throne, while you are constantly referred to 7 spiritual spheres beyond the earth, as signifying the completed number of the states through which all spirits on their road to perfect purity must pass. 7 days or epochs of creative power are mentioned in the Genesis. The seventh day must be the day of rest, and while Geology and Genesis apparently conflict, and in the letter Genesis is faulty, and so written that it suited the childish comprehension of the Hebrews, in a period of their history when they needed to be led and could not walk alone, still the institution of the Sabbath as an imperative necessity remains to-day, and will be needed until the time arrives when men and animals are alike so constantly, agreeably and yet no longer exhaustively employed, that all days will be Sabbaths, because all will be times of rest even though all are periods of ceaseless activity. True rest does not mean something synonymous with idleness, but when the faculties have been overstrained or too severely taxed, then a temporary cessation of active work is positively required, to fit the jaded form or mind for another encounter with the struggles of existence.

The French Revolutionists endeavoured to substitute one day in ten instead of one in seven, as a period of rest and respite both for man and beast; but the old Jewish legislators had probed more deeply than they into the needs of human nature, and one day in seven had to be restored as a period of rest, because the Sabbath is a hygienic, a sanitary, a physiological necessity, necessary for ox and ass, for horse and mule, as well as for son and daughter, man-servant and maid-servant; and when in olden days the Sabbath laws were most severe and were most unsparingly enforced, the wise Hebrew rulers sought to put into execution only such statutes and ordinances as contributed most effectually to the general maintenance of health and order. Their methods may sometimes have been unnecessarily severe, but times have changed since then, and we doubt very much whether the bungling politicians of the present day, could have devised better and wiser laws for the government of a people, most difficult to rule, had they been obliged to legislate in an Oriental, slave-holding country, for a people who were always prone to rebellion, and whose culture and opportunities were immensely inferior to those of modern nations, whether Jew or Gentile.

8 is always significant of good, and by many interpreters is considered as the Square raised to superior power, and therefore illustrates the two-fold idea of Brotherhood and of the Promulgation of Truth. 8 following upon 7, which signifies the spiritualization of mankind, and the attainment of perfection morally, coupled with enduring success, must have reference to such brotherhoods and methods as have for object the dissemination of spiritual knowledge; while 9 is never mentioned except with reference to angelic life, 9 choirs of angels being spoken of; but this sacred number never refers to mundane or external states of being.

The Number of the Beast is 6, and the three sixes in the entire number 666, allude to failure physically, intellectually and spiritually. Thus it is stated Kabalistically, when 666 is given as the Number of the Beast, that the powers of darkness shall not eventually triumph, though they reach to so elevated a condition, that they are apparently on the very verge of absolute conquest, but ere the moment of anticipated victory arrives the Beast is put to flight.

You have doubtless, all of you, been struck with the remarkable way in which the Beast, the Serpent, the Old Dragon and the Devil are identified. The Man of Sin, and the False Prophet, are mentioned as emissaries of the Beast, and seem to go before him, as John the Baptist prepares the way for Christ, and Elijah is said to come before the installation of the King of Glory, upon his throne of undivided power upon the earth. The dragon, serpent or beast is a very interesting subject of study, as he is identified with the devil, and hearing so much of the devil, as you all must if you are accustomed to Christian teaching, it may be interesting and profitable to enquire: Who or what is the Devil, and how best can we withstand his assaults and protect ourselves against his cunning?

Genesis says God created the heavens and the earth, all forms of vegetation, animal life and man. We are told he formed the greater and the lesser lights which shine in the firmanent above, but no hell, no devil did he create. But we are told God had made a serpent, and that serpent was more subtle than all the beasts of the field, and that serpent apparently walked upright and had the gift of speech, before he made, first Eve, and then Adam to fall into sin, and thus to forfeit paradise.

Now, a talking snake or walking serpent would be a curiosity, which would draw great crowds to a menagerie, and we are sure, if one could be found, it would be most eagerly sought after by the naturalists all over the world. Persons would even be willing to take long journeys in the interests of science, to minutely observe such a remarkable phenomenon. If there had been such a creature at Corinth in the days of Paul, surely it would have excited considerable attention, and been mentioned in contemporaneous history; but Paul tells the Corinthian Christians to beware lest the serpent which tempted Eve likewise tempt them.

What is this mysterious Serpent? It is a type of the sensual nature of man; its voice is heard in all lustful desires; the fruits of which it desires the race to partake are fruits which, like apples of Sodom, are fair to look upon, but turn to ashes in the mouth. Let every child be taught to flee from this seducing reptile, this disturber of man's peace, by holding the carnal appetites in check, and chaining the lusts of the flesh in bondage to reason and the soul. Never tell your children there is a devil outside of them, whom they need to fear; never picture the roaring lion, as the enemy of souls, seeking his prey, lurking in every corner to catch the unwary, as an external foe; but rather explain to all under your charge, that there are two natures in every human being; the one of the earth earthy, seeking to drag the spirit down to the level of the dust; the other pure, spiritual, holy, ever seeking to lift the animal nature into such union with itself that every material instinct obeys the mandate of the soul, and all material things become subservient to the sway of mind, the supremacy of Spirit.

The Serpent is evidently an ancient symbol of the material universe, and among olden philosophers it was customary to divide the universe into the Kingdom of Light and the Kingdom of Darkness: the Kingdom of Light being good, and under the dominion of Spirit; the Kingdom of Darkness being evil, and all Matter was considered evil by some philosophers. This doctrine of the goodness of Spirit and the vileness of Matter crept into the Christian Church in very early times, and was notably advocated by the Manichæans and others, who espoused a corrupt philosophy, which taught duality in quite another sense from that in which the purest and most enlightened philosophy inculcated this doctrine.

We have often told our hearers of the duality of the Soul, as something entirely different from the old Persian dualism, which tried to support the idea of rival deites, and taught of Ormuzd and Ahriman as co-equal gods; but it must be remembered that the Zendavesta declares that each of these divine persons had power to create only six gods each, and 6 is the number of the Beast, and never of the triumphant Spirit of Good. In order to divide 12, the symbol of completion, numerically speaking, into equal parts, you can only attribute failure to both contending parties; but should you grant perfection or find victory to one, allowing that its power attained the sevenfold degree, 5 would alone remain for the opposing party, and thus there would be no equal division. These old allegories, with their weird and fantastic illustrations, are all fraught with the deepest interior significance to those who have acquainted themselves with the modes adopted by the Ancients, to set forth the constant struggle incessantly waging between the powers of good and evil. But good only is eternal, primal.

absolute: good had no beginning and can have no end; evil, beginning in time, may cease to be.

Theodore Parker owed much of his success to his unfaltering faith in the essential goodness of human nature. He never looked upon any life as useless, or any condition of being as irreclaimably and absolutely bad. Thus he won the hearts as well as the ears of the multitude, and caused people to feel the truth and beauty of his philosophy, as well as to think upon what addressed itself to their intellects.

To say that there cannot be two Almighties is merely to assert a truism. How confident the author of the 139th psalm, must of been of this, when he exclaimed, "If I make my bed in hell, behold, Thou art there." Truly, that hell may have been but *sheol*, the grave, as the hell in which the soul of the just one was not left was only *hades*, or the place of departed spirits. But then there are no other hells ever mentioned in the Scripture than these two, the one, *sheol*, the grave for the body; the other, *hades*, the place where spirits yet unprepared for heaven must remain, until they are ready for the inheritance of the saints in light.

Milton sings of Lucifer, the star that fell from Heaven, and Milton became a Unitarian before he passed from earth. His own works, "Paradise Lost" and "Paradise Regained," so opened his eyes to the fallacy of the prevailing idolatry which divides the universe between God and the Devil, that he threw belief in the devil overboard, and was satisfied to trust in one only true Almighty Source of life, who can be best described in Lord Lyton's phrase, which he puts into the mouth of the Vril-ya,—The All-Good!

Astronomers may point to the asteroids between Mars and Jupiter, and imagine them to be the fragments of some disrupted orb, and there are those who have taught that the inhabitants of that lost planet are now embodied upon earth, and doing penance here for crimes committed on that other earth, which fell a prey to destruction because of the wickedness of its inhabitants. This idea has been prominently brought before the public of late, in a book entitled "Spiritual Manifestations," by Rev. Charles Beecher, a brother of the famous Brooklyn preacher, Rev. Henry Ward Beecher; and also in Allan Kardec's recently translated "Genesis." These views are considered purely visionary by many, and they are certainly of a highly speculative character, but whether right or wrong, they are an immense improvement on the old idea of a future eternity of evil, and the irreclaimability of those who have once forfeited their original paradisiacal estate of innocence.

We do not say that we fully endorse those views, but we do regard them as evidences of the progress of thought in these days, and find no fault with them on moral grounds, as their moral tendency is not objectionable; the moral tendency of every theory, which teaches the remedial nature of punishment, being upward in its tendency.

Certainly the real "Beast" or "Dragon" which we have to combat, is one we either make or encourage for ourselves, and the beast which to-day usurps the place of Deity in many quarters, even among highly-civilized and Christian peoples, is the Golden Calf, which Aaron made, symbol of that love of gold and worship of material power and state, which has caused the downfall of many an ancient people, and threatens to destroy all modern nations which feed this Beast in their midst to-day.

The Dragon, no doubt, originally signified *Draco* or *Scorpio*, the autumnal sign of the zodiac which heralded the on-coming of winter, supposed by the ignorant among the Ancients to be the season when spirits of darkness held empire over the earth. The Great Dragon, a mighty constellation or group of stars, was also greatly dreaded, and supposed to be the throne and seat of the powers of darkness, as the *Pleiades* were always described as the homes of the gods.

It is not extraordinary that people imagined day to be the work of God, and night the work of his Adversary. It is not wonderful that summer inspired men's hearts with the sense of the goodness of the Eternal, while winter suggested to their minds the thought of an avenging rival of the Infinite, who sought to frustrate his designs. Nor is it wonderful that Matter should have been considered evil and Spirit good, while the sensual nature of man is ever prone to sin and folly, and the spirit is ever urging the mind to resist the tempter.

Human nature on earth is ever poised between the powers of light and darkness, the forces of good and evil: but there can be neither positive evil nor positive darkness anywhere in the universe, as if one be absolute, infinite, and eternal, the other is not, for there can be only one Sovereign Deity: either God or Devil you may believe in, but you cannot believe consistently in both. Evil or the devil is for you the sum of whatsoever in the material world your spirit has not yet subdued or conquered. Everything in itself is good, but nothing is good relatively, when out of place, and the purpose of life is evidently not fulfilled until every material desire is completely under the dominion of the spirit.

When man is perfected on earth, then will every material propensity be legitimately employed; then will all that animal force, which now runs riot and makes such havoc in society, be reduced to order and employed in obedience to the wise dictates of the soul; then will men understand why they are on earth, and why they have been compelled to endure such manifold temptations, and in the final estate of man on earth will celestial life be expressed in material form; and if the earth is ever destroyed, unless it be by some catastrophe not in the ordinary course of planetary events, it will be with the earth as with the human body: the life will be transported elsewhere, and back again into the primal chaos or original cosmos will all the substances which now compose the earth return, until in unborn ages Spirit will again operate upon the slumbering ether, and bring into newness of being that matter or force, which ever it be, that only becomes invisible when mortal forms dissolve, and destruction seems to ensue to the eyes of man, not yet acquainted with the cause of those transformation scenes in nature, which seem to imply creation and destruction in the most absolute and arbitrary sense.

The Number of the Beast, 666, signifies the partial and apparent triumph of the power of darkness over man's physical, intellectual and spiritual nature. Before a great light breaks upon the world, how gross is the darkness which it dissipates! In the old-world centres of civilization and power, how black was the darkness which the dawn of a new era drove away! Religion was falsified and even became a sin; priests vied with each other in the perpetration of the most horrid crimes for selfish ends; faith was lost in doubt; the knowledge of immortality was lost in the darkness of an overwhelming scepticism, well nigh despair, while morals were at their lowest ebb, so that in cultured Athens, Rome and Ephesus, there were indeed beasts in the form of men who preyed upon their fellows, and perpetrated unblushing immorality, while they gloried in their superiority above the citizens of all other cities on the globe. Though a few were cultured, the many were in intellectual night, and those who possessed knowledge carefully veiled it from others, that they alone might fill honourable places, and trade upon the weakness of the ignorant, whom they purposely kept in darkness; while the neglect of sanitary laws reduced the bodily health of the people to disease, and called down upon the ungodly race what has been called the vengeance of heaven, in the shape of direst pestilence and plague.

Is there not a Beast at large in the civilized world of to-day? Are not vices being nurtured in the very cradle of modern culture? Are not the rich becoming richer and the poor poorer, under the dominion of those monopolies and governments which bend every appliance of modern genius to their own profligate and selfish ends? No country of the modern world is unstained with the Mark of the Beast. Either that mark is in the forehead or in the hand. It is in the foreheads of those whose expanded brows betoken intellectual might, unsoftened by the sweetness of love, and unmoved by the tender emotions of mercy for their less fortunate neighbours and compatriots. It is in the hands of those who do business usuriously, seeking to keep just inside the pale of civil law, while the moral law they utterly disregard.

Usury is one of the crying sins of the times. Money-lending is an abomination, as at present practised, for what is the present mode of transacting business on the market place or on 'Change, but a practical and well-considered scheme to fill the full yet the fuller, and send the hungry empty away? If one has money and needs no more to supply him with every comfort and luxury the heart can wish, he, because he has enough, can buy and sell to suit himself, can get things cheap and sell them to the poor as dearly as he pleases.

The ten kingdoms of the modern civilized world are even now, commercially, under the dominion of the Beast. It is predicted that no one shall be allowed to buy or sell unless he have received the mark of the beast. What is this but monopoly, as at present permitted by so-called Christian governments? The time has come when science has been perverted to overturn all hopes of immortality, and to devise means whereby men may oppress one another yet more cruelly, than when in barbaric times warfare was less deadly than the polished arts of war known to civilized people. The

Beast has gained dominion in the Church, wherever an established religion has meant the establishment of a favoured few, in places of emolument and power, regardless of their qualification for office, which ought to be most sacred and important. What with the hunting clergyman, who preached other people's sermons and took scarcely any interest at all in the welfare of his parishioners, by no means an uncommon feature in the clerical life of England a short time ago, and the modern minister who looks upon the ministry only as a profession, and is never anything more than a hireling wanting to divide himself between God and Mammon, and never ready to give to God even half of his energies, thinking even a tithe of the heart is too much for the Eternal,—it is not surprising that the Beast in the Church has delivered many people over to unblushing infidelity.

The present condition of many professed ministers of the Gospel, is terrible to contemplate. They dare not express their honest doubts, they dare not give up the ministry and turn to other employment, because of the influence of friends and the salary so indispensable to the maintenance of their assumed position in society; while in America the state of things is not much better than in England, for though there is no established church, no revenues derived from Government, and all denominations are on an equality before the law, still, where pews are sold at auction to the highest bidder, and men must please the fancy of the wealthy in order to retain their lucrative, and, from worldly standpoints, most enviable positions, church patronage and the sale of livings have been equalled if not exceeded in immorality, in the iniquitous system which makes worldly prestige and power the measure by which religious enterprises are to be valued.

The Beast, or the Scarlet Woman of the Apocalypse, is not the Church of Rome nor the old Roman Empire. Babylon, the Beast, the Scarlet Woman, the Man of Sin, are all typical of conditions of society which belong to all nations and societies equally, in so far as tares and wheat grow together in every field, and righteousness and iniquity stand side by side throughout the whole civilized world. Turn out the Beast from your every Church and Chapel, turn it out of your every Spiritualistic or Secularistic Society, turn it out of Synagogue, Mosque, and Pagoda alike, and when the Beast goes, mercenariness and selfishness will have to be dethroned, yea, utterly exterminated. The Beast in politics is neither Conservative, Liberal, nor Radical especially. The Beast always votes for whatever candidate is the fancy of the hour, and sees that personal and exclusive privileges are not interfered with. Whatever Mr. Bradlaugh may be as a man or an Atheist, and however we may disagree with him in his religious views, we cannot honestly refrain from pointing to him as an impersonation of a new spiritual power, which intends to level class distinction, abolish perpetual pensions, and destroy those infamous rings which hold the working classes in worse than negro slavery, in many parts of England. Bradlaugh may not be the coming man, but he is one of his heralds. Bradlaugh's work is to pull down rather than to build up, but for the uprooting of tares he is peculiarly well qualified, while Disraeli was employed by the spirit of justice, in enfranchizing the Jews and liberalizing Conservatism; and Gladstone seems moved upon to stir up strife and lead to a hatred of warfare unparalleled in the annals of history. Bright is the prophetic soul, who sees beyond war to its abolition, and esteems it a crime to take human life unnecessarily. But the present war in Egypt, disastrous and humiliating though it be, is undoubtedly one of those conflicts which has long been predicted as incident to the passage of the earth from the dispensation now closing, to that emblematized by the King's Chamber, beyond the tortuous and difficult passage-way which divides that regal chamber from the Grand Gallery, in the Great Egyptian Pyramid.

It is an old statement and a very true one, that history repeats itself. Thus, whatever may have had 1800 years ago a literal application to the downfall of Rome and the dispersion of the Tribes of Israel, may equally refer to the present crisis through which the earth is passing. The very cholera, though a scourge, is a remedial agent. The beast of disease, the beast of tyranny, of monopoly, and of every form of evil, adopts a suicidal policy. Evil is self-destructive, and thus every Apocalypse must end with the coming of a New Jerusalem, new heavens (a new spiritual order) and a new earth (a new social state); and when the power of the Beast in modern lands to-day shall have attained to such proportions that its imposing magnitude leads all who are allied with it to expect a speedy and final victory, then will the number 666 appear significantly on its every banner, which, translated into English, means what Mene, Mene. Tekel. Upharsin, meant in the days of Daniel, at Belshazzar's feast: Thou art weighed in the balances and found wanting. Thy kingdom is divided, and given to the Medes and Persians.

And who shall the successor of the Beast be? Who shall reign, when the Beast is wounded unto death, but the Child with iron rod, who shall control all nations, whose mother is the Woman clothed with the Sun (emblem of perfect spiritual light and sanctified affection), the moon (symbol of all earthly desires) under her feet, and a crown of twelve stars (the completed glories of the mind, its twelve resplendent powers in full and harmonious exercise) upon her head.

This Child, who shall rule the earth, is an impersonation of Intellectual Power, conceived in pure affection, the might of knowledge universally disseminated, not under the dominion of avarice and lust, but as the child of pure benevolence, and truly enlightened affection for all mankind.)

IMPROMPTU POEM.

THE OPENING OF THE SEALS.

TRUTH, from earth's foundations, verily, was sealed!
When the ancient Prophets only have revealed
Fragments of its glory, raylets of its light,
But its native splendour, in the heavens so bright,
Is beyond man's vision, far too bright for eyes
Trained to earthward gazing. All around you lies
A rich field of knowledge, wonders everywhere,
Could ye but discern them. But, what eye can dare
Gaze upon the glory of the noon-day sun?
It is all too brilliant: so, when day is done,
Lifting tired eyes heavenward, gazing at the stars,
Mortals ever welcome, through the misty bars,
Which conceal the heavens from the eye of man,
That mild, borrowed radiance, which, since earth began
To be fit for mortals, through the Queen of night,
Greets your straining vision, with a partial light.

One by one, the bright stars are to man made known:
One by one, the barriers are by man o'erthrown;
Nearer, ever nearer, to the perfect day,
Man is slowly treading, life's mysterious way.

John, alone on Patmos, saw an angel come
From that world of glory, which will be man's home,
When he's learned life's lessons, conquered all the clay,
Risen at length victorious into heavenly day.
One of th' ancient Prophets, was this herald true,
One who once was mortal, toiling as do you;
One who won the battle, and who wears the crown,
As ye all may wear it, when ye've earned renown.
John supposed this teacher was the Lord divine,
And would fain have worshipped at that spirit's shrine;
But the angel truly told him, man must bow
Unto God, Him only must ye serve; though now
Idols are uplifted, as in olden time,
And men worship mortals, thinking men divine;
Not rememb'ring homage must to God be given,
Who reveals himself to man, through the soul which comes from heaven.

When the Seals were opened by the angel strong,
And God's mighty purpose was revealed in song,
Sung by choiring angels, with their harps of gold,
John fell down awe-stricken, for to him was told
How fierce tribulation should to earth draw nigh,
Ere the Beast was vanquished, and the Lamb gained victory.
What means many a figure? asks the student now:
What is the Lamb's life-blood, sprinkled on each brow
Of God's chosen people? They whose names are found
In life's glorious record, where the true, renowned
In eternal story, though on earth in pain
They have cruelly suffered, crowns of glory gain.

Blood is truth celestial, and the Lamb within
Is that loving-kindness, which doth surely win
Purity's best record; they their God will see,
Whose lives are all kindness; true love is purity.

When the Seals are opened, and the Vials disclose
What men think is vengeance, God's wrath bringing woes
On a guilty people, is but wisdom, love,
Blended well together, in the heavens above.

Bright angels guide the elements, angels control the sea,
And Nature's forces are not blind, but, with vitality,
Born of the Spirit's presence, forever are they rife,
Not with the force which killeth, but brings from death to life.

The chaff may be consumed, alloy be purged from gold,
In crucibles of sorrow, the noblest hearts grow bold;
The epidemics raging, which now ye so much fear,
The pestilence, disaster, the wars ye think so near,
Are all but God's wise measures, of leading man at length,
To where, in golden ages, gentleness joined with strength,

Shall rule with rod of mercy, and yet as iron strong,
Shall be the sway of Spirit, when all the poets' song,
And all the prophets' vision, shall realized be,
In that new age immortal, when Truth gains victory!

BENEDICTION.

May the Spirit of Truth open your minds, so that every Seal of error, and darkness, and ignorance shall be shattered, and ye shall know the Truth, and the Truth shall make you free! AMEN.

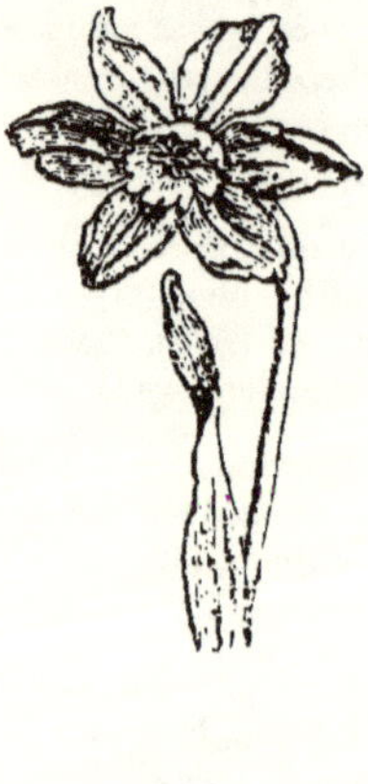

XVII.

THE SPIRIT SPHERES ATTACHING TO THE EARTH,

AND THE MISSION OF MODERN SPIRITUALISM TO HUMANITY, AS AFFECTING ALL INSTITUTIONS AND CLASSES OF SOCIETY.

WHOEVER first suggested our speaking upon the theme announced for the present lecture, must have had a rather exalted opinion of the amount of information which can be condensed in a single lecture of an hour's duration. It is needless to say that time most peremptorily forbids our doing much more than skim the surface of a subject, or rather group of subjects, which affords matter for almost infinite consideration.

We are glad the questioner has limited his desires for knowledge, concerning the Spirit-world, to the planet earth and its environment, as the immediate influx of spiritual influence now felt by mankind, certainly does proceed from those states of spiritual being which are intimately connected with the earth itself, and indeed nearly all the communications of average interest received from the Spirit-world, reach you through such intermediary minds as, by reason of their proximity to your own mental states, can easily play upon your sensibilities, and conduct their thoughts through the channels of your brains. The law of sympathy, or, as it is sometimes called, affinity, is the one great and sovereign law which renders spiritual communion possible; and neither on earth nor in the Spirit-world, can there be any communion or intercourse between spirits, unless they are in some sense kindred minds.

You all know that sympathy, or spiritual affection or union, is not dependent upon external associations, and is not governed by laws relating to earthly consanguinity. The very fact of marriage with one who is not a member of your own family circle, and the possibility of loving your wife or husband more than your brother or sister, even more than your parents, is a proof that there are ties of spirit deeper than any unions of sense. In alluding to a true and happy marriage, we are saying nothing whatever concerning those unions which are for time only, and exclusively of the senses. We mention the true marriage union as the highest, closest, holiest and most enduring of all, and all other unions. true friendships and intimate acquaintanceships, which are consummated in oneness of mind and thought, these are all practical exemplifications of the sublime fact of spiritual relationship and lasting accord.

Upon the earth the spirit is perpetually hampered and fettered by purely physical limitations, and thus scarcely any one appears as he really is. Death is the great revelator and emancipator in all instances, it strips you completely of your assumed robes, which you are often compelled to wear in the transaction of earthly business; for is there not a disguising of the true character, which cannot properly be called deception or hypocrisy? Are there not veils which you are obliged to throw over your inmost feelings, lest you should wound and annoy those around you; and does it not happen frequently that perforce you must labour at uncongenial tasks, for you are dependent upon the labour of your own hands for the bread which sustains your bodily life?

Now, the great difference between material and spiritual life is this: on earth, while in the body, you have to be actuated constantly by purely material considerations. You must have shelter, food, clothing, and money with which to purchase these things. The labour market may be in such a condition that your talents are not recognised, and the work you can best perform is not in demand. Thus very often a poet works in a coal mine, a philosopher drives a coach, a born politician is a waiter at a hotel, while persons of scarcely any qualification for the offices they hold, are drawing large salaries, and filling responsible positions, because of personal or party influence unduly exerted in their favour. One of the most painful and distressing anomalies of earthly existence, is this crowding to the front of persons who have nothing but cheek and cunning to recommend them, while the noblest. the purest, and the most talented are in numberless instances kept in the background.

Were it not for disclosures from the spiritual side of life. life would not be worth living to, at least, half the population of the globe; and so strongly is this conclusion emphasized by the experiences of the race, that we find millions upon millions of Orientals protesting that they want no immortality. Consciousness after death is not what they desire, they prefer to contemplate annihilation of individuality, for in the cessation of conscious being can they alone find rest from the troubles and woes of existence.

This condition of mind is morbid and unhealthy, and is not in accordance with Oriental philosophy, at its highest and best. It is the pessimistic hope of those who have had no experiences calculated to make them optimists. Life to them has been one long, uninterrupted round of prosaic drudgery, toiling for material necessaries only, finding no enjoyment except in sleep or indolent repose. Possessed of constitutions not naturally robust, subject to the enervating influences of a trying and unhealthy climate, they very naturally desire no prolongation of life, as they understand it. The view they take of life is, perhaps, the only one they can take, as they have no spiritual insight into the life beyond, and their religion is so mystical in its allusions to the hereafter, that though it may satisfy a metaphysician, it offers no consolation to the ordinary toiler in life's vineyard, who from day to day is doomed to the same humdrum round of labour, in which he evinces no interest, and which, in the very nature of things, is not calculated to inspire him with a sense of the value or beauty of life.

Some persons are, phrenologically speaking, incapable of looking upon the bright side of nature or taking a hopeful view of affairs in general, unless radical changes, most difficult to accomplish, are effected in their mental development; while, so long as the spirit dwells within the body, the condition of the physical frame has a great deal to do with the feelings of the individual, on the mission and purpose of his existence. A sound mind needs a sound body, just as a good performer needs a good instrument on which to display his powers; and in order to so revolutionize society, that the world shall be as close a pattern of the higher spiritual spheres as possible, it is high time that workers in the spiritual vineyard endeavoured to afford better conditions for a brighter display of spiritual light, by improving, as far as they are able, the tools and instruments which the spirits have to use in their communications with mankind.

Up to a certain point Spiritualists and Secularists can and ought to work together. Secularism maintains the necessity of physical culture and mental improvement. Many Secularists are striving earnestly to better the moral as well as the intellectual and physical condition of those around them, and it is anything but spiritual or liberal-minded to refuse the right hand of fellowship to any honest toiler in the vineyard of reform. If there is to be a great spiritual awakening in all parts of the world, and that shortly, the abolition of slums and rookeries, the cleansing of filthy alleys, the sweeping away of dens of infection and infamy, the taking of sanitary precautions against disease, the study of physiology, and the equalization of mankind, that there be no longer unjust and fictitious distinctions claimed between race and race, class and class, or man and man,—all these are works in which persons of widely different religious views may unite; and setting aside all difference of opinion on other points, it should be the steadfast aim of all noble souls, intent upon benefiting mankind, to set about the work of the reconstruction of society, in accordance with the best methods they can devise, and aided by the highest inspirations they can receive.

Spiritualism is a revelation. The facts it reveals are great and most important discoveries; but Spiritualism does not create or invent the Spirit-world, or bring its denizens to earth from far-off realms in space, where they would for ever remain disconnected with the earth, were it not for the evocatory power of Spiritualists.

Mediumship does not call up spirits from the vasty deep, or summon them from distant heavens; though it is true there is a kind of mediumship which does possess a summoning and attractive power, but that mediumship is not confined to those who go into trances, hear mysterious sounds, or see spiritual visions. You may have no mediumistic power whatever, in the ordinary acceptance of the term, and yet be a greater medium, in every practical sense, than those whose clairvoyance, or any other acknowledged spiritual gift, is a household word wherever they are known; and it is to this intuitive, impressional mediumship that we wish to turn your especial attention, when dwelling for a few moments upon the invocatory power and nature of desire, and the ability of thought and will to hold communion with the unseen spheres.

Thought-reading is now the latest craze in fashionable circles. Almost every popular newspaper devotes a considerable amount of its space to discussing the pros and cons of the theory. Mental telegraphy is admitted by many of the greatest scientists of the age, who, while they will not compromise themselves with Agnostics by admitting Spiritualism, are quite prepared to avow their belief in some subtle means of thought transfer, which Cumberland, Bishop, and other travelling thought-readers and conjurors bring into prominence before the public. Of course, such men as Bishop, Cumberland, and others are acting very foolishly when they attempt to destroy the nation's faith in spiritual communion, by their clumsy feats of legerdemain. Even when some of their tricks are cleverly performed, they do not touch the borders of genuine spiritual manifestations, as there can be no proof or test of spirit-power unless there be a display of intelligence.

When these conjurors and pretended exposers of Spiritualism, undertake to counterfeit genuine spiritual phenomena, they render themselves ridiculous in the eyes of all who know anything of genuine Spiritualism. Mr. Cumberland pretends to show how spirits materialize, by putting glycerine and muslin on his face, and dressed in a white robe, with a lamp in his hand, imitates "John King." But let him, and all who endeavour to unmask their own ignorance on spiritual matters as he does, remember that numberless spiritual manifestations have stood the closest scrutiny of eminently-scientific and highly-qualified observers, who could not possibly have been taken in by so silly and clumsy a subterfuge; and when it is remembered that persons are satisfied only with something which appeals to their inner nature, when they have solid grounds for their confidence in spiritual communion, the evidence against the conjuror as an exposer of Spiritualism, becomes stronger and stronger with every fresh investigation, until at length he is forced to retire from the field, ignominiously defeated, or become himself a convert to Spiritualism, and explain to his audiences how his own performances have compelled him to relinquish his former untenable premises.

Thought-reading is the entering wedge, the partly-opened door, which leads to a knowledge of spiritual science. Mr. Labouchere, the Editor of *Truth*, and many other popular journalists, may as yet refuse to call themselves Spiritualists, but recent articles in their journals prove them to be considerably baffled in their endeavours to explain thought-reading. If it is not a trick, then what is it? If it is an evidence of the power of minds to communicate with each other without the aid of the ordinary senses, then it goes a long way to prove the communion of minds with one another independent of the physical organism.

Thought-readers are of two classes. One class may be said to be composed of adepts, the other of mediums. Adepts are really mediums, but they are persons of unusual strength of will, and though under the influence of spirits they are not controlled to the same extent that persons of weaker will are; thus there is a difference between them, as between mesmeric operator and subject, or psychologist and sensitive. No operator is so positive that he can be operated upon by no one, still he may be beyond the reach of the mental power of his audience and their surroundings; thus though under spirit control himself, he is controlled by beings of greater will power than those in attendance upon persons whom he can subject to his will.

Theosophists and Spiritualists make a great mistake in opposing each other. It is a palpable error to suppose that either Theosophy or Spiritualism may be true, but both cannot be. A great deal of nonsense is no doubt often given off by would-be mystics and occultists, concerning Himalayan Brothers, elementary spirits, dopple-gangers, shells, astral bodies, &c., &c., but there is a very considerable residuum of sound, common sense and practical knowledge in the *Theosophist*, and other periodicals and writings which treat of the occult sciences. These sciences are not the phantastic and ephemeral absurdities most persons ignorant of the real nature of Astrology and Alchemy imagine them to be, but even Theurgy, Palmistry, and all the curious so-called superstitions of mediæval times, were founded upon a knowledge of the hidden forces of nature, and gave expression to facts relative to spirit influence which comparatively few people, even to-day, are competent to deal with, much less to explain away.

Spiritual Science must be added to material science. The supra-material sciences are as natural as the material: Theology is as natural a science as Geology; and until the public at large is willing to consider the claims of Spiritual Science, as it deals with Astronomy or Botany, Spiritualism will never be fairly treated, and the invisible world will never be intelligently understood, as a natural, objective, substantial, real world, in which force there does duty for matter here; and force is only a higher and more potential condition of being than matter. Both force and matter are emanations from Spirit, and both force and matter are at length resolvable into Spirit; as Spirit, self-conscious, self-intelligent, and eternal, is the only primal, absolute, and ultimate existence or substance in the universe.

It is customary to speak of things as real or substantial, to the extent that they are discernible by the external faculties of man. In the Spirit-world what is visible on earth is invisible, and what is invisible on earth is there visible. Thus the lens is completely reversed, and to a spiritual body matter offers no resistance, just as to a material body neither force nor spirit offer resistance.

In a recent number of *Morning Light*, a Swedenborgian weekly, the editor, while admitting that we have said many things both useful and suggestive concerning correspondence and the work and illumination of Swedenborg, charges us with having unduly confounded the natural with the supernatural. We spoke of the Science of Correspondences as a natural science. The editor of *Morning Light* says it is not a natural science, but a divine or spiritual science; and to him all things spiritual are supernatural.

It is clear to any thinker, that a great deal of such quibbling is only verbal. We think all Swedenborgians are willing to allow that there is but one God, and that everything has been created and is being upheld by his divine power. Then, if there be but one God, and the earth and the physical body are parts of his work, why make a distinction without a difference, and assign part of the universe to one class of laws and another part to totally different laws? The law of God is the law of nature: there is but one law as there is but one God, and the sooner the oneness of the universe is admitted, and the oneness of the laws that govern it, the better both for science and religion, which will always be opposing instead of friendly and allied powers, so long as things spiritual and physical are spoken of as though one were divine and the other something quite the reverse.

No more favourite mode of dealing with death is extant in

orthodox circles, than that which represents the "last great change" as one which completely and forever dissevers the spirit from all connection with the earth. And yet Jesus, whose resurrection according to Christianity brought immortal life to light, promised to be ever with his people, so that whenever two or three were gathered in his name, they might enjoy communion with his spirit. "Prepare to meet thy God!" is reiterated so constantly in connection with man's passage from earth to spirit-life, that people are all unconsciously accustoming themselves to the belief, that the future life is so entirely different from the present, that many deem it positively sacrilegious to speak of the Spirit-world except as some golden Rome or Heliopolis transferred to the unseen spheres, where Halleluiahs are to be shouted eternally by the redeemed in glory, ransomed through the blood of the lamb, from all pain and penalty forever.

This investment of the Spirit-world with such a degree of unnaturalness as to make it appear unreal and even uninviting to the majority of aspirants for immortality, is one of the most prolific sources of doubt and denial in the present day. The step from orthodoxy to infidelity is a very simple one. To give up the idea of a heaven, never more than vaguely realized, to lose faith in records and traditions, and to treat the testimony of the Ancients as a myth, is easy to many minds. Thus, from extreme orthodoxy to hopeless infidelity many pass without having realized that they have really given up much that was worth preserving. The heaven of orthodoxy is so deeply shadowed by its hell, that unbelief is a positive comfort to many deeply sympathetic natures. A God who cannot save all, cannot be Almighty; a God who will not if he can, is unworthy of our love; and the thought of spending an eternity with such a being, even though under his smile, is awful rather than satisfying to the deepest longings of the human heart.

Spiritualism has done what neither Theism, Unitarianism, nor Free-Religion could accomplish: it has effectually naturalized the Spirit-world, and has made countless human hearts rejoice in living realization of an immortality which is theirs here and now. Its phenomena appeal to the senses, while its philosophy satisfies the astutest intellect; and we need a combination of phenomena and philosophy, to reach different sections of mankind, and solve the great problem of man's nature and destiny, adequately to the comprehension of all.

We regret a tendency among Spiritualists to exalt one phase of spirit-communion above another. This tendency is no doubt natural, and is easily accounted for and explained, but it is not healthy, neither is it calculated to promote harmony or unity among common believers in the cardinal verities of the modern spiritual revelation. One person will visit London, and write to a newspaper underrating physical phenomena, and, perhaps, over-estimating the importance of philosophical addresses; another person speaks coldly, almost slightingly of what appeals to the intellect, and exaggerates the importance of sensuous demonstrations. All such comparisons are mischievous, invidious and unfair. They are, moreover, hasty and short-sighted, and do not evidence a well-balanced mind.

The needs of human nature are so varied, that all the different modes of spiritual operation now extant, are essential to the reaching of all classes of intellect, and the satisfaction of every type of enquirer. Rivalry, jealousy, these cursed tempters, are utterly out of place in a movement where all true workers help each other. Every honest medium helps every other honest medium, and those poor sensitives who are too weak to resist temptation, and so pliant that they echo the thoughts of all around them for the time being, instead of being held up to ridicule, execration and reproach, should be so kindly and tenderly dealt with, that they be induced not to err, or fall in future, as they have done in the past.

We have often heard and read the remark, that when a medium has once been caught in deception, he should be abandoned to the mercy of the cold world. Spiritualists should refuse him countenance, turn their backs upon him, show him the cold shoulder, write against him in the papers, and straightway commence vilifying him among all their acquaintances, and warning the public against him. How suicidal must such a policy be to the best interests of truth and rectitude! If you throw an easily-tempted sensitive upon the mercies of an unsympathetic world, and do nothing whatever to shelter, reform and uplift him, you are not destroying an evil, ridding society of a nuisance, or removing a stumbling-block or rock of offence out of your neighbour's way.

Unkindness never reforms, unmerciful punishment never uproots iniquity. The one you trample under foot remains the sinner he was: he is not strengthened or reformed by your cruelty and cowardice, but becomes an easier and easier prey to the wiles of those unprincipled hoaxers, who are ever ready to make use of tools for the accomplishment of their own unworthy ends. And is it to be wondered at, that when earth is constantly pouring into the Spirit-world troops of liars, thieves, adulterers and blacklegs, that these unreformed characters should still hang round their favourite haunts on earth; and as dwellers on the threshold, or earth-bound spirits, continue to infest those neighbourhoods and places of assembly where they perpetrated their crimes and follies while in the material form? Every infirmity, which is but an infirmity of the flesh, is overcome when the body dies, the weaknesses incident to an imperfect body, and the manifold temptations to which you are unwillingly exposed, are shaken off at the entrance to the immortal world. But desire is fulfilled, and wherever there is aspiration toward any state of existence, links of affinity bind you to that state, and you are, as Swedenborg has said, a denizen of hell, only, if you choose hell instead of heaven.

The visions of Swedenborg, and those of Dante, need not be called in question, because the Lutheran and Roman Catholic dogma of eternal punishment is set aside. Swedenborg was brought up a Lutheran, and Dante a Catholic. Their ideas of the everlasting perpetuity of evil were modified by spiritual revelation, but not overcome, as there are states of existence beyond the grave which temporarily answer to every mortal conception of the hereafter. The sensualist finds his harem in the invisible world, and as the Koran states, the places filled on earth by women are there filled by paradisiacal angels. Mohammed was a seer, but he saw those heavens which only answer to human avarice and lust. He dreamed a voluptuous dream which chorded well with the voluptuousness of the Orientals among whom he dwelt, and to whom his religion most forcibly appealed. The heaven of Mohammed, however, becomes a hell eventually, for those who go out from earth with no higher aspirations than those which, if fulfilled, will gratify the senses, find that at length all libertinism cloys upon the spirit, and satiety not satisfaction is the ultimate of sordid dreams of animal enjoyment.

The sensualist may hover round the earth, and still engage in midnight revelry and song. Troops of spirits, who on earth led dissipated lives, may be witnessed by clairvoyants in every haunt of gaiety and dissipation. There are their worlds, their spheres are within the atmosphere, on earth. If they have not intentionally wronged their fellows, then they are numbered among the frivolous and vain, and while their lives are most woefully empty and unsatisfactory to the higher nature, they are not in torment, neither do they experience that loneliness and depression which those must undergo whose selfishness has been such that they have never bestowed a thought except upon themselves and their own advancement.

Would that the misers and egotists of the earth could see what we have seen of the darker side of spirit life! Such revelations would surely lead them to repent of their follies ere it is too late, and sow, while here on earth, something better than wretched tares for their reaping at the harvest hour of mortal dissolution. But those who live entirely on the plane of the senses, are so steeled against warnings of every kind, that should visions ever so startling be shown to them, they would dismiss them from their minds as quickly as possible, refusing to accept the teaching they conveyed. We have known many who have had countless spiritual experiences, and have attributed them all to ill health or over-excitement, and have taken ardent spirits and sleeping-draughts, and all kinds of physic, to prevent a recurrence of those unwelcome disturbers of their peace. Among those who determinately refuse to give heed to messengers from the unseen world, no matter how vividly they make their presence known, are to be found the nineteenth-century brethren of a modern Dives, to whom it would be useless to offer a revelation, as they would not repent though one rose from the dead.

There seems reluctance to send a messenger, on the part of Abraham, in the story of Dives and Lazarus, but a close analysis of the allegory will let us see that all that its author intended to convey, was the existence of states of mind to which spiritual truths could only make a useless appeal, and because of the fruitlessness of the task it was not undertaken. The mistake is only in supposing that the task would be eternally fruitless, whereas the condition of a spirit or mortal at any given time when he may be interviewed, is no just criterion of the state he will be in, say a century, or even a year from now.

The Hindoos, who said there were fourteen spiritual spheres. of which the earth was one, correctly located the earth-bound sphere within the atmosphere of the earth itself; though, if they inferred that there were seven degrees of spiritual existence below the earth, they were astray in their calculations, so far as human spirits are concerned; for there is no retrogression in nature, and no spirit really deteriorates when passed from the body, though apparent deterioration may result from the inability of a spirit to withstand new temptations, by which he has been hitherto untried.

Spiritualism may apparently prove the deterioration of some minds in the hereafter, but in all cases where deterioration seems evident, one of two explanations will serve to show how baseless may be the assumption. There are many on earth who live outwardly respectable but hypocritical lives. They pass current in society as virtuous, but their virtue consists in nothing more than conformity to certain external requirements of a superficial state of society; polished manners, a smooth tongue, a little easy, affected charity, some degree of attention paid to religious observances, and the world caresses you with its sweetest smile. You may be a caluminator or detractor if you will, you may blacken reputations without mercy, you may amass wealth in ways that will bear no honest investigation, but so long as you keep within the bounds of the letter of human law, you are free from censure, and are indeed accounted a most exemplary member of society.

Now, in spirit life, everything goes by motive, intention, desire, thought, will; these are the realities which go to make up character; and by interior standards are you judged in the hereafter. Some one may have been badly born, scarcely educated at all, allowed to grow up like a weed without any culture. When a child he may have been surrounded with a whole host of adverse circumstances, and the power of evil pitted against his feeble strength, may have been so overpoweringly great, that it was impossible for him to withstand the power of so great temptations. He may have striven a million times to resist; he may have succeeded over and over again, but the world only knows when he has fallen. It chronicles his failures, it makes capital out of his mistakes, it holds up its hands in holy horror when the name of so great a culprit is mentioned, and yet if those who pride themselves on the easy, negative, automatic fashionable "virtue" they think so praiseworthy, had been subjected to a hundreth part of the temptation their "fallen" brother has endured, they would have sunk unmentionably lower than he, in the pit of degradation.

Your young men and women, who have never been away from home, and have known nothing of the world's seductions, are in no position to offer contrasts to those who have fallen into sin, when exposed to temptations the mere names of which the carefully-nurtured and vigilantly-protected may have never heard. It is for no man to judge his brother, and if there be one vice more hateful in the eyes of angels than another, it is that spiritual pride which so often goes before the deepest and most disgraceful falls.

In the Spirit-world every circumstance of earthly life is taken into account. When the old Egyptians graphically painted the scene in the Judgment Hall, before Osiris, they were not at all astray in their conception of the true spiritual judgment, when they weighed the actions of the departed from earth, in scales adjusted with accurate nicety. But after all, the acts are not so important as the motives, and yet from pure motives, pure acts must ever spring, so the outward and inner life must to some extent correspond, but as all have not equal light, and many sin in ignorance, the command is lawful—Judge not that ye be not judged.

We have never yet come across any one who was healthy, who enjoyed idleness, and we are certain no healthy child likes to be doing nothing. No picture of heaven can be more disheartening than that which paints it as a world of monotonous ease and listless indolence. The incessant music of heaven must be a figure of the incessant motion and activity of those who are in heaven. True music is harmony, and the perfect harmony of life within and without must ever constitute the bliss of the celestial world.

Many persons seem to think that Spirit Spheres are arbitrarily located around the earth, within a certain radius of its circumference, and though there are earth-bound spirits who are thus confined, spirit spheres, properly speaking, are strictly individual. Spirits travel in their spheres. If their spheres are bright and comfortable, then, wherever they may be, they are in happiness and peace. If their inward condition is dark and doleful, then can they rest nowhere; and should they dwell where others are in bliss, the contrast to their own condition would but add misery to their already pitiable state.

Take, for a moment, the condition of a man on earth, who owns a thousand acres of ground, possesses a stately mansion, superbly furnished and decorated; has horses and carriages at his command, and, in a word, everything the eye or ear or any of the outward senses can desire. He may be afflicted with some distressing malady, which baffles the skill of the ablest physician. He may have some secret sorrow pressing upon him, he may possess a churlish and unhappy nature, which forbids him to enjoy. Of what use are all his fair fields to him? Can his money make him happy? He who wears a diadem, surrounded by every sign of prosperity, may be far more wretched than the beggar on the roadside, who sleeps on a door-step or in a hay-loft, and dreams of angels, to wake refreshed for another day's wearisome search for bread, with an eye open to the beauties of all around him.

No place or rank can make happiness. Could mortals enter heaven through the intercession of Christ, or Mary and the Saints; could Peter be induced to open the gate of heaven, and let the suppliants in, they would not know heaven from hell when they got there, unless they developed heavenly-mindedness while passing through the gate.

Christ went to paradise, to hell, to prison all at once. He went among the dark and wretched sufferers in the earth-bound sphere, who needed his preaching and his sympathy. Could he be unhappy on a holy mission of self-denying love? Could he be thinking of the darkness and the gloom, while divine light was welling up within him, and shedding its celestial refulgence an all around? The glow-worm is never in the dark; it carries its own light with it. If your heaven be within, if your happiness depends upon what you yourself are, and not upon where you are, then you travel in heaven, and heaven travels in you, and your constant enjoyment springs from the fact of your shedding brightness wherever you go; so that if your mission be among prisoners and the distressed, you are not partakers of their misery, while you are lighteners of their woe. You are perfectly happy, just so soon as you are perfectly absorbed in works of benefaction. When the spirit really awakes to a true sense of its condition, it sees around it the results of its own labours, and for every tear that it has caused, it must needs shed one: while for every joy it has conferred, it must needs feel within itself an answering echo of pure content.

We have now just a minute in which to express our views upon the true relations of Spiritualism to all existing Institutions. That there will be a coming Religion, and a coming Church, we do not doubt; but Spiritualism, as a sectarian movement, we are convinced will never prosper, if the advocates of sectarian Spiritualism desire simply to add another to the numberless divisions into which the religious world is already unhappily divided.

Oahspe, the new bible, is one out of many endeavours on the part of the Spirit-world to effect a reconciliation between sectarian spirits, as well as among sectarian mortals. That singular compilation is the work of intelligences who now have gravitated to a common centre, from the many restrictive Oriental heavens, which for a while hold spirits estranged from each other in rival parties, as sects and parties create and perpetuate estrangments upon earth. There are Catholic, Protestant, Jewish, Mohammedan, Parsee, Confucian, Zoroastrian and numberless other heavens near the earth, and the influx from these upon receptive minds tends to build up those earthly institutions, which are counterparts of those invisible spheres. With the advancement and liberalization of the spirits forming those societies in the Spirit-world, they blend into common fellowship and become organized into communities of kindred souls, where, seeing truth from a higher standpoint than that of any of these sectaries, they comingle till they become universal in their sympathies and regard.

When Spiritualism shall have swept away the dark accumulations of error and bigotry from the Churches and Colleges of earth, then will come a day when all schools will blend in amicable union. Some may prefer the plainness of the Quaker Meeting-house, others the sumptuousness of St. Peter's at Rome: but, eventually, every Temple of Religion, of Art, of Philosophy, of Science, will become a SPIRITUAL TEMPLE, and Spiritualism will be the agent employed by the Angel-world, in bringing about that much-needed and longed-for reconciliation, which will at length make all Religions, Languages, and Peoples one.

IMPROMPTU POEM.

THE GOLDEN AGE.

THE Prophet bards of every clime
  Have sung of a Golden Age;
The Prophets have seen in a glorious dream
  The time, when the earth, grown sage
Through her lengthened discipline of strife,
  Of pain, and weary woe,
Shall lay her weapons of war aside,
  And peacefully forward go.

In the Golden Age shall the lion and lamb
  Lie down together and feed,
While the little child shall guide them both,
  And together shall sweetly lead
The strongest and gentlest, the brave and weak,
  Till the nations shall bliss have found,
When old Tubal Cain makes them swords no more,
  But plough-shares o'er all earth's bound.

From the far-off distance of buried years—
  From the cities of those plains,
Where now but the rubbish and arid sand
  Mark the seat of those old remains—
There cometh a voice, for the stones cry out,
  And make mention of days gone by,
When both hemispheres were alive at once,
  With a light that has seemed to die.

From old Egypt, now wasted with wars and years;
  From that mystic Hindostan,
Where the sacred city, Benares, remains
  As a mark of primæval man;
From Persia, Chaldæa, where buried lie
  The Soothsayer's mystic arts,
And the Magian's power to foretell events
  By the pulsing of heavenly darts;
From the buried cities of Greece and Rome;
  From Columbia's distant clime,
Where buried beneath the wigwams rude,
  Of the Indian tribes, do chime
The mystic bells of a far-off year,
When Atlantic waters were rolling clear,
Engirdling an island of vast extent,
Whose treasures to East and West were sent;—
Come mingled voices, with clearest tone,
Saying—The Past did most truly own
All your modern knowledge, and might, and power:
'Twill deliver it up at no distant hour.

Are not the nations, with one accord,
  Preparing for fatal war?
Is not your own land, even now, engaged
  In conflict with realms afar?
Are ye not on the verge of a struggle fierce,
  In which evil will surely die?
For the hand of Justice uplifted is,
  To redeem from tyranny.

Ye may sigh o'er those Nihilistic waves,
  Which sweep o'er Europa's sod;
Ye may tremble awhile 'neath the pestilence,
  Which seems as the frown of God;
But the thunders and lightnings clear the air,
  Volcanoes they ease the earth,
And diseases and sorrows, and deadly wars,
  But make way for sweet Freedom's birth.

The earth is in travail, and cries in her pain,
  Her deliverance draweth nigh;
And where now are the corpses of fallen slain,
  Will peaceful homes, by-and-by,
Rise, marking the spots where the warriors fell;
  Men shall point to them soon, and say:
Lo! there, through the horror and din of war,
  God made for new light a way.

In the Golden Age, which is coming apace,
  Shall men to make war forget;
They shall all be brothers, and form one race,
  For all peoples will become yet
One concrete Nation, wherein shall live
  The Roman, the Greek, the Jew,
The Anglo-Saxon, and every race,
  In the Race which shall earth renew.

Lay aside your weapons, O men of strife!
  And learn to control by will,—
By the power of mind, and by love's mild grace;
  Then higher up life's steep hill
Will ye mount together, as brother's all,
  And the Golden Age ye will see,
When forgetting your quarrels ye work as one,
  For Light, Truth, and Liberty!

BENEDICTION.

May the Light of Truth supernal, made manifest in Love, so infill your minds with an appreciation of true Equity, that working for each other's weal, with pure hearts and intelligent minds, ye may hasten the Golden Age, and do God's Will on earth, even as it is done in Heaven. AMEN.

XVIII.

THE LOST CONTINENT, ATLANTIS; AND THE CIVILIZATION OF THE PRE-HISTORIC WORLD.

HERODOTUS, who is popularly styled the Father of History, may indeed be the first great historian who has attempted a systematic and consecutive history of the post-diluvian world; but the history of antediluvian times is still shrouded in such deep gloom, and invested with such transcendent mystery, that very few, until quite recently, have attempted to tell the story of the world before the great and well nigh universal deluge, reference to which will be found in the histories and mythologies of all peoples.

You are probably all of you aware that the Bible is by no means the most ancient record in existence, and it does not profess to deal in any way particularly with all the differing races or varying sections of mankind. The first chapter of Genesis is a prologue, and the prophet Malachi, an epilogue to the Old Testament, while the Law and the Prophets, and the history of Israel's wars and kings, all deal exclusively with one nation (the Jewish), only telling of other peoples as their history collides with that of Israel. Every nation has its own record, and while records may dispute the palm for antiquity with one another, it is almost universally conceded by students, that the Hebrew bible is not anything like so ancient as the Vedas and other records of the far Orient.

The first chapter of Genesis may or may not be interpreted in accordance with modern facts in astronomy or geology, according as the interpreter construes the narrative. It is in its letter so vague, and deals so entirely in generalities, that nothing can be said to be plainly taught therein, beyond the general declarations that all things were created by God, and that the lower forms of life preceded the higher in their order of appearance on the earth, while man came last of all.)

Surely no one can have read this introduction to the Pentateuch, without remarking upon the saying, God made man in his own image, male and female. The simultaneity of the creation of man and woman must strike every reader very forcibly who pays any heed to what he reads, while the following chapter localizes an Asiatic paradise, as the birth-place of one peculiar and distinct race of human beings, the original progenitors of the House of Israel. With Adam the Adamic race had birth, and this race, distinct from all others, was forbidden to mingle with any other peoples. When Cain slew Abel, and wandered far from home, he found the earth peopled in those parts to which he journeyed, and these, other inhabitants than the descendants of Adam, were undoubtedly the offspring of those men and women, numbers and place of abode not supplied by Genesis, whom God created on the sixth day, mentioned in chapter one.

We merely call attention to these biblical statements, because there are not a few among our hearers who are much interested in the case of Genesis *v.* Geology, and a lecture we recently delivered in this hall, on "Evolution and Involution," called forth many comments, not only from those who heard it, but from persons across the water, who had only seen mention made of it in a few paragraphs in a London newspaper. The editor of the "Banner of Light" (Boston, U.S.A.) commented in his columns upon those paragraphs, and went so far as to say, probably they were erroneously reported, because the statement was made that Genesis and Geology were not irreconcilable. He pointed to the fact of their being two distinct accounts of creation in the first two chapters of Genesis, and styled one the Elohistic and the other the Jehovistic account. Bishop Colenso thought these accounts gave evidence of a double authorship, and that opinion is shared by many students to-day.

It is not our intention to enter into any controversy in this discourse on the authenticity of the first book of Moses, neither shall we at any time tell people to read Genesis if they wish to become acquainted with the facts of geology, or any of the natural sciences, for the Bible is no scientific text-book. Still, there is a moderate and common-sense view of the Bible, which, unfortunately, is not taken by the majority of Bible interpreters of the present day, and that is, that though the Bible came into existence in a purely natural manner, as did all other books, it was impossible in the days when it was written for any book to be produced except by the learned, or those who were singularly inspired. The Bible is the result of ancient scholarship and inspiration. It is emphatically a Jewish history written from a Jewish standpoint, chronicling those events which influenced the national life of Israel, and leaving the history of other nations alone, when that history did not run in parallel lines with that of Israel. We think we may fairly assert that the wise men of old, the most learned among the rabbins, for instance, never denied the existence of these scientific facts, known to the Egyptians and embodied in their architecture, but they did not attempt to reveal them to the people under their charge, who, for the most part, were quite unready to receive them. For a curious and interesting dissertation on the Adamic race and its origin, we refer you to the pages of a work, entitled "Genesis," by Allan Kardec, recently translated into English, and obtainable of any dealer in spiritualistic literature in England or abroad. But we must not dwell any longer upon this introduction to our subject, or we shall never be able, if we allow these considerations to divert us, to say anything we wish to say on this occasion, upon that wonderful centre of ancient learning, which fell a prey to the destructive force of the waters about 12,000 years from the present time.

A few years since, Ignatius Donnelly, of Minnesota, U.S.A., published a work of thrilling interest, entitled "Atlantis," in which he undertakes to prove that that mysterious island, mentioned by Plato as having lain in the midst of the Atlantic waters, beyond the pillars of Hercules, at the entrance to the Mediterranean Sea, was not a mere fancy of mythology, but a veritable solid reality, as much so as is the Australia of to-day.

What we have already remarked concerning a plurality of races, and all human beings not having sprung from one common forefather, Adam having been the forefather of one race only, is amply borne out by the facts of physiology, which go very far to prove this position beyond question, among students of the natural history of man. The Negro, for instance, with his thick features and woolly hair, has not only these peculiarities to distinguish him. He has a cuticle under the skin, which makes him a negro. Children born from other races, who have not intermingled with negroes, will never have this cuticle, no matter how long they may sojourn in the tropics, or how dark their offspring may become through exposure to the climate. The Malay and the Caucasian are evidently distinct races of mankind, and though they may blend in the future, and all races may at length become one, a common race, to inhabit all the earth, is rather a prediction for the future than a history of the past. But a study of races is fast leading the student to conclude, that there was a closer bond between the eastern and western hemispheres, in very ancient days, than has ever been imagined until very recently, except by a few such remarkable men as Solon, Plato and others, whose knowledge of ancient history and of the occult sciences led them to conclusions based upon actual facts with reference to the past of man on earth, which were impossible to the multitude, whose knowledge and means of obtaining information were necessarily far more limited.

Before the destruction of the Alexandrian library, under the Turks, there existed in Egypt, at Alexandria, a collection of MSS., probably the finest the world has ever known, and in these books, accessible only to the learned, intelligible only to the very few, was contained the history of the earth from the earliest times; and the history of Egypt not only 6,000 or 7,000 years ago, which is now being unearthed by modern students, but the history of Egypt contemporaneous with that of Atlantis, pre-historic America, pre-historic Australia, and pre-historic South Africa and parts of Asia.

We must now refer you to a fact in the history of the earth, *viz.*, a change in its polar axis, gradually brought about through long periods of time, and reaching a culmination at the close of every grand cycle of over 25,000 years. These vast periods of time, during which mighty changes and upheavals are outwrought, were computed by the Ancients with the same accuracy as that which attends your determining the length of the solar year, which you know to be between 365 and 366 days. The grand year of the Pleiades occupies nearly 26,000 years of earthly time, during which the sun accomplishes its journey through the twelve zodiacal signs. During this vast period, the sun's rays strike the earth vertically at different degrees of latitude, and while there is always an equator, and while there are always poles, and these poles are each 90 degrees from the equator, and while the equatorial line is always the centre of the earth, and that spot upon the earth's surface where day and night are of equal length all the year round, the equator changes place, though so slowly as be imperceptible to all save special observers.

During half the cycle, the south pole advances and the north pole retreats; during the other half, the south pole retreats and the north advances. At the present time the north pole is slowly, but surely, creeping toward you, while the south pole is retreating. The equator is travelling southward, and, therefore, in northern latitudes the climate is steadily becoming more and more inhospitable. Certain sciolists deny this. They had better save their own reputations for scientific knowledge, by accounting for facts now transpiring which prove the truthfulness of this theory, before they deny the only natural and rational explanation of phenomena transpiring under the eyes of every one, by refusing to admit the truthfulness of any theory not sufficiently small to be included in their theories, which stand them in the stead of fact.

No one looking at a map of the world, can fail to be struck with the immense preponderance of land north of the equator, and of water south of it; and no one can see the name "Greenland" applied to a desolate patch of country in the northern part of North America, without wishing to know the origin of the misnomer. Greenland was once a fertile country; while all the northern part of Asia, now called Siberia, was once a fruitful and hospitable region. The Persian records, the Zendavesta, inform you that once there was an earthly paradise, where now there are but fields of ice, and that the tradition of a forfeited earthly paradise in Asia, owes its historical value to this circumstance. Certain it is that in the northern hemisphere the climate of many lands once salubrious, is now becoming more and more inhospitable, while the heat is becoming more tempered in southern latitudes, and this because of the changing aspect of the earth to the sun.

As it would require a discourse of considerable length to fully explain this problem in science, and we have no time to deal with it now, we must refer you to the studies of specialists in this direction for further information; contenting ourselves for the present, with giving you a vague outline of the world as it was prior to the culmination of that last grand cycle of time, which must have culminated fully

11,000 years ago, the present era now closing being the fifth dispensation in the present grand cycle of time, the new era now commencing being the sixth epoch, and that during which one-half the world will attain to a civilization matchless in its importance and results.

The new era now commencing marks that period which will give to the northern half of the globe, a power and supremacy unknown save to the most privileged among the the Ancients, who were however not the recipients of the boons of culture and inspiration on so large a scale as the Anglo-Saxon and allied nations will be during the coming age, which will witness in the eastern and western hemispheres conjointly, an attainment far transcending aught that you anticipate, unless you give credence to Homeric tales, and stories of Arabian enchanters, who have filled the brain of age and youth alike with glowing pictures of a distant past, in which gods and goddesses mingled freely among mortals, and the occult sciences were something more than idle dreams or fanciful imaginings.

The modern world still believes in a golden age departed, while it also looks for one to come. Milton was not a Calvinist when he wrote his matchless verse, and sang of earthly paradises long since destroyed. Tinctured with the Puritanism which filled the very air he breathed, he doubtless was, but he echoed Hesiod and Homer, he pictured the constant strivings of deities and devils, and personified the forces of regeneration and decay in his inspired songs. To him "Paradise Lost" was a sad truth, but "Paradise Regained" was the yet truer dream. Like all great poets he was a thorough optimist, and was sorrowful and astonished at the pessimism of the world, which criticised his verse but could not understand his prophecies. The critics admired his story of a lost Eden, and greatly preferred it to his glowing prophecy of a future golden age. He lived more in the past than in the future when he wrote the "Paradise Lost," he lived in the future when he wrote his "Paradise Regained"; and he loved it best, as all true poets must, for he is not a poet but a misanthrope who sees only death. The true poet sees beyond death to the New Jerusalem, and across the Jordan, which, whelming all earthly treasures, traces, capped with living light, the glorious summits of the mountains of the Celestial City.

There is something inexpressibly sad in gazing upon a ruin, if you must feel that all the life and beauty which once woke it into birth, have gone out into the rayless night of an eternal oblivion. A buried city rising up from among piles of rubbish, the accumulations of centuries, is sad beyond comparison, if you cannot realize the truth of immortality. But when the very air around you is peopled with the impalpable forms of the departed,—when you can wander through the desolated halls and ruined temples, where once art, science, and religion adorned themselves in their most beautiful array, and summoned multitudes from far and near to witness their imperial triumphs; and wandering, musing upon these dead and gone glories, talk with the emancipated spirits of those who once woke those solitudes into every conceivable form of loveliness and grace,—you are no more despondent, for you realize in the ethereal hosts around you the victor spirits who, having done with earth embodiments, are now rejoicing in diviner worlds, reaping the fruits of their former labours, and gazing fondly on the ruined school-houses where once they gained their education; but knowing all the while that they shall each one be rebuilt, and employed by future generations for the advancement of spirits then requiring education like unto that which these ascended ones have long since gained. They can admire the dignity and utility of that law which, while it ordains the destruction of naught, makes provision that all things serve some useful end, so that when they are no longer needed in some particular form they have once-assumed, they are thrust back again into that void or chaos, whence they sprang in former ages to serve the needs of Spirit, there to lie seemingly dormant and useless, but all the while undergoing marvellous transformations, until they shall be called back again to witness new scenes of labour on the part of mind, and be in some yet undreamed-of age the very tools wherewith immortal spirits, awhile embodied in material clay, shall develop those latent energies, which only conflict with lower phases of existence can ever adequately express.

The old Jewish Sabbatic law, as it bore on the question of land, is a striking illustration in minor degree of that great law of nature which renders certain lands peculiarly fruitful for a period, and then compels them to lie waste for needed purposes of recuperation through rest. The sabbath was intended not to flatter God, but to benefit his children. The land was to be cultivated six years, and then lie fallow during the seventh, that it might again be fertilized and bear all that was needed to support life, and keep the nation in a continued condition of active prosperity.

Over-production is always the precursor of want and distress. Poor wages, little work, and general dissatisfaction always follow in the train of an overstepment of the law of prudence in matters pertaining to labour. Work yourselves incessantly without rest, year in and year out, and you disease your bodies till they are unfit for further exertion, or you paralyze your brains and end your days in a madhouse, or as a drivelling idiot, harmless, indeed, but utterly incapable of enjoying any of the blessings which would have accrued to you had you taken a less feverish and more common-sense view of life, and the number of hours that should rightfully be devoted either to physical or mental labour.

Not only does man need periodic rest, but all sentient creatures need it, and they suffer accutely when deprived of it; and not only do all living creatures need it, but the earth itself needs it, for whenever a land has been peculiarly prolific, and has been the scene of unparalleled achievements, the time surely comes when it becomes unfit any longer to bear the strain of such high pressure, and enters upon a state of senility, and ultimately apparent death. Having passed its meridian, it begins slowly yet surely to decline the hill which it once ascended.

But what is one's loss is another's gain. When the sun shines brightest in England, through the long summer days, the winter reigns at the Antipodes. When it is high noon in one hemisphere it is midnight in another. There is never a withdrawal of light and heat from one portion of the globe, without a conference of the same upon other sections of the world. It is always summer somewhere, and it is a beautiful thought, entertained by many optimistic philosophers, and in no sense disputed by the facts revealed by strictest physical research, that every summer is in some sense more beautiful than its predecessor, that with every succeeding year the world becomes more widely adapted to human life in its highest forms, and that the ultimation of the world will most probably be something far different from the catastrophe predicted by theology. For instead of a final conflagration, while yet it is inhabited, the hope of the true philosopher, founded upon reason, observation, intuition, and spiritual revelation alike, is that the time will come when every form of life will be perfected on earth, every noxious and ravenous form of life outgrown, and where now the deadly upas tree sheds its fatal shade, the healthful fruit will hang ripe and rich on the bending boughs of the trees, which will then be in its place. Where now nations are embroiled in perpetual conflict peace will reign supreme, and where now life is felt a burden almost too heavy to be borne, want, wretchedness and despair will have taken their final flight, and the earth will have reached its meridian splendour, and bask in the noonday-glory of its long-promised golden day.

The world is still young. It is only a growing child; it is still in its adolescent period; and has not yet settled itself to enjoy a maturity of peace and prosperity, of which there is ever promise and indication in the nature of the earth itself, despite the wailings of the pessimism which to-day is possible because optimism is true, rather than from any other reason. The general cry of to-day is: the world is getting hopelessly bad; things are going from bad to worse; immoralities and crimes are on the increase; and we shall soon be hurried into perdition. The storm-clouds of God's righteous anger are gathering thick about our heads, and unless we instantly repent we shall all miserably perish. Such lamentation as this shows nothing more than a quickened conscience, a yearning for something higher than is yet attained; while the voice of conscience ever spurs us on to nobler achievements, by making us discontented with our present, leading us out of evil by impressing upon our minds the hideousness and danger of all evil courses.

England is not now what Atlantis was in the palmiest days of her most brilliant and glorious career. She is not in specific directions even what Greece and Rome, Egypt and India, were in their brightest and now far-distant days. But we seriously doubt if there ever was a time in the history of the earth, no matter how old the computations of geologists may cause it to appear, when there was a prospect of so rich a harvest of literature, science, religion and the arts as there is in the modern Europe and the modern America, with which you are all more or less familiar.

No student of ancient history can fail to see in the significant signs of these present times, a nearing recapitulation of events which transpired in the dim distance of pre-historic ages. North of the Equator is now the scene of the greatest mental and physical achievements of the race, while there are colonies of English-speaking people at Cape Colony, in Australia and Australasia. Still, the population increases slowly there in proportion to the increase here, and progress towards the cultivation of the entire ground, nominally possessed by the descendants of European races, is still very slow.

Formerly Australia was joined on to the southern parts of Africa, and the island of Atlantis was the bridge between the two hemispheres, so that by means of Atlantis a constant system of communication was kept up between Asia, Africa and the southern part of Europe on the one hand, and the American continent on the other. The northern part of the modern world was, in the days of Atlantis, buried beneath the waves as the waters now cover Atlantis and many a land and fruitful island connected with her, prior to the time of her being swallowed by the ocean when Atlantis sank. Then northern climes arose from their long sleep beneath the waves, for whenever one part of the world becomes a prey to the waters, other lands are released, for the sea never encroaches in one place without receding in another, or recedes somewhere without encroaching somewhere else. But the days will come when the earth has reached the zenith of its perfection, when literally as well as figuratively there will be no more sea, *i.e.*, there will no longer be vast continents of water acompanied by vast deserts of sand elsewhere. Land and water will be equally divided. Land will all be watered and therefore all fruitful, while the waters will be broken up into many rivers and inland seas, lakes, brooks, and running streams; and the ocean, which is only a barrier between land and land, will disappear.

It is computed that now the waters cover about two-thirds of the surface of the globe. Tradition says once they covered all the land, and dry land appeared so soon as the waters subsided. They will continue to subside more and more, until they occupy only one-half the territory of the earth; and in that day, when land and water are equally divided on the globe, both hemispheres will be civilized and prosperous together, and from pole to pole the earth will not contain one barren or unfruitful spot, neither will it sustain a single poisonous plant, noxious reptile, savage beast, nor brutal man.

Whenever a section of the earth attains to its temporary zenith, that section of the world is the scene of a perfect state of society, so far as perfection can obtain on earth, and it is undoubtedly from this perfection of old-world centres of prosperity, that the poets and philosophers, the fanciful historians and compilers of mythologies, have gathered the data from which they have been enabled to erect that stupendous pile of mythologic lore, which is to-day the wonder and the pride of the student of classics, the poets and the great thinkers of every ancient clime and period.

As you have no doubt all heard of Plato's faith in Atlantis, though comparatively few have probably read his story of that mysterious land, it may not be uninteresting to this audience if we briefly summarize the information we have gathered from various sources, Platonic and other, concerning the physical, social, political and religious condition of that far-famed and highly-blest land.

Atlantis, as we have already told you, lay between the shores of the eastern and western world, from which it was divided by narrow and easily-navigable waters; the art of navigation being very ancient, and the Atlantians being well versed not only in this but indeed in all the arts and sciences, ignorantly supposed to be modern, when they are so ancient no scholar can determine when they originated; and so great a man as the Astronomer Royal of Scotland (Professor Piazzi Smyth) supposes them to have originated in very early times, by direct revelation from heaven to Melchisedek, or whoever may have been the mystic architect and designer of the Great Egyptian Pyramid. But if the Great Pyramid was not erected till 2,170 B.C., it is comparatively speaking a new building, and all that can with any show of reason be assumed concerning the date of its erection is, that it could not possibly have been later than that time. The astronomical reasons for assigning that date as the time of its completion, can also be brought forward in support of its erection at a much earlier time, and many who do not take the real antediluvian world into consideration at all, refer that celebrated pile, justly called a miracle in stone, to 3,500 or 3,700 B.C.

But recent excavations in Central America have led to disclosures concerning the monumental remains there, which led to the publication in a London paper some years ago, the fact of there having been discovered at Pueblo, in New Mexico, a pyramid of much larger dimensions than that of Gizeh, in Egypt; the Mexican pyramid covering over forty acres of ground, while the Egyptian structure covers not more than about thirteen-and-a-half. The Mexican pyramid, scholars decided, must have been in existence fully 7,000 years, and how much longer no one seems prepared to decide. The realm of discovery in the Western world is even richer for future generations than in the East, as it marks a period in history completely ignored by Herodotus, and all historians since his time, and opens up a marvellous field of exploration to all who care to enquire systematically into the origin and blending of races, religions and languages.

Some very strong reasons for belief in the reality of Atlantis, we will now adduce, before giving you, as the climax of our recital, a brief sketch of the internal condition of Atlantis, and the state of her people spiritually as well as materially.

We have already noted the mythologic argument; and allow us here a word concerning myths. They are invariably fanciful histories, as well as speculations, concerning the contending forces of good and ill. Astronomical myths are very frequently alluded to at present, and many if not all which can be legitimately included in the astronomical category, had for their object the preservation and transmission of astronomical facts. which were kept secrets among the learned. Socrates drew down upon him the ire of the Athenian monopolists, when he endeavoured to unveil the Mythos, as Galileo, Bruno, Copernicus, Columbus and many others drew down upon them the anathemas of Christian bigots, because they dispelled the Ptolemaic illusion which kept the masses in ignorance, though there never was a time when secret Orders, possessing knowledge on these subjects, did not exist.

Historical myths are of another class, but not of a widely differing one, for in order to veil yet more carefully the esoteric meaning from the "vulgar," and preserve it for the initiated only, astronomical facts were fancifully represented, and thrown round the heroes and heroines of antiquity, when they were made to pose as gods and goddesses in the temples and traditions of the classic lands. All the nations whose territory borders upon the Hellenic seas, are peculiarly rich in mythologic lore, and a modern examination of this goes very far to prove the fact of there being personal histories behind these wild, fantastic tales. The gods and goddesses of old were not always spirits who communed with seers and sybils in the mystic shades and mountain fastnesses of the classic world. They were quite as often the great and mighty potentates and priests, the prophets, seers, and judges of a by-gone age, around whose memories countless legends had gathered, as Strauss, and Kant, and other German authors of the life of Christ, say that through the centuries since his time, there has been a gradual development of mythology around Jesus as a centre.

The celebrated myth, Prometheus, is now considered by many *savans* to be a fanciful biography of Pythagoras, the celebrated sage of Samos, and so mystic has become the record of the life of this great man, that it is quite as difficult to clearly prove his personal existence to-day, as it is to prove that of Jesus of Nazareth, simply by reference to contemporaneous history. If the mythical personages around whose names such weird, awful, and beautiful legends have gathered, were really the personal dwellers on some long-lost island, the princes in some great monarchies, long since defunct, the presidents of some glorious republics, after which the modern world can only, as yet, feebly copy,—how easy it is to read between the lines the history of the career of religious ideas, and see how intimately associated with Theism, and how subordinate to it, has been that universal tendency to a belief in divine incarnations, and all the countless divinities of Polytheistic systems; while above all, in solitary grandeur, as one superb mountain towering over every neighbouring hillock, and making them appear but ant-hills by its side, has been the sublime and unquenchable faith in one only Supreme Being, whom all nations have adored even though afar off, and have in some manner worshipped, even though, ofttimes, very ignorantly.

Paul at Ephesus, seeing an altar to the Unknown God, and saying to the citizens—"Whom ye ignorantly worship, him declare I unto you," reminded these so-called Pagans that their own poets had always taught them of one Deity, infinitely beyond all lesser lords, whose offspring we all are.

Judaism, rigidly monotheistic though it is and ever has been, has never denied that there are many gods, but only one, Jehovah, to whom all gods must bow. These gods of the nations David did not ignore. He mentions them constantly in his Psalms, but he styles that idolatry, which gives to the creature the homage due to the Eternal only, and denounces the setting up of idols in the temple dedicated to the only Infinite and Holy One, whose name is Jahveh, he who ever was, now is, and ever will be.

A review of Ignatius Donnelly's work, which we mentioned with approval at the outset of our lecture, furnishes the reading public with the following facts concerning Atlantis, which are extremely interesting and especially pertinent to our subject. A reviewer, mentioning the fact of Egyptian navigators being sent out in the reign of Pharaoh Necho, to explore the seas surrounding Africa, tells of their having, after sailing for some considerable distance, found the sun north of them. They were doubted in their day, as all discoverers ever were and always will be by the ignorant, for ignorance engenders doubt, and nothing but knowledge can supplant it, unless it be unreasoning belief, blind gullibility, than which doubt is far preferable. To-day these men, who found the sun north of them when journeying southward from Egypt, can only be looked upon as discoverers who antedated Vasco de Gama, the reputed finder of the Cape of Good Hope. This man was a discoverer relatively. The knowledge of the Cape of Good Hope was lost to the people with whom he mingled, but we very much doubt whether either he or Vespucci or Columbus were not in possession of some secret history of the olden world, not accessible to the multitude, when they set forth on their long and perilous voyages in ill-manned ships, to find those mystic lands which lay beyond the devil-occupied seas, where superstition, ignorance and priestcraft had invented devils to act as scare-crows to drive off inquiring minds from the fields of corn and fruit, which the ecclesiastics preferred to claim as theirs and theirs only.

The fact of the existence of Atlantis as a centre of civilization, and a great seat of commerce between the eastern and western hemispheres, can alone satisfactorily account for the wonderful resemblance between the extant traces of antique civilizations on both sides of the world. It will.

moreover, unveil the mystery of the Mound Builders, those mysterious people to whom science has paid of late no inconsiderable amount of attention. It will explain the origin of the hieroglyphics in the far-famed cave of Elephanta, and will throw an immense amount of light upon the origin of the North American Indians, as well as upon that of the Aborigines of Australia.

The American Indians are by no means the debased people many think them to be. Those who know them truly can never call them rude barbarians. Of late they have decreased in numbers and increased in barbarity, and why? but because the American Government, that of the United States, has treated them meanly and dishonourably. They are called by every harsh name, because they fight with spears and tomahawks against the cruel aggressors, who, calling themselves civilized and Christian, think it no shame to destroy mercilessly the Indian's wigwam, and thrust him forth without food or shelter to die by the wayside, while the march of civilization tramples him under its iron heel, and calls such brutality and injustice the way of God and the march of progress. The Canadian Government, which has been far kinder and juster to the Indians than has been that of the United States, has avowedly had much less trouble with them. The true, manly, independent Yankee, a lover of freedom and a respecter of the rights of others, would never oppress the Indian. The kinsmen of Garrison, Wendell Phillips, Longfellow, Emerson, Parker, and a host of worthies time forbids us to mention now, are always protesting against atrocities committed by stronger peoples to subject weaker races to themselves, and then exterminate them. The enlightened, liberal, loyal American Press has never sanctioned outrages or any depredation committed upon the Indian reservations; but the mere money-grubber, the mere fortune-hunter has ever boasted of his superiority to the race on whose every right he has mercilessly trampled, and pointed to those whom he has cruelly oppressed, as being unfit to live. Such barbarians are they, because they would not lie down and be crushed out of existence without making a desperate effort to defend themselves and those they held most dear.

Many Indian tribes are characterized by their intelligence, refinement, and spirituality; notably on the Pacific slope are there tribes of Indians who boast an illustrious pedigree, and are the direct descendants of once powerful races, whose territory embraced Mexico, Peru, and indeed all the region now called the Central American territory. These races were in constant communion with the Eastern world, by means of Atlantis, and the very striking resmblance, existing palpably to all archæologists, between the remains of Oriental and Occidental civilizations of days gone by, prove beyond a peradventure, that there must have been a bond of union between the "old and new" worlds, such as Atlantis could only have afforded.

The traditions of the Indians are in many instances evidences that they were once in communion with Egypt and other Oriental climes. You may say in their faith in a Great Spirit, and in the conscious existence of the human spirit after the death of the body, and in rewards and punishments in the hereafter, they simply share with all tribes who can boast any civilization at all. But the religious resemblance by no means ends with these fundamental generalities. Many striking resemblances can be traced, in instances so eminently particular, that identity of origin is very powerfully established. For instance, Volney says, "In the Greeks of Homer I find the customs, discourses and manners of the Iroquois, Delawares and Miamis" (Indian tribes). He futher says, the tragedies of Sophocles and Euripides paint almost literally the sentiments of the red men (Indians) respecting "necessity, fatality, the miseries of the human life, and the rigours of blind destiny."

The Oneidas (another tribe of Indians) claim descent from a stone, and did not the Greeks trace their origin to the stones of Deucalion? The snake locks of Medusa are represented in the snake locks of an ancient hero of the Iroquois. The translation of men to heaven bodily is a feature of the American Indian as well as of the Hindoo races. Longfellow tells us of "Hiawatha" rising to heaven and vanishing from sight, amidst sweet music. These admissions prove no doubt more than orthodox Jews or Christians wish to see proved, for while they point to a far-off origin of Indian and Atlantian, Greek and Hindoo Myths, they treat the Old and New Testaments as only two out of an immense collection of records, all couched in similar language, and all expressive of the oneness of symbolism common to the pre-historic as well as to the classic world.

If time permitted we would gladly pursue our theme much further, as we hope to do in subsequent discourses at no distant date, but though we have said but little on this fascinating branch of our subject, we venture to believe we have said enough to let you see that the story of Atlantis is founded on something far more solid than the phantasmagoria which many persons consider stands as a wild and fanciful legend, in the stead of any actual historic fact.

Another class of evidences are purely physical, and to these we can now allude but for a moment; but we should not be doing anything like justice to our theme did we fail to appeal to the ocean itself, to confirm the assertions of Solon, Plato. and the ancient seers at large, who wrote so eloquently and instructively of this strange, buried land.

Deep-sea soundings, recently made by ships of various nations, conspicuous among which were the British ship, "Challenger," and the U.S. vessel, "Dolphin," have gone very far to sustain our conclusions, by discovering in the bed of the ocean, immense deposits of lava and volcanic *debris*, extending over thousands of miles of what evidently once was land. The peaks of the Azores are exactly in the spot where Plato located Atlantis, and Solon, who had travelled in Egypt, and possessed himself of much information while there, soon grew into perfect accord with the learned there, that popular histories only touched upon very recent events compared with those which were amply chronicled in Egypt in Solon's day.

Solon's opinion was, that 9,000 years had elapsed then since the sinking of Atlantis, and Solon lived about 2,300 years ago. Add these numbers, and you have something over 11,000 years. We have already referred you to the duration of the Grand Cycle, as a period extending between 25,000 and 26,000 years, and have told you that this period is divided into 12 almost equal portions, called eras, ages, or dispensations, each one occupying about 2,150 years or thereabouts. We are now just at the dawn of the sixth division of the present Cycle, thus, multiplying 2,150 by 5, we get 10,750 years, and allowing for the fact that numbers in these cases have only an approximate accuracy, we find the testimony of the Grecian sages agreeing perfectly with the events of to-day, spiritually interpreted.

How account for the story of a universal deluge, without giving heed to the story of Atlantis? Noah's flood, of 4,000 years ago, was a very local matter, while every record called sacred on the earth, from those of Hermes and the Vedas to those of Scandinavia, all contain a narrative of a universal flood. This tradition of the deluge is scientifically explained by that revelation which the bed of the sea is now making to the world, concerning the once populous and fruitful lands it now covers, while, east and west, stones are literally crying out in the revelations given to all who study them, by those marvellous monumental remains which contain histories, far more glowing and imperishably written, of nations long since gone out of earthly existence, than are to be found in any parchment scrolls or printed records.

In closing we can only add, that Lord Lytton's "Coming Race" can well be read as a reminiscence of the past, as well as a dream and prophecy of the future. Time was when the powerful Atlantian race was as glorious as Lytton's Vril-ya. Aerial navigation, the use of wings as mechanical appendages. were among their triumphs relating to the comforts and amenities of civilized life, while during the later and most glorious portion of their career, they had outgrown warfare, and had triumphed over those innumerable stumbling-blocks in the way of a nation's progress, which are yet perplexing the statesmen of every land beneath the sun.

Their religion was a simple confidence in the All-Good. Their rites and ceremonies were those from which the magnificent conceptions and glowing imagery of the early Egyptians sprang. They were the originators of those Schools of the Prophets, of which the Ancients speak so much, while having attained to an almost inconceivable spiritual altitude, their spiritual faculties became so alive to the realities of the realm of spirit, that their land was verily the abode of gods. Theirs was the original of Arcadia, Olympia, Hesperides, and every charming resort of divinities pictured to you in Homeric verse and Platonic philosophy. Spirit communion, purified from sensuous dross and devoted to pure and benevolent ends, revealed to them the certainties of life immortal; while education was the substitute for punishment, moral suasion and intellectual might were in the stead of carnal weapons of defence, while their land, charmingly situated, perfectly watered, thoroughly under cultivation, yielding every fruit of the earth man could desire, in rich profusion; surrounded by easily-navigable seas, across which access to other lands was constant, conspired to render the Atlantians the favoured race, because the most moral, intellectual and healthful. Disease, poverty, crime and painful death became almost outgrown, ere the hour drew nigh for the land to become the ocean's prey, and having flowered out into such luxuriant beauty, to decline suddenly when its inhabitants were prepared to quit the earth, and their spirits to be transported to another planet. A few were saved from the fate which overtook their land. These mingled with the life of both hemispheres, some escaping to America, and some to Asia.

When, in 2,000 years from now, the belt of civilization again puts a girdle round the earth, in more than name or pretence, a greater race, a larger one, covering wider territory than the Atlantian, will have been formed, and the new millennium will be more glorious than the Golden Age, so deeply mourned, so soon to be recovered and transcended, when the paradise to be gained will far transcend in glory the paradise the old world lost.)

IMPROMPTU POEM.

THE REAL AND THE IDEAL.

SURELY, things IDEAL after all are REAL!
  And things the most Ideal are the most Real,
Because the Soul discovers the Ideal,
  And purblind sense deals with the earthly Real.
The poor, worn body, in th' embrace of death,—
  This, mortals ever seem to think the Real:
The happy Spirit, fled from scenes of dust,
  To them is only fancy, the Ideal!

The Artists' paint a glorious sunrise,
  A lovely sunset, showing all the scene

Where earth and heaven meet in sweet accord,
  As though estrangement they had never seen.
The colours, true to life, which greet his eye,
  He puts upon the canvas in his joy;
The splendours all around him he reveals,
  And men declare 'tis but Ideal employ!

The Poet sings a song of fadeless love,
  Undying fealty to a loving heart,
And tells a tale of constancy divine,
  In which no shade of doubt can bear a part.
The real writer says, It is not true;
  The prosy reader says, Can never be;
Such deep devotion for such loyal love,
  Say men, the world of mortals ne'er can see.

The Christ of Gospels, and of painter's art,
  Who loses life and all the world counts dear,
To save his brethren from sin's bitter fruit,
  Is but a myth, for surely none so clear,
So free from stain, so noble and so great,
  Could ever dwell upon the shores of time:
Men cannot see, that what is great and best,
  Is true forever, e'en on earthly clime.

The sputtering candle, and the broken mug,
  The ragged urchin gamb'ling in the street;
The haggard face, the listless indolence,
  Which every passer-by must often meet;
The fish, the worm, the fire, the grate, the cat,—
  These things are true to nature, they are Real;
But, verily, the commonplace of life
  Is not so real as the great Ideal.

These little things, these phantoms of an hour,
  Will be unreal to-morrow, fled and gone;
While all the visions of the starry night,
  The Artist saw, will still be shimmering on;
The Poet's love, the true historic Christ,
  Will be alive when baubles are no more,
And every high ambition of the soul,
  Will live and triumph when all earth is o'er.

That is the Real which shall longest live,
  The Ideal world is the most real far;
The sun, the moon, the mountains towering high,
  The peaceful valleys, and each blazing star,
High hopes, pure loves, deep sentiments most wise,
  Ardent ambitions, and the Eternal State,
Man's immortality,—these will remain;
  Though all things petty soon shall meet their fate,
And be dissolved in elemental strife,
  All that is great, and beautiful, and true,
Must live and reign, co-eval with its God,
  And every day appear in some sweet fashion new,

Though seemingly it dies; for what is death
  But that transition which doth free the soul,
And let the ideal nature freely fly,
  Until the Spirit doth all earth control.

O Poet! Artist! Singer! Sculptor! Scribe!
  Though men deride ye for your loftiest dreams;
Go, tell us more of Heaven's immortal dower;
  Go, tell the world how great to you it seems,
This mystic universe of stars and suns.
  And while the world, in market-place and stall,
Will barter chattels for a mite of bread,
  Go ye, and summon angels, men, to all
Proclaim the fact, while ages roll along,
  The Ideal world doth the most Real be,
Because it is the region of that Cause,
  But whose effects on earth the noblest see.
Go, tell the world that every ardent hope,
  And every dream of truth and love remains
A living entity, when earth is dead;
  And that we live for aye in God's domains!

BENEDICTION.

May the sublimities, the Eternal Realities, of the Immortal World, so vividly impress the likeness of themselves upon your every mind, that, in the pursuit of what is truly Real, ye realize the blessedness of the Ideal, even the fulness of Life and Joy Immortal! AMEN.

FINIS.

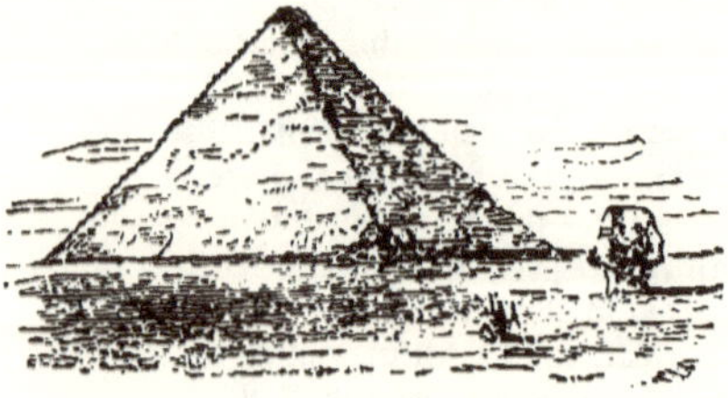

www.ingramcontent.com/pod-product-compliance
Lightning Source LLC
Chambersburg PA
CBHW020946030726
47496CB00005B/1375
* 9 7 8 3 3 3 7 1 7 1 4 1 4 *